NF

BEVERIDGE AND SOCIAL SECURITY

BEVERIDGE
AND
SOCIAL SECURITY

An International Retrospective

Edited by

JOHN HILLS, JOHN DITCH, AND
HOWARD GLENNERSTER

CLARENDON PRESS · OXFORD
1994

Oxford University Press, Walton Street, Oxford OX2 6DP
Oxford New York Toronto
Delhi Bombay Calcutta Madras Karachi
Kuala Lumpur Singapore Hong Kong Tokyo
Nairobi Dar es Salaam Cape Town
Melbourne Auckland Madrid
and associated companies in
Berlin Ibadan

Oxford is a trade mark of Oxford University Press

Published in the United States
by Oxford University Press Inc., New York

British Library Cataloguing in Publication Data
Data available

Library of Congress Cataloging-in-Publication Data
Beveridge and social security: an international retrospective/
edited by John Hills, John Ditch and Howard Glennerster
p.   cm.
Papers (except chapter 3) selected from a conference on "Social Security Fifty Years
After Beveridge" held at the University of York, Sept. 1992
Includes bibliographical references
1. Great Britain. Inter-departmental Committee on Social
Insurance and Allied Services—Congresses.   2. Social security—
Great Britain—History—Congresses.   3. Beveridge, William Henry
Beveridge, Baron, 1879–1963—Congresses.   I. Hills, John.
II. Ditch, John, 1952– .   III. Glennerster, Howard.
HD7165.A72B42   1994   93-39182
368.4'00941—dc20
ISBN 0–19–828806–9

1 3 5 7 9 10 8 6 4 2

Typeset by Selwood Systems, Midsomer Norton
Printed in Great Britain
on acid-free paper by
Bookcraft (Bath) Ltd., Midsomer Norton, Avon

JK

PREFACE

The papers contained in this volume (with the exception of Chapter 3) are drawn from those on a broadly historical theme originally presented at a conference on 'Social Security Fifty Years After Beveridge' held at the University of York in September 1992. The conference was jointly organized by the Social Policy Research Unit and Department of Social Policy and Social Work at the University of York, and the Welfare State Programme, Suntory-Toyota International Centre for Economics and Related Disciplines at the London School of Economics. It was the annual colloquium of the European Institute of Social Security, and was organized in association with the Foundation for International Studies in Social Security.

The editors are very grateful to all those involved in organizing the conference, particularly Jonathan Bradshaw, Sally Baldwin, Gary Craig, Han Emmanuel, Jane Falkingham, Hilary Holmes, Denise Marchent, Janet Moore, Nicola Tynan and Jef Van Langendonck. They are also very grateful for financial support of the conference and the work associated with it from the Economic and Social Research Council (under Programme Grant X206 32 2001), the Joseph Rowntree Foundation, the European Commission, the Department of Social Security, the Benefits Agency, the Information Technology Services Agency, the International Social Security Association, Prudential, the Council of Europe, and the Social Policy Association.

The chapter by Jose Harris was originally delivered as a Public Lecture at the London School of Economics in December 1992, on the fiftieth anniversary of publication of the Beveridge Report itself.

Finally, the editors are especially grateful to Jane Dickson, who prepared all of the typescripts for publication and ensured that they could be presented in a consistent format.

London School of Economics　　　　　　　　　　　　　　　　　　J.H.
University of York　　　　　　　　　　　　　　　　　　　　　　J.D.
March 1993　　　　　　　　　　　　　　　　　　　　　　　　H.G.

CONTENTS

LIST OF CONTRIBUTORS

BRIAN ABEL-SMITH is Emeritus Professor of Social Administration at the London School of Economics. His extensive publications on social security, public health-care policy, poverty, and distribution over four decades range from *The Reform of Social Security* (1953) to *Cost Containment and New Priorities in Health Care: A Study of the European Community* (1992). Current activities include advising the Government of Tanzania on health policy and the European Community on pharmaceuticals policy.

PETER BALDWIN is Associate Professor of History at the University of California, Los Angeles. He is the author of *The Politics of Social Solidarity: Class Bases of the European Welfare State 1875–1975* and editor of *Reworking the Past: Hitler, the Holocaust and the Historians' Debate*. As part of a larger study of state intervention, he is currently working on measures taken against contagious disease in Europe during the nineteenth and early twentieth centuries.

BETTINA CASS is Professor of Sociology and Social Policy at the University of Sydney. She is also Commissioner (part-time) on the Australian Law Reform Commission and was the Director of the Australian Social Security Review, 1986–8. She is author of a number of books, reports and papers on the history and contemporary politics of the Australian welfare state. She has strong research interests in social security, employment and unemployment, housing policy, and the politics of gender.

JOHN DITCH is Assistant Director of the Social Policy Research Unit at the University of York, where he directs the social security research programme. He is the author of *Social Policy in Northern Ireland 1939–1950*. His current research interests include a comparative study of child support, the European Community's social policy, and an investigation of changes in circumstances among Income Support recipients in the United Kingdom.

ABRAHAM DORON is Professor at the Paul Baerwald School of Social Work at the Hebrew University of Jerusalem. His main research interest is social security and health care policy in Israel and in cross-national comparative perspective. Recent publications include *The Welfare State in Israel: The Evolution of Social Security Policy and Practice* (co-authored with Ralph Kramer). He is currently studying the privatization of social welfare services and its effects on underprivileged population groups.

TOR ERIKSEN is Managing Director of Regional Social Insurance in Värmland, Sweden. He has previously held positions at the Swedish National Social Insurance Board and the Swedish National Insurance Inspection Board. He is the author of a number of publications on Swedish pensions and other aspects of social insurance, including *What Can We Learn from our Neighbours? The Swedish Pension System in a Nordic Perspective* and *What Do We Want our Social Insurance For?* (both in Swedish).

MARTIN EVANS is a Research Officer with the Welfare State Programme at the London School of Economics. Publications include *Squaring the Circle? The Inconsistencies and Constraints of Beveridge's Plan* (with Howard Glennerster). Research interests include postwar housing subsidy and rent policy in Britain and social assistance in Britain and Europe. He is currently investigating the distributional impact of the 1988 social security reforms in Britain.

JOHN FREELAND is a Senior Lecturer in Social Policy at the University of Sydney. He is a member of the Australian Government's Employment and Skills Formation Council and Commonwealth Employment Service Advisory Committee, and has participated in a number of major government reviews of labour market programmes, training, and youth policies. He is the Australian Council of Social Service's policy co-ordinator on employment, education and training. He has written extensively in these areas.

HOWARD GLENNERSTER is Professor of Social Administration at the London School of Economics. He is the author or editor of numerous books and articles on social policy, including most recently *Paying for Welfare: The 1990s*. Current research interests include the private returns to education and training, the impact of health service reforms in Britain, and changes in the delivery of community care.

FRITZ GRÜNDGER is Professor of Social Policy at the Berlin Protestant School of Social Work and Social Education. Among his publications, mainly in German, are a comparative study of investment planning in the health and education sector, a textbook on social policy (co-authored with Jürgen Zerche), and several contributions to social economics. His special interests are the economics of human services, and the history of economic thought.

JOSE HARRIS is a fellow of St Catherine's College and Reader in Modern History at the University of Oxford. She is the author of *William Beveridge: A Biography*, *Unemployment and Politics: A Study in English Social Policy 1886–1914*, and *Private Lives, Public Spirit: A Social History of Britain 1870–1914*. She is currently working on the 'intellectual history' of social policy and the welfare state.

JOHN HILLS is Co-Director of the Welfare State Programme at the London School of Economics, and is Programme Advisor on income and wealth to the Joseph Rowntree Foundation. He is author of *Unravelling Housing Finance: Subsidies, Benefits and Taxation*, and editor of *The State of Welfare: The Welfare State in Britain Since 1974*. His research interests include housing finance, social security, taxation, and the distributional and life-cycle effects of the welfare state.

TEUN JASPERS is Professor of Labour and Social Security Law at the State University of Utrecht. He has a particular interest in international and European labour and social security law. He is a member of the Social Security Panel of the Social Economic Council in the Netherlands, and of its working groups on subjects including the social dimension of Europe and equal treatment of men and women.

He is also a member of the Committee of Independent Experts for the European Social Charter of the Council of Europe.

SASKIA KLOSSE is Lecturer in Labour and Social Security Law at the State University of Utrecht. Her research interests and publications concern the effects of regulations leading to the re-entry of disabled people into employment in the Netherlands and in Germany, as well as European social security law.

RODNEY LOWE is Reader in Economic and Social History at the University of Bristol. He has published widely on the history of British welfare policy. Books include *Adjusting to Democracy*, *The Welfare State in Britain Since 1945*, and two major guides to documents at the Public Record Office, *Economic Planning 1943–51* and *The Development of the Welfare State 1939–51*. He is currently working on the replanning of the welfare state between 1957 and 1964.

JOHN MACNICOL is Reader in Social Policy at Royal Holloway University of London. He has published extensively on the history of social policy, including *The Movement for Family Allowances 1918–45: A Study in Social Policy Development* and (as co-editor) *Aspects of Ageing*. He is completing a study of the politics of retirement and state pensions in twentieth-century Britain, and is also working on a history of the idea of an 'underclass' in Britain and America.

EDWARD PALMER is Adjoint Professor of Social Insurance Economics at the University of Gothenburg and Head of Research at the Swedish National Social Insurance Board. Publications in English on various aspects of social security include 'Social Insurance and Saving in Sweden' (with A. Markowski) in *Social Security versus Private Saving* (edited by George von Furstenberg), and 'A Macroeconomic Analysis of Employer-Contribution Financed Social Security in Sweden' (with M. Palme) in *The Political Economy of Social Security* (edited by A. Klevmarken and B. Gustafsson).

JOHN VEIT-WILSON is Emeritus Professor of Social Policy of the University of Northumbria at Newcastle and currently a Principal Research Associate of the University of Newcastle upon Tyne. He has written chiefly on the development and types of poverty theory and research measures from the work of Seebohm Rowntree onwards, and on the making of British social security policy for the poor. He is currently studying the minimum income standards used by governments in other countries to evaluate the adequacy of their income maintenance provisions.

MIES WESTERVELD is attached to the University of Utrecht as lecturer in the field of Labour and Social Security Law. She is preparing a thesis on social security pensions in widowhood and old age in the Netherlands, the United Kingdom, and Germany. She is also deputy judge at the Administrative Court for Social Affairs in Rotterdam.

MACIEJ ŻUKOWSKI is *adiunkt*, teaching and researching at the University of Economics in Poznań, Poland. His research includes a comparison of public pension schemes for employees in Britain, Germany, and Poland, and a study of the relationship between social insurance and other sources of income in old age. He is the translator into Polish of Nicholas Barr's *The Economics of the Welfare State*.

1

Introduction

JOHN HILLS, JOHN DITCH, AND HOWARD GLENNERSTER

In December 1942 queues formed outside the government stationery office as people waited to buy a densely written three hundred page official report. Its title—*Social Insurance and Allied Services: Report by Sir William Beveridge*—was not one we would expect to see in the best-sellers' list today. Its reputation, if not its direct influence, became world-wide. Fifty years later many details of the British social security system continue to reflect the Report's recommendations. It is still taken as a benchmark against which to measure reform proposals both in Britain and in other countries.

This book contains a series of papers looking back from the vantage-point of the 1990s to what the report said, how it came about, the social, political, and economic pressures under which it was written, what happened to its recommendations, parallel developments abroad, and its influence on them.

In Chapter 2 Brian Abel-Smith tells the story of how the Report came about and the extraordinary impact which it had at the time. A committee which had been intended by the Government to be a relatively 'harmless' tidying-up exercise was effectively hijacked by its Chairman, Sir William Beveridge, to produce a report which talked in terms of policies which would defeat the 'five giants on the road to reconstruction'—Want, Disease, Ignorance, Squalor and Idleness. Instead of simply sticking to the details of social security benefits, Beveridge emphasized the dependence of his recommendations on three key 'assumptions'—children's allowances, a comprehensive health service, and maintenance of full employment. He used the media of the time effectively to appeal above the heads of the Government, outflanking both the Treasury and the Prime Minister, Winston Churchill, in presenting his vision of the postwar world, and his detailed ideas for building it. How the Report was implemented, and whether its recommendations really achieved what was claimed for them, is the focus of the subsequent chapters.

Jose Harris, Beveridge's biographer, looks in more detail at the philosophy lying behind the Report. She stresses that it would be a mistake to think of Beveridge as a straightforward orthodox reformist liberal. On the contrary, by the late 1930s his views had moved through several stages to a point where he believed the free market was unworkable and that large-scale state intervention was needed. Social insurance—even with the wider agenda of the three 'assumptions' visible in the Report—was only the tip of a much greater iceberg of intervention, which would involve nation-alization of land, state direction of labour and control of investment. But, as she explains, he was not arguing for a 'Santa Claus state'. In his vision, social insurance underpinned good citizenship, and was austerely structured to ensure that 'rational economic man' would opt to work—if the state organized the labour market to ensure that work was available. Meanwhile the position of women within his plan reflected his ideals and beliefs about family life and partnership in marriage, progressive for the time, but which led to a structure ill-adapted to the way in which women's roles have actually developed since the War.[1]

Peter Baldwin looks at why Beveridge's reputation has endured. Should he be seen as 'the father of modern British social policy', or were his principles ones which had already been implemented elsewhere, with many of his recommendations in fact ignored? He discusses the influential role played by T. H. Marshall's gloss on the report in 1949, in which the 'social citizenship welfare state' as outlined by Beveridge and implemented by the Attlee government was seen as the culmination of centuries of social progress, an event of equal stature to the French or Russian Revolutions. But the reputation also rests on the balance that Beveridge struck, using social insurance, between collectivism and individualism. In what Baldwin labels the 'Struwwelpeter' approach, Beveridge expanded the group over which risks are pooled to the whole community, a universalism which marked his approach out from the narrower industrial groups sharing risks in the Bismarckian model. In this system the idea of financing from contributions as opposed to general taxation meant that all were to become 'upright, self-maintaining citizens', giving legitimacy to the system and to claiming from it. Today, with growing holes in what is covered by social insurance, with the retreat from the social citizenship model, and with increasing emphasis on private provision, it is the individualistic parts of Beveridge's thought, and the limits which he wanted to place on state action, which may continue to give his ideas contemporary force.

The origins of those holes in social insurance lie in the Report itself, and are examined by Howard Glennerster and Martin Evans in their chapter. The appeal of Beveridge's vision was one thing; the success of his detailed recommendations in meeting it quite another. In essence, Beveridge was trying to square a circle in claiming that social insurance benefits, financed

---

[1] See the papers in Baldwin and Falkingham (forthcoming) for a discussion of the problems caused for social insurance by changes in demography, the labour market, the role of women, and family structure.

by flat-rate contributions and heavily constrained by what could be negotiated with the Treasury, could abolish 'Want', in the sense of reducing to
minimal levels the numbers who would need means-tested additions to
reach subsistence. Beveridge rested his claim on findings from Rowntree's
latest (1941) survey of poverty, which showed that five-sixths of poverty
resulted from 'insurable contingencies'. Flat-rate benefits paid to those
facing these contingencies could then cope with most poverty. But as he
tried to apply this model it began to unravel. The unsolved 'problem of
rent' meant that flat-rate benefits—unless very generous indeed—could not
guarantee subsistence without means-tested top-ups. Flat-rate contributions,
an essential part of Beveridge's vision, limited what benefits could be paid.
His view of the position of married women—seven-eighths of whom he
thought would 'follow no gainful occupation' in peace-time—resulted in a
system which catered for widowhood as a contingency to be covered, but
not divorce, lone-parenthood or caring, and which was ill-adapted for a
world where the majority of married women do have earnings. He compromised with the Treasury in excluding the first child from family allowances.
The uniformity of benefit levels was broken by higher rates for industrial
injury benefits. The general level of benefits eventually set after the War did
not, in fact, equate to Rowntree's poverty lines after allowing for inflation.

The end result, Glennerster and Evans argue, is that British social
security's true legacy from this period is not National Insurance. Rather it
is the notion of a national minimum income safety net covering all,
implemented through means-tested National Assistance and its successors,
but stigmatized by Beveridge as being a residual provision for 'cripples, the
deformed, ... and moral weaklings'.

In Chapter 6 John Macnicol looks at what was the largest spending item
in the Beveridge plan, and which remains the largest part of social security,
the state retirement pension. He sets Beveridge's recommendations for the
pension in the context of the political debate of the previous seventy years.
Beveridge's pensions—contributory and tied to a retirement condition—
contrast with the tax-funded pensions paid at age 70 with restrictions related
to means, rather than to retirement, established under the 1908 Old Age
Pensions Act. The Treasury had sought from the passing of that Act to
shift pension finance onto a contributory insurance basis, succeeding in
1925 in making sure that the extension of pensions to those aged 65–69 was
contributory, and designed eventually to replace the 1908 scheme. Macnicol
argues that, in effect, the Beveridge Report marked the culmination of that
campaign. Not only were pensions contributory, but Beveridge agreed with
the Treasury that, in contrast to other benefits, the new levels should be
phased in over twenty years. In his eyes this followed the logic of benefits
reflecting past contributions; in the Treasury's it contained costs, at least in
the short term.

In his recommendations Beveridge was not simply following the consensus
of those giving evidence to his committee; nor did his proposals meet
with universal adulation. The National Federation of Old Age Pensions
Associations' (NFOAPA) newspaper argued that the Report offered
'present day pensioners nothing'. The phase-in period meant that, in contrast
to other groups, for pensioners the principle that benefits should cover
subsistence was being abandoned. In the event, under pressure from Ernest
Bevin, pensions were brought in at their full rate immediately. Had the
Report's proposals been implemented as they stood, millions more pensioners would have remained dependent on means-tested National Assistance (many still did, as a result of factors like rents). Rather than being
seen as a radical document, Macnicol suggests that the Report emerges as
a very successful bulwark against the radical demands of organizations like
the NFOAPA for unconditional pensions from the age of 60.

John Veit-Wilson advances the prosecution case against the Report on
the grounds that it stifled debate about the adequacy of benefits to prevent
poverty for the following two decades or more. Beveridge claimed that
benefits would be 'sufficient without further resources to provide the
minimum income required for subsistence in all normal cases'. But, Veit-
Wilson argues, what constituted subsistence rested on confusion in Beveridge's mind about the meaning of the various income measures used by
Rowntree. Rowntree had developed one income level—the 'P1 measure'—
needed to meet purely physiological needs, as a device for counting the
numbers in 'primary poverty'. He set a second, higher level—the Human
Needs of Labour scale—including the income needed 'for the development
of mental, moral and social sides of human nature'. Beveridge, despite the
misgivings Rowntree expressed to him, took rates based on little more than
the P1 scale, but continued to describe them as being 'enough to live on'.
The result of this, Veit-Wilson concludes, was that people living on benefit
scales derived from the Report's recommendations were in fact condemned
to deprivation, while the authoritative reputation of the Report led to their
benefit levels being thought to be adequate, and to a lag of twenty years
before the 'rediscovery' of poverty in the 1960s.

Rodney Lowe asks whether Beveridge's principles were ever, in fact,
implemented in Britain. He examines what the Report described as the six
key elements of social insurance and the 'blueprint for national life' on
which they were based. First, adequacy of benefits 'in amount and time'
was not implemented. Not only were there the problems outlined above
with the definition of adequacy, and with the allowance made for wartime
inflation in setting benefit rates, but also the long-term unemployed were
excluded from Unemployment Benefit and would have to resort to National
Assistance. The second recommendation—'unification of administrative
responsibility'—took twenty years to be achieved, and then very imperfectly,

in the form of a Ministry of Social Security. Flat-rate benefits and contributions were implemented, but abandoned in stages through the late 1950s and 1960s. From 1971 higher rates of benefit were paid to some, long-term, claimants than to others. The introduction of the ability to 'contract out' from part of state pensions in 1959 breached the principle of universality. Only the technicality of 'classification' of insurance groups remained, and even this was modified in the 1970s. Given the rejection of these detailed proposals, Lowe argues that it was unsurprising that Beveridge's wider vision of a postwar society was also rejected.

Lowe puts forward two reasons for the rejection of Beveridge's principles. First, despite the concessions made to the Treasury in whittling down the commitments made, there remained in Lowe's words: 'at the heart of Whitehall, interests fundamentally opposed to the spirit of the Report'. Second, as described in the earlier chapters, the Report itself contained many internal contradictions in respect of its technical proposals and underlying philosophy, which made its recommendations impractical. The Report may have been successful in expressing ideals, but it was much less so as a practical blueprint for the postwar welfare state.

What of Beveridge's influence abroad? Fritz Gründger compares and contrasts the development of Germany's social insurance system, based on foundations laid by Bismarck, with that of Britain, and examines the contemporary response to the Report. Given the War, it is hardly surprising that the Report was comprehensively attacked in the German press at the time, although the prominence of the attacks says something about the realization of its propaganda importance. In public the recommendations were described as showing that Britain was fifty years behind German social insurance, and as being a fraud on the British people. Secret documents, however, described the plan as being 'superior to the current German social insurance in almost all points'. As Gründger describes, all of this was especially galling to Dr Robert Ley, a man who had been working on a comprehensive reform of German social insurance for the Nazi government, but whose work was stopped in January 1942.

After the War, the allied powers worked towards introducing a unified social insurance system, which would break away from many of the traditions established by Bismarck, and leave something closer to the Beveridge model. However, German public opinion wanted those traditions restored, and by the time Four Power co-operation broke down, the western allies declared social insurance an internal matter. In the 1950s, the opposition Social Democrats put forward reform ideas for pensions which incorporated 'Beveridgean' ideas, and a high-level delegation visited Britain to look at the British system. But by the time the Pensions Reform Act was passed in 1957, the moment when Beveridge might have taken over from Bismarck had passed. German pensions and social insurance remained firmly based on income-related contributions and benefits. Indeed, it was Britain which was to follow behind Germany as it gradually abandoned Beveridge's flat-rate principles.

What happened in Poland after 1945, as is described by Maciej Żukowski, illustrates a different outcome to the conflict between 'Bismarckian' and 'Beveridgean' principles. Between the wars, Polish social insurance had been gradually evolving from the German and Austrian systems applied in parts of the previously divided country. In its separate regimes for different groups and in its earnings-related structure, it clearly followed the Bismarck model. After the War, several of the changes made by the communist government mirrored the Beveridge Report's principles, although there is no evidence of any direct relationship. These changes included: the focus on establishing a common minimum income for all citizens, instead of on income replacement and protection of accustomed living standards; centralization of administration; and the major role of the state. However, except for a short period in the late 1940s, pensions were income-related, not flat-rate, and successive reforms were aimed at addressing the problem of the relatively low level of pensions of those who had retired earlier, and whose pensions were therefore based on a lower level of income than those of more recent pensioners. There was no role for the private provision which Beveridge stressed in addition to the basic state pension, and the lack of employee contributions ran completely against his principles as described above. Solutions advocated by Beveridge were adopted only where they suited the aims of state policy, and if any influence existed, it was not admitted.

Saskia Klosse, Teun Jaspers, and Mies Westerveld also look at a system which they describe as 'a Bismarck building with a Beveridge façade', the Dutch social security system. Some of Beveridge's ideas were incorporated into the Dutch system after 1945, notably the universalist idea that the role of government was to guarantee protection against hardship for all citizens. As in the British system, married women were treated separately, with the 'family principle' assuming that provision would be made by their husbands. However, following the German system, contributions remained income-related, as did most benefits.

The authors go on to ask whether the 'Beveridge façade' of this system can survive. The Dutch system, like others in Europe, is under pressure from three directions: the rising dependency ratio and worries about costs; concerns about competitiveness, if the system is more expensive than others within the European Community's single market; and the need to comply with Community legislation on equal treatment of men and women. The first two of these could result in pressure to move towards a 'mini-system', with Beveridge-style flat-rate benefits. The third has already caused changes in the system, removing elements of the family principle. The authors conclude that if Beveridge is to have a 'second youth' under European pressure, his principles will have to have a face-lift.

The Report had a more direct effect in Israel, as described by Abraham Doron in the next chapter. It was translated into Hebrew in 1943, and was followed by a spate of plans for social insurance. Shortly after the establishment of Israel in 1948, the Report's translator, I. Kanev, first produced an unofficial social insurance plan for the new state, and then chaired a committee making official recommendations. An immediate parallel with Beveridge was to undertake such an ambitious venture at a time of national hardship and austerity. A Beveridge-style old age and survivors' insurance scheme with flat-rate benefits and the intention of near-universal coverage was introduced in 1954. In contrast to the British scheme, the contributions financing it were earnings-linked from the start, making it highly redistributive. However, the pensions actually paid have gradually fallen back in relation to average earnings. As this has happened, the flat-rate pension has gradually lost its relevance for the influential middle classes, a process which was, if anything, accelerated when increases in pensions were made on a selective basis in the 1960s, breaking with the tradition of universality. By the 1990s, explicit means-testing was firmly on the agenda. Doron concludes that both the Kanev and Beveridge models were essentially backward-looking. In both countries it was a flaw to fail to integrate national insurance pensions with occupational schemes; and the failure to do so has meant the end of universal support.

Tor Eriksen and Edward Palmer also focus on the development of state pensions, in their case in Sweden. Beveridge's principles of a minimum level of public assistance supplemented by private schemes were supported by the responsible government minister of the time, at least as far as sickness and health care were concerned. However, they did not command support from the Social Democrats as a whole, and in the 1950s Sweden's state pension was developed along earnings-related income-replacement lines, with the essentials of the current (ATP) system introduced in 1960, and containing important features such as the 'best fifteen years' rule to protect the position of women. Today, however, that system is under severe stress. Demographic changes imply a rapidly rising dependency ratio. The linking of the ceiling on contributions into the scheme to prices rather than earnings means that if incomes do grow, the scheme will effectively become flat-rate. On the other hand, if real income growth is low, the implied contribution rates also become unsustainable. Analysing likely reforms, the authors conclude that the redistributive element in the system will lessen in the future, with a more explicit link between contributions and benefits (something of which Beveridge would have approved). The losers in this will, however, be those without steady earnings patterns, particularly women.

Finally, Bettina Cass and John Freeland look at social security in

Australia from the perspective given by Beveridge's second great report, *Full Employment in a Free Society*, full employment being one of the three key 'assumptions' on which the 1942 report was based, and which underlay the postwar 'Keynesian settlement' in both Britain and Australia. They trace the development of the Australian welfare state in relation both to the labour market and the wider economy, and to the political process. In contrast to the contribution-based social insurance models of either Beveridge or Bismarck, the Australian model is based on tax-financed social assistance and minimum wages. Recent analyses have stressed that it is misleading to characterize this as a straightforward 'liberal' regime. However, the authors conclude that the alternative, 'radical redistributive', characterization does not fully capture the distinctiveness of the model which has emerged from the alliances that have shaped Australian public policies. Rather, the two characterizations represent the ideological boundaries within which current arrangements are being contested.

What, then, are we to make of Beveridge's legacy, fifty years on? As the chapters of this book make clear, it is crucial to distinguish between Beveridge's vision and the rhetoric with which it was expressed, and the practical details of his proposals.

The vision, of adequate universal coverage defeating the giant Want, was one which captured the imagination of the public in Britain and of reformers abroad. However, what has actually evolved in Britain neither matches Beveridge's blueprint, nor meets that vision. It is true that British social security still bears the traces of the 1942 report in many of the more obscure provisions of contribution conditions and the like. But with many of the contingencies which cause poverty today not catered for by National Insurance, and with a radically different labour market from that of fifty— or even twenty—years ago, it can hardly be claimed that the national insurance system meets Beveridge's aim of covering all normal needs without recourse to a means-test—as is witnessed by the more than eight million people receiving means-tested Income Support in 1992.

Abroad, the model of non-means-tested flat-rate insurance benefits has not become the norm; still less has the model of flat-rate contributions. But it is from abroad, in the shape of the European Community, that the debate has returned to the Report's most lasting contribution—its concern with a national minimum. If, as envisaged by the Social Chapter of the Maastricht Treaty, Community countries are to ensure a minimum income for their citizens, how is this to be done? In one direction lies a means-tested safety net as exemplified by British Income Support. In another lie alternative non-means-tested ways of ensuring a national minimum (Atkinson 1993). The resolution of this debate may determine whether Beveridge's ideas will be thought to be relevant in another fifty years' time.

REFERENCES

Atkinson, A. B. (1993), 'Beveridge, the National Minimum, and its Future in a European Context', Welfare State Programme Discussion Paper WSP/85. London: LSE.

Baldwin, S., and Falkingham, J. (eds.) (forthcoming), *Social Security and Social Change: New Challenges to the Beveridge Model*. Hemel Hempstead: Harvester Wheatsheaf.

Rowntree, S. (1941), *Poverty and Progress: A Second Survey of York*. London: Longmans, Green.

UK
N44
H55

2

The Beveridge Report:
Its Origins and Outcomes

BRIAN ABEL-SMITH

In the middle of the Second World War, during the period when Britain was left alone to fight Hitler's Germany, the Beveridge Report was published. It was seen by many throughout the world as the dawning of a new age to replace the prewar horrors of mass unemployment, inability to afford health care and poverty in sickness, widowhood and old age. The language was confident and grandiloquent:

The plan for social security is put forward as part of a general programme of social policy. It is one part only of an attack upon five giant evils: upon the physical Want with which it is directly concerned, upon Disease which often causes Want and brings many other troubles in its train, upon Ignorance which no democracy can afford among its citizens, upon Squalor which arises mainly through the haphazard distribution of industry and population, and upon Idleness which destroys wealth and corrupts men ... (Beveridge 1942: 170).

The proposals in the report are concerned not with increasing the wealth of the British people, but with so distributing whatever wealth is available to them in total, as to deal first with first things, with essential physical needs .... The object of government in peace and in war is not the glory of rulers or of races, but the happiness of the common man .... The purpose of victory is to live into a better world than the old world. (Beveridge 1942: 171)

Such was the message transmitted throughout the world. The fact that the report was in many ways flawed and failed to live up to its promises was not at that stage the important point. It was the statement of intent which was heard and understood by people crouching over their radios to hear the BBC throughout occupied Europe, by British armed forces throughout the world, and by those manning the munition factories at home. According to the British ambassador in Washington it was 'the most effective British propaganda for US consumption'. It showed 'the everlasting stamina of the British people' (Chapman 1991: 148), not that they were going communist, which might have been the reaction some ten years later. Even the Germans feared the Report and ordered their press to avoid mentioning it (Chapman 1991: 64; see also Chapter 9).

Though Beveridge himself never used the term, the idea of the 'Welfare State' was to become the stock-in-trade of many politicians courting popularity throughout the world, and even of military dictators. Social policy reformers in other countries were inspired by whichever underlying themes seemed most appropriate to their own countries. One major theme was that social security could be stretched to cover everyone, not just those in regular employment; and many ingenious devices have been put in place since to approach this ideal. Another was that there were economies and greater equity in unifying social security funds—an idea which influenced France, though it was never fully put into practice. A third was that health care could be made the right of all citizens, a principle now put into practice in Scandinavia and five of the twelve countries of the European Community, with a sixth to follow in 1994, and others already very near 100 per cent coverage. A fourth was the idea of an active labour market policy to combat unemployment—no longer as fashionable as it once was. A fifth was the idea of a national minimum income, which is now part of the European Community's social charter.[1]

Thus the Beveridge Report was an important international testament, not perhaps for what it actually did for Britain, but for what it said could be done by governments throughout the developed world. The occasion where this chapter was first presented, when so many people from all over the world gathered in York, the site of pioneering studies of poverty, to commemorate the anniversary of Beveridge's famous Report, was long enough afterwards to tell the story as it really happened. For things were not quite what they may have appeared to have been to the world outside.

The chapters that follow deal with the detail of what Beveridge was proposing. My task is simply to set the context for the discussion by giving, in a brief sketch, the answers to a number of obvious questions. Who was Beveridge? How did he come to write his Report? What was expected of him compared with what he did? How far did the Report actually fulfil his planned objectives? And what happened to his Report in practice?

WHO WAS BEVERIDGE?

Beveridge's life is admirably described in the biography by Jose Harris (1977). The son of a British judge in India, Beveridge got his degree at Oxford in mathematics and classical studies, and then studied social conditions in the poor eastern part of London at Toynbee Hall, a foundation to do social

---

[1] 'Persons who have been unable to enter or re-enter the labour market and have no means of subsistence must be able to receive sufficient resources and social assistance in keeping with their particular situation' (Commission of the European Communities 1989: cl. 10).

work and befriend the poor. He then became a journalist on a quality newspaper, where he propounded the solutions to unemployment of labour exchanges and unemployment insurance; and from there he was brought into government as a civil servant working for Winston Churchill, then Minister responsible for Trade, to help put his ideas into action. Thus he played a major part in introducing the first statutory scheme of unemployment insurance in the world in 1911. During the First World War he worked as a civil servant on manpower mobilization for the War, and later as the head civil servant in charge of the new Ministry of Food responsible for the rationing programme.

After the War he accepted the post as Director of the London School of Economics, where his energy and fund-raising skills enormously expanded that institution, and thus the role of the social sciences in Britain. Among his academic staff were Clement Attlee, to become in 1945 the Labour Prime Minister who introduced the Beveridge plan with important modifications; and Hugh Dalton, who served as Chancellor of the Exchequer in the same government. He then moved on to become Master of one of the Colleges at Oxford, and during the Second World War found his way back to the Ministry of Labour where Ernest Bevin, previously secretary of the largest trade union, became the Minister in Churchill's coalition government. There Beveridge was not slow in pushing for the *dirigiste* policies he had favoured in the previous War, showering the Minister with unsolicited memoranda.

Though at times attracted by socialism, he never joined the Labour Party or became a Fabian. Throughout his life he remained a liberal in politics. His thinking went through major changes at different periods of his life. He developed strong beliefs in central control and planning in each of the World Wars; but between them he was much more inclined to leave the market to do its own work.

He did not, however, abandon his interest in social security after helping to pioneer unemployment insurance. In 1924 he produced rather hastily for the Liberal Party a pamphlet called *Insurance for All and Everything* which had within it the germ of his later Report. He favoured the unification of social insurance contributions, but only envisaged modest benefits below subsistence level, as a threshold for voluntary saving. There was no mention of family allowances and little concern about unemployment. Despite the *All* in the title, it was a scheme to be confined to people below a certain income level. From 1934 he became part-time chairman of the Unemployment Insurance Statutory Committee, established to advise the Minister and to suggest changes in the level of benefits and contribution which would maintain the solvency of the Unemployment Insurance Fund. This task gave him an intimate knowledge of the current working of this scheme.

Beveridge married for the first time eighteen days after his famous Report was published. His wife had been a life-long friend and partner, working closely with him from the LSE to University College, Oxford, where she moved into his home 'outraging the lady censors of the university world' (Harris 1977: 362). He did not marry Mrs Mair until her first husband, Beveridge's cousin, had died. His arrogant personality and autocratic style of leadership did not go down well either in the civil service or the LSE, where his staff were seldom consulted on his decisions. Mrs Mair was an even less popular figure in either of his university jobs.

THE ORIGIN OF THE REPORT

The committee was set up in response to complaints by the trade unions in February and March 1941 about the bewildering variety of different provisions for sickness and disability, and their relationship to other social security provisions, and a request for a properly balanced scheme for the insured person (Chapman 1991: 6). Each benefit had grown up on a separate basis. There were three different and mutually exclusive benefits for unemployment, and three different types of pension for old age. Sickness benefits were provided to insured persons only by non-profit insurers, the so called 'approved societies' who could add additional benefits to the minimum if money was available; there were different schemes for the blind and for the disabled, and a scheme had been superimposed for civilians injured by enemy bombing. Provision for industrial injuries was through private profit-making insurers who tried to buy off their claimants with inadequate lump sums, and it required legal proceedings to try and get a square deal—the so called 'forensic lottery' (Ison 1967). The benefits and pensions were at different rates and some made provision for dependants and others did not. Seven different government departments were involved in these complex arrangements.

In the middle of the War it was important for the Government to make some concessions to the trade unions. A small increase in sickness and disability benefits was announced, and a promise made to introduce an enquiry which would lead to reform after the War. The Treasury, fearing an expenditure commitment, wanted the committee kept secret, but the trade unions had only accepted the small concession on benefits because of the promise of an enquiry which their members would need to see announced in public (Chapman 1991: 39). The Treasury fought to see that the terms of reference of the enquiry were kept as narrow as possible. They were:

to undertake, with special reference to the inter-relation of the schemes, a survey of the existing national schemes of social insurance and allied services, including workmen's compensation, and to make recommendations. (Beveridge 1942: 5)

In other words it was intended (at least by the Treasury) to be a 'tidying-up operation', not a complete review (Harris 1977: 386). According to a senior Treasury civil servant, the terms of reference were 'as harmless as they can be made'. For this purpose the committee members, other than the chairman, were to consist only of civil servants. Most of them were the middle-level civil servants dealing with the various schemes with, of course, an added Treasury watchdog. The Treasury wanted as a 'safe' chairman Sir Hector Hetherington, who had started a review of workmen's compensation which was wound up at the start of the war. Ernest Bevin, Beveridge's Minister, was at first against any enquiry at all, until the idea was put to him of making Beveridge its chairman; and he then favoured the enquiry as a way of getting the pushy Beveridge at last out of his Ministry (Harris 1977: 376). In this way the Government unknowingly released what the Treasury was to find later on was a formidable bombshell. Such was the strange and inauspicious origin of what was to become a world-famous report.

Beveridge realized that he was being sidetracked from the war effort and accepted his appointment with tears in his eyes (Harris 1977: 376). The omnipresent Mrs Mair claims to have talked him round to believe that this was a 'heaven-sent opportunity' to bring his work of forty years to a triumphant conclusion (Beveridge 1954: 106).

THE WORK OF THE COMMITTEE

The committee was set up in June 1941. For the first six months Beveridge was busy with other tasks, while the civil servants prepared memoranda on the existing schemes and outside evidence was awaited. But in December 1941, after receiving only one of the 127 pieces of written evidence which the committee was to receive, Beveridge prepared and circulated a long paper which contained the essence of the final Report. The various schemes were to be unified, with flat-rate benefits raised to subsistence level and continued while the contingency generating entitlement, including sickness and unemployment, lasted. Unification meant the end of the role of the approved societies in sickness insurance. Benefits were to be paid for by flat-rate contributions divided between employers, the insured, and the state. Virtually the whole population would be covered compulsorily, and the means test would be abolished for all who could be covered by contributions. Unification was not just to apply to National Insurance, but to Social Assistance as well. No longer would any of the task of providing income to the poor be left to local authorities. Instead this function would become the responsibility of a central government agency, which would become a residual safety net.

Included in the paper were the three assumptions which stretched the terms of reference to the limit: family allowances, a free health service available to all, and full employment (Chapman 1991: 42). Beveridge by this time had come to see family allowances as essential above all else to preserve incentives to work, by making a gap between low earnings and benefits if the latter were to be raised to subsistence level. This was a key point which Beveridge had come to appreciate during his work monitoring unemployment benefit. A free health service was needed to prevent medical bills eroding subsistence; and full employment was essential if the insurance basis of the scheme were to be protected.

The Treasury watchdog reported these vast public expenditure commitments (calculated to double public spending on social security) to his Minister, and Beveridge was asked to withdraw his three assumptions. This, to his credit, he refused to do. He was then curtly told that the Report would be signed by him alone, and the civil servants would not be associated with its recommendations (Chapman 1991: 44). This decision rebounded on the Treasury as he now had no need to pay much attention to the views of the other members of the Committee. However, this does not mean that none of them sympathized with his aims: both the Home Office representative and the Ministry of Health representative pointed out in their memoranda the many failings of the schemes they were administering.

Much of the evidence, which came later, did in fact support Beveridge's general approach; and as Chairman he made no secret of his own views in interviewing witnesses which inevitably led to press reports about what was likely to emerge. He took great trouble to bring the trade unions round to his precise position, and in this he succeeded, except in the case of workmen's compensation. Further broad hints of what was in his mind came in his broadcasts and articles in the press. All this broke with convention as public opinion knew largely what was in the offing before the government was in a position to consider it. This did not win him friends among the Ministers.

Perhaps the most important recommendation was that both benefits and contributions should be flat-rate. The alternative of benefits related to earnings was put to the committee by the International Labour Office, but was brushed aside by Beveridge as being damaging to personal saving. The idea of flat-rate benefits paid for by earnings-related contributions was also put to him both by the approved societies and the research body PEP, but he also discarded this approach as breaking the essential link between contributions and benefit. Flat-rate benefits and contributions were therefore recommended, rather than the Bismarckian alternative. This was partly because this was how National Insurance had developed in Britain, following voluntary health insurance, in which it was impractical to relate contributions to earnings as the employer did not contribute. But it was also because Beveridge, the liberal, wanted the maximum scope for private provision above his minimum.

The most expensive recommendation, however, was that benefits should be raised to subsistence level and include family allowances. The litmus test of social security had come to be seen as how far it reduced poverty, not how far it maintained the standards of living of the worker as on most of the Continent. By this time poverty research in Britain had grown into a major industry, with enquiries conducted over the previous fifty years in London, Liverpool, Sheffield, Plymouth, Southampton, York, and Bristol. To define subsistence Beveridge drew on this expertise and appointed a subcommittee consisting of York's poverty researcher Seebohm Rowntree, Bowley the statistician, and a doctor and nutritionist from the British Medical Association. The definition of subsistence which they produced was not generous. While there was a margin for 'inefficient spending', nothing was allowed for beer, tobacco, newspapers, books, or the cinema (Chapman 1991: 76). But the real difficulty with flat-rate subsistence benefits was that rents varied widely. A benefit purporting to be at subsistence level would be unnecessarily high for some families with low rents and not high enough for other families with higher rents. Rowntree suggested that a subsistence level might be given in the form of a flat-rate benefit plus actual rent, but this was eventually ruled out by Beveridge as infecting the scheme with the taint of a means test. A two-tier scheme, paid for by earnings-related contributions, consisting of a flat rate plus an earnings-related element, could have eliminated more poverty than a flat rate alone. But this did not fit Beveridge's preconceptions.

The second key issue was how to cover nearly everyone and make the scheme comprehensive, as he claimed it would be in a scheme firmly based on insurance. In the attempt to do this, married women were given a bad deal. He did not expect the wartime trend for married women to take paid work to continue after the war, and refused to recommend that married women should be put on the same footing as men, since the vast majority were, or perhaps should be, dependent on their husbands. Those who did work after marriage were to be given 'special treatment'. They were to lose on marriage whatever entitlement they had earned to the full rate of sickness and unemployment benefit, and only receive about 75 per cent of the usual rate. They were to be denied dependency additions for their husbands unless the husband was incapable of self-support. Their pensions as a result of marriage were to be cut to about 60 per cent of the rate paid to men or single women. Thus their own contributions could only earn them a further 40 per cent of the male rate. And they were to be given an option not to contribute at all, which was to seem the more sensible option to most married women, in view of the bad deal they would get by contributing and the uncertainty of whether they would in fact earn the extra 40 per cent of the usual rate (Abel-Smith 1983). And, surprisingly, he did not question the decision that women could draw their pensions at 60 while men had to wait until 65. This had been introduced only two years earlier as a 'cheap dodge' to ward off a demand by the trade unions for higher pensions (Walley 1972: 69).

Other groups who could not be fitted into an insurance scheme were deserted and separated wives, and unmarried mothers, where Beveridge finally admitted defeat. One-parent families were to grow rapidly in the years to come. An additional worry were spinsters caring for aged parents—the so called 'domestic spinster'. The further problems of school-leavers, those disabled before working age, and women re-entering the labour force were not given any special attention.

In March 1942, Beveridge wrote to Maynard Keynes, now installed in the Treasury, asking for his advice on the financing of the scheme. Keynes immediately became an enthusiastic supporter. So did Lionel Robbins, another distinguished academic economist, at this time temporarily installed at the Economic Section of the Offices of the War Cabinet. Keynes calculated that if Beveridge could cut £100 million off the cost of pensions he would have 'a pretty plausible tale to tell'. The top of the Treasury, however, considered the draft plan 'a political broadsheet', the sentence 'A revolutionary moment in the world's history is a time for revolution' particularly raising official eyebrows (Chapman 1991: 55); and a series of recriminatory notes passed between the top of the Treasury and the Economic Section.

After a series of behind-the-scenes negotiations with Keynes, Beveridge compromised by agreeing to omit the first child from family allowances and to postpone full subsistence pensions for the aged for twenty years with moves towards this level in a series of steps every two years. With these key amendments the Report was completed.

Despite these concessions the Treasury as a whole was far from being appeased. Nor was Churchill, who was irritated by the press leaks of what was in the Report. In his view nothing should be done until after the War and a general election (Harris 1977: 424); if he had been able to have his way he would have stopped publication (Bullock 1967: 62), but this was impossible in view of the undertakings given earlier. At first the War Cabinet refused to allow Beveridge facilities to publicize his report, but at the last moment there was a change of heart, which was reversed after a few days, during which the damage had been done.

THE RECEPTION OF THE REPORT

The report was finally published, then, on 2 December 1942. Its reception was euphoric. There was said to be a queue a mile long at the government bookshop (Beveridge 1954: 114). Some half a million copies were sold: quite unprecedented for a technical government publication of this kind which ran to nearly three hundred closely-printed pages. About fifty thousand copies sold in the United States (Harris 1977: 427–8). The reception in the press was rapturous; Beveridge became photographed wherever he went (Beveridge 1954: 118). Churchill, the Treasury, and many Ministers had failed to realize how far public opinion had moved in the three years of the War.

Many reasons can be given for the sea change in public opinion. The high taxation to pay for the War, full employment, and rationing had brought a much greater degree of equality of income. All social classes had had to share the same air raid shelters. Some hundred thousand persons had been killed or seriously injured by Nazi bombs (Chapman 1991: 31). Some eight million persons were in the armed forces, the Home Guard or Civil Defence. And the patriotic fervour of the War to which all contributed had created a new sense of 'equality of sacrifice' and 'fair shares' for all citizens.

Moreover, policy developments had not stood still while the Beveridge Committee was sitting. The Treasury had been forced by parliamentary pressure to publish a paper on family allowances. And in June 1942, a resolution favouring family allowances was carried by a large majority in the House of Commons. As a result the Chancellor of the Exchequer had conceded in June 1942 that family allowances would be introduced if the trade unions favoured it, Beveridge recommended it, and the economic situation permitted it (Macnicol 1980: 181). The first of these conditions was met in September of the same year.

Secondly, during the first four years of the War, free care in hospital was extended from air-raid casualties and servicemen to munition workers, certain chronic sick, and eventually to all manual workers in the industries of wartime Britain and others waiting for hospital care. It proved impossible to draw a line between those who were and those who were not contributing to the war effort. In October 1941 the government announced that after the War there would be 'a comprehensive hospital service' for all who needed it.[2] Thus by the time his report was published, Beveridge was giving no more than a push forward to a movement which had its own momentum, not least through pressure from the medical profession.

---

[2] House of Commons, *Official Report* (Hansard), 9 Oct. 1941, col. 1116.

THE GOVERNMENT'S RESPONSE

These developments did not mean that the Beveridge report was to have an easy passage in Whitehall. After publication a committee of civil servants was established to study it and make recommendations to the Government. This committee proposed to cut the level of family allowances by 37.5 per cent so it would not 'pretend to be a subsistence rate', justifying this by the addition of services in kind whose value was known not to make up the difference (Macnicol 1980: 189). The report of the committee also tended to favour an income test for these allowances. On the other benefits, it pointed out that a universal scheme involved giving money to many people who did not need it. Subsistence pensions for the aged were not needed, as pensioners had had time to save (Chapman 1991: 83). It opposed the idea of unemployment benefits continuing while unemployment lasted. The Treasury put its own memorandum to the Cabinet arguing that the report could not be afforded, though this was challenged by the Economic Section of the War Cabinet behind the scenes.

As a result of pressure from Mr Bevin, long an advocate of decent pensions for the aged, the idea of increasing pensions over twenty years was rejected when the report of the civil servants was considered by the Cabinet. He also opposed the indefinite payment of unemployment benefit. It was decided by the Cabinet not to give support to the key subsistence principle, or to commit the government to legislation during that parliament to implement any of the recommendations. But the presentation of the government's position in Parliament seemed so negative that 121 members voted against the government and many more abstained. There was thus a serious risk of the breakup of the coalition Government in the middle of the war over the attitude to be taken to the Beveridge Report. The senior politicians in the Government had in fact been upstaged by Beveridge, and they never forgave him. Churchill was 'reported to have taken strong exception to the Report, to have refused to see its author and forbidden any government department to allow him inside its doors' (Bullock 1967: 226).

Within a week the Government had reversed its position and accepted that there could be legislation during the war. In a broadcast four weeks later Churchill himself seemed to come out in favour of the Report in principle. 'The time is now ripe', he said, 'for another great advance, and anyone can see what large savings there will be in the administration once the whole process of insurance has become unified, compulsory, and national' (Churchill 1944: 181). This resolved the political crisis, but the wording carefully made no commitment to abolish want.

Detailed plans were prepared and published in 1944 with the War still in progress, for a national health service, for family allowances, and for national health insurance. The Government, however, still refused to accept the subsistence principle. Though the proposed rates for sickness and unemployment benefits were those recommended by Beveridge, they had by then been overtaken by rising prices. The proposed rates of pension for the aged were lower than the rates for sickness and unemployment. The other amendments to Beveridge agreed by Cabinet soon after the Report was published were still retained. The Government's proposals were this time well-received in Parliament. Few criticized the failure to implement the subsistence principle. Those who did included Beveridge himself, elected to Parliament in 1944 as a Liberal.

IMPLEMENTATION

The actual implementation of the Report fell to the Labour Government elected after the war. The rates of benefits and pensions were unified at a slightly higher level than the sickness and unemployment benefits proposed by the coalition Government. The Government told the House of Commons that these rates of benefit could be 'justified broadly in relation to the present cost of living.... I believe we have in this way endeavoured to give a broad subsistence basis to the leading rates'.[3] No doubt many Members of Parliament assumed that the principle of subsistence benefits was being implemented.

But the actual rates chosen were about 31 per cent above those recommended by Beveridge in 1938 prices. This was in line with the rise in the cost of living index, and the Government had undertaken to keep it at this level; but the index measuring the cost of living had been fiddled by both governments. The prices of sub-items which figured in the index were held down, while comparable items were allowed to increase in price. By the time the full scheme was introduced in 1948, wages had risen by 76 per cent and prices had in fact risen by 72 per cent which meant that the benefit rates were nearly a third below what Beveridge had recommended as necessary for subsistence (Abel-Smith 1953: 3). Moreover, the index used understated the increase in prices for those living on a low income. And there was no provision for indexing benefit levels: they were to be adjusted every five years. More important, they were only just above the level of social assistance payments to which those applying for assistance normally had their full actual rent added. This attracted little attention at the time; but it has remained more or less the case ever since. In so far as freedom from want is attained in Britain, it is by undergoing a means test, not through National Insurance. Beveridge's residual safety net has grown to

---

[3] House of Commons, *Official Report* (Hansard), 6 Feb. 1946, cols. 1741–2.

become the key agency providing ultimate protection to over eight million persons. Paradoxically, an important achievement of the Beveridge Report was to establish a right to a means-tested minimum income for those not at work (other than dependent wives) which the European Commission is in the process of trying to get introduced in those member states which do not have it.

In retrospect, Beveridge had been unwise to chase the hare of subsistence by academic enquiry. If, instead, he had focused his recommendation on bringing benefits up to the level used for social assistance, plus a generous allowance for rent, he would have given governments less chance of fudging the key subsistence issue later on. This point had been put to him by the Assistance Board in its evidence to his enquiry. 'If benefit rates do not, in the great majority of cases, at least approximate to the corresponding assistance rates (which in the nature of things must be true subsistence payments), there is a risk of supplementation of benefit by way of assistance occurring on a scale which may undermine public confidence in the insurance scheme' (Chapman 1991: 81). Beveridge had failed to take notice of these prophetic words. He would have done well to study and consider more carefully some of the evidence he was given.

REFLECTIONS

How does one sum up this history of the British experience? Some would argue that the Treasury had been right all along. No government could have afforded subsistence benefits immediately after the War on top of the need to build houses, extend education, and give free health care to all, which cost much more than even the Treasury had estimated during the war (Abel-Smith and Titmuss 1956: 2). Others might argue that this history shows that it is really the Treasury civil servants who rule Britain, whatever the government. A further view, however, might be that Beveridge missed the opportunity to build up a strong and wide constituency for social security, such as is to be found on the Continent, by continuing contributions and benefits on a wholly flat-rate basis. Certainly his flat-rate contributions lasted for only thirteen years, when earnings-related contributions started to be introduced. But his flat-rate benefits left room for massive supplementation by sick pay and occupational pensions. Thus, for most of the middle classes, social security became only a small and almost unnoticed top-up to their major provision, which came through tax-subsidized employers' schemes or private insurance.

The fact remains that Beveridge did make a major contribution to world thinking about social security by setting out a bold, comprehensive, and integrated strategy. For this we are right to commemorate the publication, fifty years ago, of a report which perhaps influenced events more outside than inside Britain.

REFERENCES

Abel-Smith, B. (1953), *The Reform of Social Security*, Fabian Society Research Series 161. London: Fabian Publications.
—— (1983), 'Sex, Equality and Social Security', in J. Lewis (ed.), *Women's Welfare and Women's Rights*. London: Croom Helm.
—— and Titmuss, R. M. (1956), *The Cost of the National Health Service in England and Wales*. Cambridge: Cambridge University Press.
Beveridge, J. (1954), *Beveridge and His Plan*. London: Hodder and Stoughton.
Beveridge, W. H. (1924), *Insurance for All and Everything*. London: Daily News.
—— (1942), *Social Insurance and Allied Services*, Cmd. 6404. London: HMSO.
Bullock, A. (1967), *The Life and Times of Ernest Bevin*, ii: *Minister of Labour*. London: Heinemann.
Chapman, R. P. (1991), 'The Development of Policy on Family Allowances and National Insurance in the United Kingdom'. M.Phil. thesis, London.
Churchill, W. S. (1944), *Onwards to Victory: War Speeches by the Right Hon. Winston S. Churchill, CH, MP*. London: Cassell.
Commission of the European Communities (1989), *Community Charter of the Fundamental Rights of Workers*. Brussels: CEC.
Harris, J. (1977), *William Beveridge: A Biography*. Oxford: Clarendon Press.
Ison, T. G. (1967), *The Forensic Lottery: A Critique on Tort Liability as a System of Personal Injury Compensation*. London: Staples Press.
Macnicol, J. (1980), *The Movement for Family Allowances 1918–1945*. London: Heinemann.
Walley, J. (1972), *Social Security: Another British Failure?* London: Charles Knight.

3

Beveridge's Social and Political Thought

JOSE HARRIS

[handwritten: (Sir) William Beveridge B31]

When I first began to think about what I might say in the lecture on which this chapter is based, I mentioned to a class of undergraduates that I was taking part in various anniversary celebrations for Beveridge and his report: and it was obvious that most of them were politely puzzled about who Beveridge actually was. It turned out that two had never heard of Beveridge at all: the rest were divided between those who thought he had passed the 1944 Education Act, and those who thought that he had personally introduced the National Health Service. All of them believed that he had been a minister in the Labour Government of 1945.

I assume that none of this confusion is shared by those reading this chapter, and that readers are broadly familiar with the main landmarks of Beveridge's public career: as a young man down from Balliol, Beveridge served an apprenticeship in the study of social problems with Canon Barnett at Toynbee Hall; he helped Winston Churchill to found the first labour exchanges and unemployment insurance; during the First World War he became the youngest-ever permanent secretary of a Whitehall department; from 1919 to 1937 he was the director of the London School of Economics in its stormy golden age; above all, he was the author of the Beveridge Plan of 1942—a document still widely regarded as the Magna Carta of the British welfare state. Readers may also know something of Beveridge's personality and character—his reputation for intolerable rudeness and irascibility towards his peers, combined with immense kindness, generosity, and capacity to inspire devotion among his juniors and subordinates; his high-handed mandarin autocracy in administrative affairs, combined with a quite unexpected, almost uncanny, knack of mass communication with the ordinary public.

In this chapter, however, I am not going to set out the details of Beveridge's public life, nor will I attempt to conjure up the endless idiosyncrasies of his complex and stormy personal character. I want instead to analyse and pin down some of the main characteristics and contours of Beveridge's public doctrine. I want to look at his ideas in the Beveridge Plan in the context of his wider views on state, society, economy, efficiency,

gender, psychology, and personal freedom. As will become clear, I do not
want in any sense to claim that Beveridge was a great systematic political
theorist after the manner of Bentham or Hobbes. But I do want to suggest
that a precise understanding of the nature and content of Beveridge's
political thought is quite important: it is important because of the almost
mythic status that Beveridge has acquired, for good or ill, as the fountain-
head of much of our fundamental thinking about modern social welfare.
At the 1992 congress of the International Social Security Association in
York, where more than 500 people came together from many countries to
mark the achievements of Beveridge, it was apparent that he was widely
regarded as a kind of international version of Rousseau's divine lawgiver—
as an inspired and charismatic figure who had flown in from space during
the early days of the welfare state and carved its fundamental principles on
tablets of stone, before mysteriously disappearing to another planet. Such
prophets are notoriously dishonoured in their own countries: but even in
hero-despising modern Britain Beveridge constantly crops up in the discourse of both right and left in a wide variety of semi-mythical guises—in
accounts that have nothing in common except the assumption that Beveridge
and his report are still somehow fundamentally important to 'the way we
live now'. This is true not only of those who see Beveridge as the founding
father and patron saint of our social system, but of those who see him as
its demonic evil genius. One hears, for instance, from certain critics on the
right like Correlli Barnett the claim that Beveridge was a sinister and
sentimental political idealist, whose grandiose vision of state abolition of
poverty and unemployment was directly responsible for Britain's postwar
economic decline and for the corruption of the mass of the British people
into a 'segregated, sub-literate, unskilled, unhealthy and institutionalized
proletariat hanging on the nipple of state maternalism' (Barnett 1986: 304).
But equally one hears from others who claim to have been close to Margaret
Thatcher that her guiding principle in social policy was to cure the evils of
the modern welfare state by a systematic slimming diet of 'return to
Beveridge' (Harris 1992). Similarly, one hears on the left much talk about
reversing the decline of the welfare state by a return to the more generous,
universalist, and socially sharing 'spirit of Beveridge'. And yet one also
hears innumerable complaints from leftish academics that Beveridge and
his report were full of flaws and inadequacies: inadequacies that are
perceived to range from Beveridge's very spartan definition of subsistence-
level poverty, his obstinate attachment to regressive flat-rate insurance, his
recessive and patriarchal conception of women—through to the claim that
the Beveridge Plan from its outset was never designed to do any more than
to thwart and ward off radical social change by propping up inequality,
individualism, and competitive market capitalism (Cutler *et al.* 1986; Melling
1991; Veit-Wilson 1992).

Such controversies bear witness to (if nothing else) the lasting potency of the legend of Beveridge. Yet both historians like myself, who wish to understand the past, and practical citizens, concerned with the urgent plight of modern society, want to know a little more than this—we want to know which, if any, of these differing accounts are 'true'. Would a back-to-Beveridge system, if such were conceivable, mean a return to a much more basic and limited welfare system than the one we have now; or would it mean a return to one that was much more generous, egalitarian and comprehensive? Did Beveridgism mean frugality and economy in public expenditure, or profligate extravagance? Did the Beveridge Plan, as some appear to believe, 'save capitalism', or did it, as others claim, give capitalism the kiss of death? If the principles of Beveridge are indeed the stone tablets of the modern welfare state, both here and in other parts of the world— then let us read precisely what is written upon those stone tablets before we decide whether we should, or indeed whether we can, choose in some way to 'return' to them.

Before I analyse Beveridge's thought in detail, I want to make a few initial points about Beveridge's general intellectual outlook. The first of these points is that there was no single great thinker, no paramount influence in Beveridge's intellectual life, by reference to whom his ideas about politics and welfare can be explained and decoded. By this I mean that there was no unique influence in Beveridge's life comparable with, say, Jeremy Bentham's influence on Edwin Chadwick, R. H. Tawney's influence upon Richard Titmuss, or F. A. Hayek's influence on the modern radical right. On the contrary, throughout his life Beveridge's frame of reference was a highly idiosyncratic and eclectic one. There are references and resonances in his writings—often simultaneously and inconsistently—to such diverse theorists as Plato and Comte, Sir Henry Maine and T. H. Green, Marx and Mill (and, indeed, to Bentham, Tawney, and Hayek), but there is little evidence of Beveridge ever using their ideas in any systematic way, rather than as a rhetorical magpie looking for picturesque similes to illustrate and reinforce his own preconceptions. The sole thinker of any stature to whom Beveridge paid more than lasting tribute was the Victorian biologist T. H. Huxley; and many of the lurking tensions in Beveridge's political thought may perhaps be heard as an echo of Huxley's famous Romanes lecture of 1893, which warned that social and moral progress might at some stage prove to be in fundamental conflict with biological efficiency and survival (Huxley 1894). But Beveridge was in no sense a personal disciple of Huxley; and Huxley's practical influence was most clearly apparent, not in Beveridge's theories of welfare, but in his approach to the methodology of social research—in his belief that the processes of discovering and analysing social facts were identical to those of investigation in geology and biology (Harris 1977: 42–3; 284–7).

The second preliminary point I want to make is that never at any time in his life, not even in 1942, did Beveridge view himself primarily as an expert on what is commonly thought of as 'social welfare'. Rather he saw himself as an all-round political economist in the old-fashioned sense of that term—as someone who was going to promote individual and collective welfare, not by purposive acts of policy, but by the discovery and enforcement of regular and universally valid socio-economic laws. Once such laws had been discovered, he believed that the day would come when rational individuals and governments would be able merely to observe those laws, with the result that such devices as state insurance or poor law schemes would become unnecessary—they, and the whole structure of remedial social administration, would simply wither away. Such, he hoped, would be the outcome of his famous history of prices from the twelfth to the twentieth century—a project which was designed to reveal the hidden causes of inflation, unemployment, collapse of credit, and all other forms of economic dislocation—and to his dying day Beveridge believed that it was his history of prices rather than his report on social insurance which would in the long term prove to be his main contribution to the understanding and betterment of the modern world (Harris 1977: 468).

Beveridge's obsession with understanding money and prices seems perhaps rather less eccentric in the 1990s than it appeared to many of his contemporaries between the two world wars. Nevertheless, I think most people would agree that it is in his role as a 'social reformer' that Beveridge's interest mainly lies; and it is to his thinking on social welfare policy that I want now to turn. There is a fairly familiar, and in my view erroneous, folklore image of Beveridge's place in the history of social policy (a stereotype which, I confess with some annoyance and chagrin, all my careful work in the archives has singularly failed to dislodge). He is still viewed as a fairly straightforward and orthodox reformist liberal, whose ideas in the Beveridge Report developed in a logical progression from his career as a social worker at Toynbee Hall forty years before; and he is often portrayed as personally embodying the half-way house between individualism and collectivism supposedly characteristic of the welfare state—as one of the twin icons, along with J. M. Keynes, of the 'middle ground' and the 'mixed economy' (Addison 1975; Williams and Williams 1987; Melling 1991). In reality, Beveridge's views on politics and welfare were much more complex and variable than this view would suggest. In my biography of Beveridge I suggested that his underlying philosophy might be divided up into three chronological phases: phases that were in many respects quite distinct from and contradictory with each other. To confuse these three phases seems to me potentially highly misleading, and at least partly explains why polemicists in all quarters are able to mobilize Beveridge as a witness for the defence or prosecution on so many different issues.

The first major phase in Beveridge's political thought covered the Edwardian period and lasted until the end of the First World War, and was more or less in tune with the widespread reformist optimism of the prewar era. During that early period Beveridge believed in far-reaching bureaucratic intervention in many spheres of the nation's social life, without any fundamental structural modification of private enterprise and the free market economy. Indeed, during this early period most of his social policy proposals were quite specifically designed to use state intervention to make the market economy work more smoothly and efficiently; goals that were very clearly spelt out in his pioneering study of *Unemployment: A Problem of Industry* (1909). Thus his policies for the decasualization of dock labour and the wartime dilution of skilled engineering labour were meant to deploy the resources of the labour force more rationally and productively than the somewhat sticky cake of Edwardian industrial custom would allow. Contributory unemployment insurance as introduced in the National Insurance Act of 1911 was designed not merely to relieve poverty but to prevent physical and psychological deterioration among valuable skilled workers during periods of recession. And labour bureaux and employment exchanges were meant to embody in concrete institutional form the nineteenth-century economists' ideal of a perfectly mobile, fully informed, and totally rational market for labour. So 'the young Beveridge' of the Edwardian years, like the Benthamite utilitarians seventy years earlier, saw the aim of social policy as being, not so much to displace the free market, but to sweep away obstructions to the free market and to make it stronger, more effective and more rational than ever before (Harris 1977: chs. 5–10).

The second phase in Beveridge's thinking about social policy emerged at the end of the First World War, and dominated his outlook for much of the interwar years—this being also the period in which he was the director of the London School of Economics. In this second phase Beveridge did not wholly abandon his earlier faith in the reformist administrative state; but he became increasingly pessimistic about how far rational social reform was compatible with either sound public finance or popular democracy. The seeds of this second phase were sown in the aftermath of war, when, as Permanent Secretary of the Ministry of Food, Beveridge was in charge of famine relief programmes in the successor states of the Austro-Hungarian empire; and he discovered in 1919 what many have rediscovered in the 1990s, that there is nothing like a visit to a collapsing eastern Europe for converting one overnight to the virtues of sound money (Harris 1977: 245–50). From this time onwards Beveridge appeared increasingly troubled by the fear that well-meaning public philanthropy might subvert rather than strengthen economic revival; and the second edition of his book on *Unemployment*, which appeared in 1930, differed totally from the first edition by suggesting that long-term economic stability could only be secured by maintaining a fixed ratio between currency and gold (Beveridge 1930). These shifts in his economic views were paralleled by developments in his views on social welfare. During the late 1920s and early 1930s we find him referring to 'the whip of starvation' as 'a necessary precondition of economic advance'; and he was extremely pessimistic about the public works/deficit spending cure for unemployment being advanced by Keynes and Lloyd George. In the mid-1930s he made a special study for the Rockefeller Foundation of Roosevelt's New Deal legislation, and concluded that it was a 'mass of contradictions and inhibitions' which was threatening to destroy American liberal democracy (Harris 1977: 327). He appears increasingly to have believed that there were only two stark alternatives open to makers of policy: either a pure free market softened only by a residual welfare safety net, or a totally regulated economic and social system on the model of the Soviet Union. At a purely theoretical level, Beveridge was increasingly intrigued by the phenomenon of Soviet-style planning; but in a British context he was totally sceptical of the various early-1930s movements for planning, corporatism, and finding a middle way between capitalism and socialism—all of which he saw as wholly unworkable without loss of personal liberty and totalitarian enforcement. In fact, much of Beveridge's social thought during the interwar years centred upon an almost total rejection of the *via media*, mixed-economy, liberal-collectivist principles that were later to be seen as the characteristic hallmarks of 'Beveridgism' and of the British welfare state (Harris 1977: chs. 13, 14).

The third phase in Beveridge's approach to social policy came when he shifted to the view that the free market itself had in turn proved unworkable, and that not merely social but economic policy needed large-scale intervention by a centralized collectivist state. The reasons for this shift were indissolubly linked to the context of war—to Beveridge's growing belief in the late 1930s that only a planned economy could fight against Hitler—and to the actual impact of the war itself, which brought with it willy-nilly all the paraphernalia of planning, sharing, public services, and centralized command over resources that in the 1930s had appeared to him politically unthinkable. In the context of 1940, all Beveridge's earlier doubts about whether planning and state intervention were compatible with liberty and democracy simply vanished virtually overnight; and this released in him a pent-up tidal wave of intellectual energy on a vast range of social and economic questions that drove him like a daemon throughout the Second World War. It was this burst of frenzied creativity that formed the background to the famous Report on Social Insurance and Allied Services on which this book is focused. And it is on the intellectual background and content of the Beveridge Report that my reading of Beveridge most clearly deviates from much received opinion on the subject—in that, on the evidence of both public records and private archives, I do not think the conventional image of the Beveridge plan as an innocuous synthesis of progressive liberalism and administrative collectivism is wholly correct. Beveridge was writing his report for a predominantly Conservative coalition government, and he was under strong pressure from the Treasury to confine the budgetary aspects of his proposals within the very narrow limits that it was believed the postwar economy would be able to sustain. It is clear, however, from Beveridge's memoranda and private correspondence that the Social Insurance plan formed merely an iceberg tip—and in Beveridge's view perhaps the least important tip—of the very much more ambitious and far-reaching programme of social reconstruction that he had in his mind at the time. This programme—spelled out very much more fully in Beveridge's papers for Sir William Jowett's Home Affairs panel and in Beveridge's later *Full Employment in a Free Society* (1944)—went far beyond the spheres of health, insurance, and social welfare; it included such possible objectives as the nationalization of land and housing, national minimum wage legislation, public ownership of up to 75 per cent of industrial production, a public enterprise board to direct both public and private investment, and permanent state control of incomes, prices, and manpower planning. Such proposals were only hinted at in the text of *Social Insurance and Allied Services*, but they were part of the invisible undercarriage of political thought that supported Beveridge's proposals on the future of social policy throughout the Second World War.[1]

I have set out so far a very condensed and superficial account of some of the main chronological shifts in Beveridge's social and political ideas. I now want to take a slightly different approach, and to ask whether any consistent principles underlay the rather dramatically changing contours of Beveridge's thought—principles that amount to some kind of general theory or philosophy of social policy or social welfare. Beveridge as a student at Balliol had spent several years studying both classical and modern philosophy; but nevertheless he was in no sense a philosopher by vocation, nor was he even—for all his quick-witted brilliance in many spheres—a very systematic thinker; and it is in many ways much easier for the armchair historian to expose the contradictions in his thought than to piece them together into a coherent pattern. However, I think that Beveridge's views on welfare, and on society in general, did at a certain level come together around certain common themes—themes that tell us quite a lot that is significant not merely about Beveridge himself but about the wider evolution of social policy in the early twentieth century—and which may perhaps also tell us something about our own society and how it relates to Beveridge after the passage of fifty years.

---

[1] BP 8/45: minutes and papers of the Advisory Panel on Home Affairs, Apr.–June 1942. Ibid. ixa. 13–16: Employment Investigation minutes and papers, 1943–4.

The first and perhaps most basic theme that I want to emphasize is Beveridge's lifelong belief in rational economic man (and, indeed, rational economic woman), who with few exceptions would work if it were in his or her financial interest to do so, and would not if it were not. In spite of his large share in the dismantling or humanizing of the Poor Law, Beveridge fully endorsed the basic New Poor Law principle that social welfare benefits for those capable of work should always be less than what they could get in wages—and that they should in some sense be subject to a test of willingness to work. This belief was as central to Beveridge's views on welfare in the period of the Beveridge Plan as it was in his earlier period of support for the free market. It is important, however, to get this principle in the right perspective. Beveridge was not someone who denounced the unemployed themselves as incipient scroungers and loungers; and in his Social Insurance inquiry of 1942 he amazed witnesses from the Co-operative Congress by suggesting that if a man with a family to support could get more from the dole than he could get from wages, then it was not merely economically rational but his positive moral duty as a citizen and responsible parent to apply for the dole.[2] What he did condemn, however, were politicians and administrators who allowed such a poverty trap to come about—thereby, so he argued, allowing social policy to fly in the face of human psychology, to undermine economic incentives, and to demoralize both those who did and those who did not apply for welfare support. His views on the question of how adequate incentives and differentials between wages and welfare were to be maintained varied at different times in his career. In the 1900s he appears to have thought that most wages were too low, whilst in the 1920s he undoubtedly thought that many benefits were too high; but in the 1940s he had come to the conclusion that the best way to deal with the problem was by means of a family allowances scheme, operated quite independently of both wages and social security. Family allowances, payable whether the breadwinner was in or out of work, were in Beveridge's view to be a major weapon in the war against child poverty. But they also had the major secondary advantage of overcoming the anomaly that benefits took account of family size while the wage system did not: so in other words, they were an important means of buttressing what Beveridge saw as the perfectly legitimate and, indeed, indispensable principle of so-called 'less-eligibility' (Macnicol 1980).

A second characteristic of Beveridge's social philosophy was that he saw social welfare as fundamentally bound up with ideas about good citizenship: indeed, he saw consolidation of citizenship as being in some sense a *more* fundamental goal of social policy than relief of need, though he would also

[2] PRO CAB 87/77: Social Insurance Committee (hereafter SIC) minutes, 11 Mar. 1942, p. 11.

have seen the two as closely bound up with each other. Now what exactly did Beveridge mean by 'citizenship', that concept so dear to the hearts of many late-Victorians and Edwardians, and once again newly fashionable in the social welfare discourse of the 1980s and 1990s? I think he meant by it a vision of political behaviour that had deep roots in British social and intellectual history going back to the time of the English Civil War and beyond: a vision that entailed economic independence, moral virtue, self-discipline and self-policing, active rather than passive participation in a self-governing polity.[3] All these virtues Beveridge saw as quintessentially embodied in the Victorian self-governing friendly societies and benefit-paying trade unions; and both in 1911 and in 1942 one of his central aims as a social reformer was to protect and nurture that ethic of private citizenship—not to replace it by mechanical state provision, but to harness and integrate it into the structure of public life (Harris 1992). The reason why Beveridge hated the Poor Law, selectivity, and all forms of means-tested benefits was not because he saw them as harsh or inefficient (on the contrary, he conceded that they were often cheaper in aggregate and more generous to individuals than universalism). Rather it was because he saw them as fostering an ethic of clientage, concealment, and calculated improvidence among those whom they relieved—an ethic that he believed ultimately corrupted the whole of wider society, both receivers and givers. The belief in both voluntary and compulsory insurance as a kind of pattern of civic virtue explains many features of Beveridge's thinking that later commentators have often found irritating or obscure. It explains his obsession with the contributory principle as, in Beveridge's eyes, the structural embodiment of active, concrete citizen-obligation (on a par with the payment of taxes in older manifestations of the civic virtue tradition). It explains his determination to defend flat-rate insurance, and to promote the role of the self-governing friendly society as the philosophical partner of the universalist state. And it explains also his very chilly response in 1942 to the role of the commercial insurance companies: bodies whom he saw as having crept into the body politic under the cloak of citizen participation, but who since 1911 had worked systematically to undermine and destroy that ideal.[4]

[3] Beveridge's views on the links between citizenship and insurance contributions can be found in many sources. They were most systematically expressed in his journalistic writings of the 1900s; but the same theme was a continuous thread of his draft papers and cross-examination of witnesses for the Social Insurance committee in 1942. See his 'The Question of Disfranchisement', *Toynbee Record*, Mar. 1905, pp. 100–2; leading articles in the *Morning Post*, 25 Dec. 1905, 19 Feb. and 11 May 1906, 27 Nov. and 14 Dec. 1907; and 'Basic Problems of Social Security with Heads of a Scheme' (PRO CAB 87/76: 11 Dec. 1941).

[4] PRO CAB 87/77: SIC minutes, 16 June 1942, QQ. 4001–346; CAB 87/78; SIC minutes, 26 Aug. 1942, QQ. 7668–8103. Those commentators who would have us believe that the main aim of the Beveridge Plan was to 'save' private capitalism must surely find some explanation

A third fundamental characteristic of Beveridge's thinking about social welfare was that he was always much less interested in the relief of poverty *per se* than in the kind of restructuring of the labour market that he hoped would ultimately make relief of poverty unnecessary. His 'ideal type' of a social welfare client was not the long-term social dependant, but the independent worker, normally in regular and well-paid work, whose need arose from various kinds of temporary 'interruption of earnings'. Throughout his life he clung to the view that having a stake in the labour market was social normality, and that people who did not conform to this model could for the most part be made to do so by wise social administration. For instance, casual labour as Beveridge saw it was caused not by any inherent incapacity for work but by lack of proper labour organization; unemployment among the long-term disabled was the result of lack of proper schemes for special training; sweated labour and low pay were things that should be legislated out of existence—to the accompaniment of the compulsory retraining and redeployment of those whom such legislation might be expected to displace. Even the National Health Service—even that famous Assumption B for comprehensive health care which many would see as perhaps the most important single item in the Beveridge Plan—was very specifically envisaged as 'rehabilitation services for prevention and cure of disease and restoration of capacity for work': in other words, the prime function of the NHS was to be a gigantic service and refuelling station for the nation's labour market. Above all, the whole of Beveridge's social security system was predicated on the assumption that there was to be work for all whether they wanted it or not; that neither private work incentives nor the overall financial viability of the social security system could be maintained for very long without controls over the labour market to maintain full employment (Beveridge 1942: paras. 440–3).

Beveridge's emphasis on work and citizenship seem to me all-pervasive in his writings throughout his career; but there was nevertheless another fundamental aspect of his thought with which these principles were in latent conflict, and that is his attachment to a certain ideal of family life and in particular his views about the role and status of women. There has been much discussion recently about those aspects of the Beveridge Plan which assumed that the vast majority of women were dependants of their husbands, and that married women within the labour market should be given the option of more limited insurance than was available to male contributors. There is clearly much in this which is out of tune with the ethic of the present day. I do not myself agree, however, that this implies that Beveridge was guilty of a peculiarly benighted form of welfare patriarchalism. On the

for Beveridge's quite savage attacks on one of the major heartlands of private capitalism—namely, commercial insurance companies.

contrary, Beveridge's views were largely in accord with those of the majority of the organized women's movement in Britain in the 1930s and 1940s (Pugh 1992); and it seems to me futile and somewhat patronizing to berate both him and them for failing to think what they *ought* to have thought from the vantage-point of the 1990s. Where I *do* think Beveridge may be legitimately criticized, however, is for insisting upon a certain conception of social insurance *and* a certain conception of women and the family, and yet evading the issue that, even within the context of his day, these conceptions were in certain respects at loggerheads with each other. Beveridge's views on women may be summarized as follows. Throughout his life he was a strong supporter of the enfranchisement of women, and an even stronger supporter of the view that they should take a prominent and equal role in public life—as guardians, local councillors, Members of Parliament and members of political parties.[5] He was a consistent promoter of women in administrative and professional careers. At the same time, however, he cherished a very high ideal of women as makers of the home and bearers and rearers of children—a view that he claimed was shared by the vast majority of married women themselves, since in peacetime seven out of eight married women in Britain were not in regular work.[6] It was a view perhaps also coloured by the fact that, until his marriage to Mrs Mair at the age of sixty-three, Beveridge spent much of his life in fruitless pursuit of an ideal wife who might share his home and children (Harris 1977). It was the role of women as home-makers, Beveridge argued, that gave them just as much right as men to citizenship and a share in public life (though he did not deny that some women might also acquire such rights through paid work and through professional careers). He also argued that the work of women in the home was of great economic value to the nation, and gave women no less than men an entitlement to a share in universal social insurance: 'you have to recognize the function of housewife as an essential national service'.[7] Beveridge's problem, however, was that he was *also* committed to certain beliefs about the nature of citizenship and about the primacy of the labour market: to the views that, in the context of social insurance, *contribution* was the indispensable badge of citizenship and need was a problem of *interruption of earnings*. The logic of Beveridge's position required that the labour of citizen-carers in the home should in some sense be rewarded or credited with payment, from which they could make contributions into a fund that would support them when for some reason their earnings were 'interrupted'—whether by sickness, unemployment, childbirth, or old age. It is, I think, to Beveridge's credit that he did at

[5] *Morning Post*, leading articles, 18 June and 19 Nov. 1906, 15 June 1908.
[6] PRO CAB 87/76: 'Basic Problems of Social Security with Heads of a Scheme', 11 Dec. 1941, para. L.
[7] PRO CAB 87/77: SIC minutes, 6 May 1942, Q. 2267.

times see precisely this point,[8] and a great deal of time and effort was spent both by Beveridge himself and his committee in trying to devise practical ways by which social insurance could be made to cover all the women whom Beveridge thought should be brought in: not just mothers and carers of small children, but the woman looking after elderly parents or sick relatives, the woman needing 'refitting benefit' to enable her to resume a career, and the woman who suffered what Beveridge called an 'industrial accident' in the occupation of matrimony in the form of separation, desertion, or divorce.[9] In no area of the Beveridge Plan were greater efforts made to squeeze the knobbly foot of society into the narrow glass slipper of contributory social insurance; but it has to be said that in many respects these efforts failed. They failed, in my view, not because of Beveridge's outmoded patriarchalism, but because he was simultaneously committed to two ideals—both of which were widely popular with both sexes in the 1940s—but which were ultimately to prove in tension with each other: the ideal of the economically independent citizen and the ideal of the indispensable mother in the home.

A final aspect of Beveridge's approach to welfare was his belief that an adequate system of social insurance and social security could not operate without a framework of disciplinary constraints. This may seem a surprising point in view of Beveridge's well-known dislike of means tests and his emphasis on replacing discretionary benefit with contractual entitlement— and also in view of his recommendation that there should be no fixed time-limit to long-term insurance claims. But in fact Beveridge was convinced that the more comprehensive and adequate a system of welfare became, the greater the need for disciplinary policing of that system—not by cutting off benefit from those deemed likely to abuse it, but by compulsory retraining of the long-term unemployed, state control over deployment and direction of manpower, and strict limitation of the right to register for work in one's past line of trade. 'Conditions as to the acceptance of suitable employment will be *more* stringent than at present,' he wrote in one of his draft papers; and 'any scheme which makes those assisted unamenable to economic rewards or punishment while treating them as free citizens is inconsistent with the principle of a free community.'[10] One reason why he saw the friendly societies as so greatly superior to mere insurance companies was because the former practised fraternal policing of sick and out-of-work members, whereas the latter had no control over misuse of their funds.[11] A'

---

[8] Over 30 years earlier he had argued in the *Morning Post* (18 June 1906) that the 'economic basis of motherhood' was the 'central issue of feminism'.

[9] PRO CAB 87/77: SIC minutes, 6 May 1942, Q. 2268; CAB 87/78: 31 Aug. 1942, QQ. 8270–82.

[10] PRO CAB 87/76: 'Basic Problems of Social Security with Heads of a Scheme', paras. 16, 42.

[11] PRO CAB 87/78: SIC minutes, 26 Aug. 1942, QQ. 7853–8062.

similar point may be made about Beveridge's view of the overall organization of the economy. As I have already suggested, Beveridge did not really believe in 1942 that there was some kind of permanent half-way house between economic liberalism and thoroughgoing collectivism. Quite the opposite: he thought that once the automatic, self-activating discipline of the market had been abandoned, it had to be replaced by an artificial framework of discipline imposed by the community and the state. It was largely for this reason that, at the time of writing his report on Social Insurance, Beveridge appears to have believed that all major domestic economic relationships—such as fixing of profits and prices, collective bargaining, deployment of labour, and levels of investment—should be permanently subject to centralized public control (Harris 1977: chs. 16, 17).

What does Beveridge's social and political philosophy offer to those who are looking for a 'return to Beveridge' in 1992? It offers, I think, very little to those who would see social security as merely the buffer zone of an otherwise unregulated free market economy, since the whole of the Beveridge Plan was premised on the assumption that large parts of the social arena traditionally occupied by the market would henceforth be under rigorous state control. On the other hand, it offers equally little to those who have ambitious views about how far state welfare might be expected to lift long-term beneficiaries not merely out of primary poverty but into full participation in the lifestyles enjoyed by those in regular work. Beveridge in the cross-examination of witnesses before his committee constantly emphasized that social security was not a 'Tom Tiddlers Ground', and that he was not in the business of building a 'Santa Claus state'.[12] Far from being the bonanza of extravagance that some have imagined, the Beveridge report in its benefit provisions was a markedly austere document, geared to sound money, budgetary purity, limited contractual entitlement, a spartan subsistence minimum, and firm behavioural controls. Much of its popularity lay in the very fact that it was so closely in tune with the wartime ethic of bread for everyone before cake for anyone—or, as one TUC spokesman put it, 'the stockpot for everybody ... a dessert or sweet afterwards is something over and above'.[13] Its underlying political vision was in many respects neither capitalist nor socialist nor even particularly liberal but 'classical-republican': it envisaged a society in which all citizens would actively participate in regular work, modest rewards, moral cohesion, family life, communal provision against need, stoic virtue, and mutual self-policing. Its utopianism lay not in its specific proposals but in the tacit assumption that much of the wartime framework of austerity, sharing, discipline, and

[12] PRO CAB 87/77: SIC minutes, 25 Feb. 1942, p. 28; CAB 87/78: SIC minutes, 17 June 1942, Q. 4720, 4726.
[13] PRO CAB 87/77: SIC minutes.

social solidarity—the institutional embodiment of the so-called 'Dunkirk spirit'—would continue indefinitely into the era of peace.

REFERENCES

Addison, P. (1975), *The Road to 1945: British Politics and the Second World War*. London: Cape.
Barnett, C. (1986), *The Audit of War: The Illusion and Reality of Britain as a Great Nation*. London: Macmillan.
Beveridge, W. H. (1909), *Unemployment: A Problem of Industry*. London: Longmans.
—— (1930), *Unemployment: A Problem of Industry (1909 and 1930)*. London: Longmans, Green.
—— (1942), *Social Insurance and Allied Services*, Cmd. 6404. London: HMSO.
—— (1944), *Full Employment in a Free Society*. London: Allen and Unwin.
Cutler, T., Williams, K. and Williams, J. (1986), *Beveridge and Beyond*. London: Routledge and Kegan Paul.
Harris, J. (1977), *William Beveridge: A Biography*. Oxford: Clarendon Press.
—— (1992), 'Victorian Values and the Founders of the Welfare State', *Proceedings of the British Academy*, 78.
Huxley, T. (1894), *Evolution and Ethics and Other Essays*. London: Macmillan.
Macnicol, J. (1980), *The Movement for Family Allowances, 1918–45: A Study in Social Policy Development*. London: Heinemann.
Melling, J. (1991), 'Reading Beveridge: Recent Research on Pre-war Social Policy', *Social Policy and Administration*, 25/1.
Pugh, M. (1992), *Women and the Women's Movement in Britain 1914–1959*. Basingstoke: Macmillan.
Veit-Wilson, J. (1992), 'Muddle or Mendacity: The Beveridge Committee and the Poverty Line', *Journal of Social Policy*, 21/3.
Williams, K., and Williams, J. (eds.) (1987), *A Beveridge Reader*. London: Allen and Unwin.

UNPUBLISHED SOURCES

BP: Beveridge Papers (British Library of Political and Economic Science).
Papers of the 1941–2 Committee on Social Insurance and Allied Services (PRO CAB 87/76–8).

4

Beveridge in the Longue Durée

PETER BALDWIN

I come neither to bury Beveridge nor to honour him, although the temptation to strive for one or the other of these two extremes is great at the half-century mark after his most lasting achievement.[1] Any retrospective evaluation not wholly in thrall either to ritual encomium or denunciation is likely to hover ambiguously between honouring and burying. Examining Beveridge and his influence in the comparatively *longue durée* we have put behind us since the publication of *Social Insurance and Allied Services* is no exception. The *longue durée* is a concept usually attributed to the French historian Fernand Braudel. It marks an attempt to situate historical events in their broadest possible context, in a flow of time that is almost geological in its imperceptible movement. Such an analysis has the advantage of allowing the historian to separate out the important from the trivial, the durable from the ephemeral. But at the same time, of course, when regarded from such Olympian heights, all mortals are but dust. If we combine one of Keynes's better known maxims with Braudel's historical philosophy, we may quickly agree that in the *longue durée* we are all dead—Beveridge as much as lesser mortals. Any retrospective must fairly balance two rival historical claims. On the one hand is Beveridge's tremendous reputation at the end of the Second World War as the father of modern British social policy and as one of the main international architects of what has been called the social citizenship model of the welfare state. On the other are the factors that lessen the otherwise extraordinary prominence of his place in social policy history. These include the length to which some of the principles often associated with his name had in fact been implemented already, earlier, in other nations, the extent to which the planks of his platform have subsequently been abandoned in British social policy, and the degree to which his influence abroad has been less than it seemed in the first flush of the Report's publication.

[1] I am grateful to Claus Offe, Ramesh Mishra, Deborah Mitchell, Julian Le Grand, Theodore Marmor, and, above all, Jonathan Bradshaw for advice and wherewithal in the preparation of this paper.

THE BEVERIDGE MYTHOLOGY

Let us begin with the aura. The nebula of charismatic authority surrounding his reputation sets Beveridge apart from all other social politicians. His name, even today, evokes metaphors of founding fatherhood of the welfare state and a reverence for the possibilities of statutory benevolence that has otherwise been lost in the nasty battles following the cutbacks of the 1970s. Old age pensioners may have thanked 'that Lord George' when they began receiving benefits after 1908, but Lloyd George's historical reputation obviously rests more firmly on his other accomplishments. Bismarck is perhaps the only other figure in the development of the welfare state with a reputation equal to Beveridge's, but his place in history also rests only marginally on social policy endeavours and then not in a very positive sense. The Beveridge Report has become a benchmark in the annals of social policy history, although, like Masters and Johnson in its year of publication, it was probably the most-sold, least-perused book of 1942. Beveridge's only rival among state papers, in public impact if not piquant detail, was the Denning Report on the Profumo scandal (Kincaid 1973: 45). To sense this aura surrounding the Report and its author, all one need do is to compare *Social Insurance and Allied Services* to the other wartime blueprints for welfare reform: Marsh, Wagner, van Acker, van Rhijn, Parodi, D'Aragona. Where are they now? These were all social politicians with a local reputation and a plan for change to their name, but none of that transcendence evoked by Beveridge.

The heightened fervour of the wartime years certainly contributed to Beveridge's appeal. James Griffiths described the Report as manna falling from heaven, and that was in the sober retrospection of his memoirs a quarter-century later (Griffiths 1969: 70). The hyperbole at the time was, if possible, even greater. Even the enemy took notice, with the Nazis piqued that, by promising the state's concern for the material wellbeing of its citizens, Beveridge had appropriated what they regarded as one of the propaganda feathers in their cap. That the Report was published just after victory at El Alamein, seen even then as a turning point, and thus coincided with a hopeful sea change in the public mood at the War's prospects was a fortuitous coincidence. At a moment of blood, sweat, and tears rhetoric, the stuff of the Report may not appear to have been the kind of subject to send adrenalin coursing through the collective veins, but in fact Beveridge had managed to hook his concern with the nuts and bolts of social policy to more elevated and inspiring themes. The Atlantic Charter of the previous year had held out social security as one of the postwar era's ambitions. Beveridge fleshed out such lofty promises, providing the details of what was expected by many to be a new order. Rhetorically, Beveridge was adept at emphasizing the broader social themes embodied in his particular suggestions. His was not the average Command Paper; it was part legislative proposal, part visionary philosophy.

To such specific considerations comes a more general way in which the wartime circumstances of the Report's publication added to the jubilation of its popular reception. Several scholars, especially Richard Titmuss and Arthur Marwick, have made their reputations suggesting and elaborating the idea that the War encouraged a general sentiment of social solidarity. The events of the hostilities, especially the bombings, nourished the perception that all citizens shared many risks in common, and fostered a heightened sense of community. The War, so the argument runs, allowed a solidaristic conceptual breakthrough, a partial renegotiation of the social contract. All citizens, even those who had formerly thought they were capable of managing without the state's aid, now found themselves facing the same major risks on a largely similar footing. All were in the same boat. Rawls's veil of ignorance descended for a short but significant time on British society and citizens who now approached their fate with apparently similar chances were persuaded that solidarity was the social virtue to characterize postwar reforms. All citizens were to be treated equally, not just in the formal terms of civil and political rights, but also in the more bread-and-butter measure of an equal claim to basic subsistence. Seen in this broader context of common threats to all, charity became mutual self-help based on individual self interest.

Finally we have what is an historiographical reason for Beveridge's reputation: the gloss put on the Report by T. H. Marshall. In a sense, Beveridge found his historian already during his lifetime, indeed at the peak of his influence. Their relationship was not that of Johnson with his Boswell, providing posterity with intimate details that would otherwise have got lost, but rather more like Robespierre with his Marx. In his renowned Cambridge lectures in 1949, just a year after the main reforms of the Labour Government, Marshall elaborated a powerful, plausible, world historical perspective by which to judge the measures that Beveridge had been so instrumental in prompting. Marshall's grand teleology of an historical progression through a trinity of modes of citizenship, from civil, to political, and finally to social rights, portrayed the Beveridge/Labour reforms as the culmination of a centuries-long process, and imbued them with a transcendent importance that carried them, in terms of their role in history, far beyond what a framework of social policy legislation would otherwise have aspired to. Marshall's account of these postwar reforms as marking a significant change not just in the provision of social benefits, but in the very nature of the social contract, has guided the hand of textbook writers and general commentators ever since; it has set the tone for an interpretation of the welfare state that has proven enormously influential down to the present day.

What Marshall and this school of thought did was to make of the social citizenship welfare state, as embodied in the Beveridge/Labour reforms, the historical answer in Western European history to the Russian Revolution and the birth of socialism in the east. Marshall provided a reformist, social-democratic alternative to the Marxist reading of modern European history. In the Marxist historical analysis, feudalism had given way to capitalism and the reign of the middle classes during the bourgeois revolution in 1789. The next step was to be another shift in power between rising and declining classes, as the proletariat took the reins from the bourgeoisie, installing itself in power and allegedly abolishing the whole process of class antagonism. The nations of Western Europe waited in vain, however, for this subsequent progression. Instead, what some of them got, in Marshall's account, was a shift to the social citizenship welfare state. This may not have been the revolution expected on the far left, but at the same time it represented something more than just a reformist adjustment to the ruling order. The social citizenship welfare state capped the evolution of civil and political rights with their meat-and-potatoes equivalents. Material well-being even in times of personal misfortune, something that had not yet been included in the definition of citizenship, an element that had been left to the market place for adjudication, now became part of what it was to be a member of the community. Equality was not to mean just the right of all, rich and poor, to personal freedoms, the vote and the privilege of sleeping under bridges, but to a certain modicum of well being, a basic civilized level of income.

The fact that the apparently main historical route through the socialist revolution, to which the social citizenship welfare state provided an alter-native, has collapsed in the meantime certainly does not detract from the allure of the Marshallian reading of Western European developments. The point worth underlining here in this well known story is the extent to which the Beveridge/Labour legislation was lucky enough to find its world his-torical interpreter just as it came to fruition. Marshall made dramatic, but plausible and well argued claims for the reforms. He made of them, in effect, an historical event equivalent in importance and stature to the French or Russian Revolutions, and that was no mean feat for what was basically a series of laws on social insurance.

BEVERIDGE'S BALANCING ACT

And yet, the wartime aura is not enough to explain Beveridge's elevation to whatever pantheon social policy possesses. Many things seemed important in the heightened atmosphere of wartime and the years immediately fol-lowing and none the less vanished once the humdrum everydayness of postwar life set in again. The belief that the Resistance could be the basis of a political renewal for France is perhaps the most sobering example. Moreover, it is clear that the wartime spirit of social solidarity can only partially explain the popular resonance of the Report. Many countries, after all, had been at war, their citizens subject to the same mortal risks, but not all nations emerged apparently prepared to legislate on the basis of an expansive sense of inclusive communality. There were obviously qualities to what Beveridge proposed and what Labour sought to implement that had an appeal of their own, regardless of the immediately surrounding circumstances.

What made the Beveridge Report and the reforms associated with it remarkable was the manner in which they balanced on a knife edge both the collectivism and the individualism inherent in any social policy. Beveridge formulated an ideology of collectivist social insurance, and thus advocated the full realization of the reconciliation between community and society that insurance makes possible. One of the main themes of François Ewald's brilliant book, which deals with the welfare state in its broadest sense, is the extent to which insurance—and especially social insurance, with its broadening of the risks and groups covered—perfectly embodied the reforming liberal's hope of harmonizing the need for the community's solicitude and intervention with the individual's autonomy and insistence on personal freedom (Ewald 1986). Ewald manages to accomplish the unlikely task of turning the invention of the actuarial table and its ability to map the regularities of misfortune and mortality that lie beneath the flux of individual fates into an historically pathbreaking step in the evolution of modern society. Given an ability to predict the usual occurrence of various forms of mischance, society could, with minimal compulsion and regulation, now help individuals by ensuring that they never need suffer more than the cost of an average burden. Insurance promised individuals that they would have to endure no fate greater than the average, at least to the extent that misfortune could be pecuniarily compensated for, and social insurance guaranteed that the bulk of society enjoyed the benefits of such risk equalization.

Two extremes of possible human social experience were in this way avoided: on the one hand, the medieval view of society as something like a family writ large, hierarchical, paternalist, communal; on the other, the extreme liberalist view of society as a mere conglomeration of autonomous, individualistic monads, brought together only incidentally in their pursuit of self interest. With the redistribution of the costs of risk allowed by the science of probability, actuarial mathematics, and the development of insurance techniques, a middle ground was staked out between these extremes that embodies what Ewald sees as the essence of the modern social contract. The individual was allowed personal freedom and autonomy and yet did not have to forgo the advantages of communal solidarity, the help of the group in times of need. Society became seen as the largest possible risk pool, and the citizen as a policy holder. Quetelet, the Belgian astronomer and mathematician who popularized the use of averages and means in the taming of social problems, was thus canonized as the patron saint of modern society in this liberal reforming vision that Ewald traces as the philosophical core insight behind the welfare state. Quetelet elevated the average human, *l'homme type*, a statistical abstraction which was now treated as a social reality, as the common benchmark against which the deviations of life outside the actuary's tables were measured (Hacking 1990: 105–14). It was not classes struggling with each other for mutual advantage that primarily characterized modern society, but rather the equalization of each individual's risks with the group—a fundamental base of equity, in other words, that permitted the inequalities of the market free rein in other realms.

Much of this will seem commonplace to those familiar with such subjects. But it is worth reminding ourselves of the potentially solidaristic impulse behind social insurance, especially given the generation or so of interpretations that has emphasized the extent to which certain varieties of social insurance can be applied to much less enlightened or liberating goals. Most obviously, the Bonapartist ambitions pursued by Bismarck with his welfare legislation are hard to fit into an Ewaldian conception of social solidarity. Given this background, it is one of the major reasons for the positive response to Beveridge that he was able to capture or recapture the solidaristic element of social insurance underlined by Ewald. Social insurance before Beveridge had not fulfilled its solidaristic potential. On the Continent, where the technique had first and foremost come to fruition, social insurance was still organized in a corporatist manner during the interwar years. It had started out in the late nineteenth century largely limited to the manual working class. From here, it had expanded by degrees, sometimes taking into the system groups on the margins of the industrial proletariat, as with agricultural workers. Sometimes it had created new systems for new groups, as in Germany when salaried employees were insured apart from the manual workers with whom they did not wish to share an actuarial fate. Social insurance remained balkanized; it had managed to achieve only partial solidarities, to spread risks only within groups that were socio-economically quite homogeneous.

More importantly, large segments of society, in some cases a majority, were not yet regarded as needing this sort of communal solicitude. It was assumed that they were capable as individuals of coping with whatever misfortunes came their way. They were independent, both as a sociological classification and as indicative of their lack of participation in any risk pool. Large parts of society, especially among those who were not wage earners and who still made up half or so of the economically-active population in most Continental societies, did not belong to anything but the most rudimentary forms of private insurance. Because of such exemptions, the presumption remained that social policy was a concern only for the dependently employed, and especially workers; that it was something that solid citizens, the good burghers, did not need and would seek to avoid. Social insurance in its pre-Beveridgean incarnation was thus not a matter of interest to the citizen, but to the economic producer as a member of particular classes or economic groups.

This attitude is what Beveridge helped change. His clarion call was for a universal approach to social insurance, his aim to expand the risk pool from being limited to particular classes to embracing all citizens, his hope to make the redistribution of risk a reflection not of the needs of isolated groups, but of all mortals, of the whole community. This universal embrace that was now to characterize an enlightened application of social insurance lay at the heart of the concept of social citizenship as elaborated by Marshall. Just as personal liberties and then political expression had gone from being the preserve of some to the right of all, so, too, social rights were to be expanded. Not only the fortunate and prosperous were now to enjoy necessary medical care, a working life of uninterrupted income, or a dotage of comparative comfort. A minimum level of material well-being, basic protection against the vicissitudes of mortality and the inequities of the market, was now, like the vote, to be every citizen's birthright.

Because all citizens were to belong to the social policy system, the stigma that had earlier been attached to receiving support from the state, to being unable to maintain oneself without outside assistance, would be dissolved. The War had shown that all were in the same boat when it came to the basic risks of life and death. Universalist social insurance continued and extended this wartime insight to the everyday risks of postwar existence. Because all members of the community were now recognized as being equivalently dependent on the state's aid, the stigma of help from the community that had formerly affected only those who were not autonomous was to be erased by enrolling all citizens in the risk pool, making all equally reliant on society. The universalization of risk-sharing that was the hallmark of Beveridge's reforms removed the stigma of dependence through what might be called the Struwwelpeter approach. In *Struwwelpeter*, Heinrich Hoffmann's collection of admonitory children's stories, a group of white boys who make fun of a black are dipped into an inkwell, turning them as dark as the object of their ridicule. When even the millionaire queued at the post office for his pension, the less well endowed would feel no shame in collecting theirs. That was the logic of the universalization of dependence that enrolling all in the social insurance scheme entailed.

Each citizen was to belong to social insurance and contribute for the risks that afflicted them. Not all were, of course, treated in precisely the same manner: housewives were not expected to insure against unemployment, although civil servants, who also suffered little from this risk, were. But all were to belong and no one was measured by his or her particular risk-proneness; each contributed according to the average risk and received according to their needs. Beveridge in this way heralded the fulfilment of the solidaristic potential of social insurance. The quarantining of certain groups within their own risk pools, the excusing of the wealthy and fortunate from sharing burdens with the harder pressed: these characteristics of the old style of social insurance were now to be superseded.

It was this universalist ambition that became the hallmark of the Beveridge reforms and that anchored his reputation in other nations. An all-inclusive embrace for social insurance was one of the most important characteristics of the social policy legislation proposed in France immediately after the war by Parodi, Croizat and Laroque. French reformers disagreed with Beveridge on plenty of other points, but they regarded the inclusion of the entire population as the surest way to achieve national solidarity. In Germany, one of the main debating points between the Christian and the Social Democrats turned precisely on this question of making social insurance a concern for all citizens. The right wished to retain the old system of socially-divided arrangements, while the left sought all inclusive and universalist reforms on the Beveridgean model. Neither set of reforms on the Continent achieved their ambitions at the time, and it was not until two decades later and then under very different circumstances that measures which captured some of this solidaristic wartime spirit were implemented here (Baldwin 1990: chs. 3, 5).

Beveridge did not, of course, single-handedly invent this universalist version of social insurance. Other nations had already implemented various measures adumbrating the social citizenship approach. Australia and New Zealand had introduced all-inclusive measures in the interwar years and had, partially as a consequence, attracted the attention of European, especially French, socialists as a model to follow. England's own 1908 pension scheme was not limited to any particular social class. Much of such legislation, however, resembled old-fashioned poor relief more than it did social insurance. Benefits were often conditional on criteria of worth and worthiness, and thus universal only in the sense that they were the right of all respectable poor, regardless of what class or social group they might originally have been born into. The closest precursor to Beveridge's proposals were therefore the Swedish pensions of 1913, the first example of 'people's pensions' that, in return for contributions, gave all citizens a modest benefit regardless of class or income. Even reforms like the Swedish were, however, partial measures, limited to one form of social protection or another. Beveridge's aim, and the reason for his enduring reputation, was more ambitious. He advocated something not yet attempted before: not just a universal embrace for one branch of social policy or another, but a comprehensive, complete system of social insurance in which all citizens found their place. It was the totalizing ambition of his Report that made its proposals so striking: the complete coverage against all risks for all people. All for one and one for all. The Three Musketeers meet the Government Actuary.

THE LIBERAL VISION

The universalist aspect of his proposals was, however, only half of Beveridge's philosophy of social policy: the other half takes us away from the collectivist, solidaristic vision and towards the liberal bent of his ideology. The most important means by which Beveridge infused an otherwise solidaristic approach to welfare with a bedrock assumption of individualism and liberalism came with his emphasis on the insurance and contributory aspects of reforms. One way he hoped to eradicate the inherited stigma of dependence on statutory help was to enrol all citizens, and thus make all equally dependent, taking the Struwwelpeter approach. The other arrow in Beveridge's quiver was to make universal not just membership, but also the contractual legitimacy of benefits that a contributory approach allowed. All citizens were to become recipients, but at the same time all were to become contributors to the social insurance system. By universalizing social insurance all citizens, even those who had formerly been self reliant, were now made dependent on the state. By upholding the contributory, insurance side of provision, in contrast, the vast majority of recipients, even those who had formerly been regarded as incapable of contributing to their own upkeep, were now expected to become upright, self-maintaining citizens. Beveridge's two-pronged approach to legitimizing the welfare state at one and the same time made the rich dependent and the poor respectable contributors.

Contributory social insurance had, in theory, no great advantage over tax financing; in and of itself it freed up no new resources to fund social policy and, from an Olympian vantage point, whether financing was assured through taxes or earmarked contributions was a bookkeeping distinction, or at best a question of which method seemed politically most astute. The advantage of a contributory system was psychological and thereby political. In an economic system otherwise saturated by market principles, the legitimacy of benefits that appeared to be paid for by their recipients' contributions was much like that of any other commercial transaction. Being the purchaser and not just the consumer, the recipient claimed a right to benefits through ownership, thus needing to make no apologies for their collection. Beveridge's concept of citizenship made benefits contingent on contributions, but at the same time, it expected almost everyone to be a contributor. The Beveridgean welfare state was based on a nation of contributors, an underwriter's paradise.

By taking the contributory tack, Beveridge helped set the course of future welfare policy also for nations other than Britain. British social politicians had been converted, after the dead end of the 1908 pensions, to a contributory approach following Lloyd George's famous pilgrimage to Germany that summer. None the less, it still remained a debating point, one that largely separated the left from the centre and right, whether welfare policy should be financed out of general taxes or through earmarked contributions. The Webbs, in their minority report for the Royal Commission on the Poor Laws in 1909, had opposed a contributory approach because they believed that workers could not afford it. Three decades later, Beveridge was convinced they could. On the Continent, a heavily tax-financed system was never realistically on the agenda—in Germany because of long contributory traditions, in France because the precarious fiscal system could not have handled it. Even in Sweden, where disputes similar to the British were fought out, a heavily tax-financed approach was progressively abandoned starting in the 1950s in favour of much greater reliance on contributions (Rodriguez 1982).

To the extent that social insurance was erected on an orthodox actuarial basis and that contributions paid for at least a significant fraction of benefits, the stigma of dependence was sidestepped. It was avoided, however, not because a new attitude which accepted that all were ultimately dependent on the community's aid had come to permeate society, but, quite the contrary, because the old virtues of individual self-reliance and independence were now made the hallmark even of statutory provision against risk. The more heavily the contributory principle was emphasized, the more social insurance was made to seem like private insurance, the more the state became just another, although larger, insurance broker. Beveridge's concern with eradicating means tests was indicative of this fundamentally contractual philosophy. The stigma of means tests demonstrated the extent to which, in a market system, benefits received without preconditions other than need were regarded as socially disabling. The distaste associated with means tests, and the insistence on a contributory and partially contractual basis for benefits, revealed a political and psychological resistance among most Britons to the logical consequences of social rights, the receipt of aid solely on the basis of citizenship and need.

Contributory social insurance by its nature considers most of its members to be capable of self-help, and limits the state's role to organizing such bootstrap measures. It thus presupposes a fundamental homogeneity in its client population in at least two senses. First, it assumes that the risk pool is wealthy enough to eradicate poverty among some members by distributing income from others. Beveridge claimed in the Report that poverty was a problem of distribution, no longer of production. Workers as a group now had sufficient income that no-one need live in poverty if only resources were properly allocated. Second, a system of contributory social insurance assumes that the members of society's actuarial risk pool are generally fully-employed income recipients who may suffer occasional or, in the case of old age, foreseeable interruptions of normal revenues, but who are otherwise in a position to be full contributing members of the insurance system, not just in terms of their income, but also in those of their mode of life. Social insurance is not so much designed to redistribute income vertically between social groups as horizontally across gaps in income receipt over the course of the individual's lifetime. In his 1924 pamphlet, *Insurance for All and Everything*, and in the Report, Beveridge emphasized the concept of 'interruption of earning' as the factor that linked together all the different contingencies that insurance could relieve. His scheme was designed for 'perfectly normal persons' facing 'disorders endemic in modern society,' and took little account of the deviant, the incurable, and the down and out (Harris 1977: 350). Unlike charity or poor relief, social insurance, in Beveridge's view, was geared to the needs of the majority, not to an atypical minority; the focus was not on the margins of society, but the mean.

Beveridge's reliance on the insurance principle was part of his strategy for turning social policy from a form of state charity accompanied by the stigma of dependence into a right of citizenship, earned by the contributor. By insisting that everyone, even those who had formerly been considered incapable of thus participating, become contributors and thus earn the complete rights of social citizenship, Beveridge expanded the circle of full members of the community at the same time that he enlarged the nature of citizenship. Simultaneously, however, as a consequence of this approach, he drew the boundaries around full citizenship in a more exclusionary manner. Non-contributory, means-tested and therefore stigmatizing benefits had been received by a larger part of the population before the War than Beveridge intended would be the case after his reforms. Means-tested benefits were to be limited to an irreducible minimum, given only to the residual element of those who could not function in a contributory system. The rest of the population was assumed to share the characteristics of contributory citizenship. The insurance principle thus presupposes a fundamental degree of homogeneity within its target population, and it was on this homogeneity that the concept of social citizenship was founded: the citizen as contributory participant.

This basic assumption of the Beveridgean social citizenship welfare state has left its operating premises open to at least two sorts of criticism. First has been a new variant on the inherited social control critique. The old version was a political attack on social policies' ability to smother impulses that might otherwise lead to radical reform. Welfare measures were mere amelioratives, Band Aids on festering sores, that took the edge off the worst misery, but in so doing prevented concerted efforts to root out the fundamental causes of social inequity. The new version, which relies heavily on Foucault's theories of social discipline, is a more culturally-oriented criticism. It accuses the welfare state of imposing norms, of being a method by which the average middle-class virtues are turned into benchmarks for the conduct of all groups and classes. It attacks, in other words, the presumption that all citizens must share the characteristics of contributory participation in order to enjoy the status of social citizenship.

Some of this criticism, when it is levelled against Beveridge, amounts to little more than an attack on him for being the child of his time, for not being able to transcend the prejudices of his period and station—an accusation to which, in the *longue durée*, we must all plead guilty. That the majority of women would fit into Beveridge's scheme as housewives—not as individuals, but as part of the family unit—is but the most obviously dated of his assumptions and has been subject to deserved attack (Jordan 1991: 18). More overarching is the critique of social insurance's presumption that the middle-class virtues of thrift, prudence, abstemiousness, sobriety, and regular work constitute the code by which all classes must live in order to be social citizens. Janet Beveridge, who had a knack for putting in the baldest terms the ideas that lay more implicit in her husband's writings, encouraged him to set as one of his three main policy objectives 'education of those not yet accustomed to clean careful ways of life' (Harris 1977: 387). This line of attack meshes well with postmodernist critiques of the welfare state, whereby the Beveridge vision is regarded as a relic of Enlightenment notions that there is one standard applicable to all citizens. Quetelet's *l'homme type* and his claim to have charted the predictable fluctuation of averages around the mean to which human diversity can be reduced in an actuarial sense, is declared dissolved in the allegedly multicultural brew of modern societies.

The second line of attack to which Beveridge's emphasis on the contributory principle has left him open is more concrete. The nature of poverty and therefore of participation in the system has turned out to be different from Beveridge's expectations. Much poverty has been increasingly caused by conditions that social insurance cannot cope with. There is a growing group of people who have never been and are unlikely to become regular contributory members of social insurance: the permanently unemployed, single mothers, those bypassed by the educational system, the urban underclass (Jordan 1991: 21). Few of these have hopes of being integrated into a social insurance system intended for the regularly-employed 'normal' working population. The role of means-tested and targeted programmes for the poorest has remained much more important than expected by Beveridge, and has, indeed, grown since the 1970s (Parry 1986: 162). More generally, Beveridge's prognosis that poverty was something that could be cured with the resources at the disposal of social insurance's client pool has not proven correct. Primary poverty has once again become a hurdle for a significant group of society in a way that did not seem likely in the economically heady decades after the War.

The universality of measures that assumed each citizen also to be a contributor has been undermined. With the tattering of this defiant banner of the Beveridgean vision, it has become increasingly clear that the whole notion of universality presupposes a society sufficiently homogeneous for all to be on a similar footing. Positive discrimination, targeting of benefits, increased usage of means tests and similar changes indicate that this is no longer the case. Socially speaking, if the economic disparities between middle and lower classes are too great, the social policy system will not be able to embrace them both, at least not given an ethos of contributory participation, on the same terms. Instead, there will develop social insurance for the better-heeled, and some variant on a new poor law for the worst-off. Culturally speaking, to the extent that society fissiparates into balkanized subgroupings, the question becomes, will each accept membership in the system on the same terms? Will the Algerian schoolgirls in France who refuse to attend class unless veiled be willing to belong to the social insurance system without conditions? Universality may have been an illusion born of the temporary sense of community during the war or one fostered with the greatest success in the uncharacteristically homogeneous societies of northern Europe, but not necessarily one that is practicable, at least not in its postwar formulation, in circumstances of economic decline or in increasingly heterogeneous societies.

SOCIAL CITIZENSHIP

This brings us to the ambiguity at the heart of the concept of social citizenship as put into practice by Beveridge and then given its world his-torical inflection by Marshall: the potential contradiction between being a citizen and being a contributor. If all cannot be contributors, can they be citizens? Civil and political rights are generally accepted as unconditional, with a few obvious exceptions usually involving pyromaniacal loudmouths in crowded public spaces. Social rights, in contrast, are not. Social citizenship, in Marshall's formulation, claims to be an enlargement of earlier and more restricted forms of citizenship. Citizenship in its civil and then political versions is an unmitigated right. Citizens, by virtue only of their membership in the community and regardless of their other virtues or lack thereof, possess civil rights. Even bounders, cads and hooligans are thus protected. Political rights, above all the vote, are similarly founded. Regardless of merit, education, intelligence, virtue, tax status or most other attributes, all have the right to express their political choice. *Inskribiert und nicht krepiert, heißt promoviert* was the way that wags once described the criteria for the doctoral degree at one of the dissertation mills of the nineteenth century, the University of Erlangen. To be immatriculated and not yet dead were the only requisites for the Ph.D. Civil and political rights have a similarly unqualified nature. Social rights, with the exception of the NHS and perhaps the educational system, are less absolute, more contractual in nature. They are coloured by the market and do not completely supplant its criteria for the distribution of resources; they are founded on an extension of the fundamentally exchange-based nature of property rights to welfare benefits.

Moreover, social rights, whatever their nature, were not a simple expansion of their civil and political antecedents. Political rights had indeed been based on and had enhanced civil rights, at least in the sense that the former presupposed the latter. It was unlikely that someone should have political, but not civil rights. One exception was perhaps a German Socialist between 1878 and 1890 who would have been allowed to vote, but not to organize. Social rights, in contrast, are often not an elaboration of these previous levels of rights, but may, in fact, be an alternative to them. It is increasingly characteristic of modern societies that there are many who have social rights and yet no political ones. Turkish 'guest workers' in Berlin, with claims to a pension but no hope of the vote, are perhaps the extreme example. They may, in fact, be bought off, as it were, with more social rights, given a special allowance to return home and effectively abandon any political claims they might have had. The United States is usually criticized as providing examples of the opposite extreme: an impoverished underclass with more civil and political rights than social ones. But even here, there are, for example, immigrants who arrive outside the law with not even the right to residence, but none the less claims to coverage of certain basic expenses: housing, food, and medical care for their native-born children and therefore also for themselves. As under Bismarck, social rights can still serve as substitutes for political and sometimes civil claims. The core to citizenship continues to be founded on political rights. To be a contributor is not the same as being a citizen.

The grand and whiggish teleology of Marshall's vision of citizenship, coming to fruition over several centuries and culminating in the postwar reforms, is a powerful part of the Beveridge mythology that is undercut by an historical look at the actual genesis of social rights. As Gaston Rimlinger, among others, has pointed out, there was no such heroic progression. Like most accurate historical pedigrees, the family tree of social rights was more mongrel than purebred. Social rights were first broached and accepted in the late nineteenth century for a wide variety of motives. In Germany, they were prompted by unabashedly Bonapartist aims, as a substitute for civil and political rights, not as their expansion. In Britain, issues of national efficiency encouraged the propertied and business classes to support some variety of social rights. Social rights were here welcomed as strengthening, as much as they were feared for encroaching on, property rights (Rimlinger 1983).

The central ambiguity of social rights is the potential contradiction between citizenship and contributorship. The bedrock rights, civil and political, are founded on the sheer fact of citizenship alone, while social rights involve a heavy element of market logic, of contractual ownership. Robert Pinker pointed out some time ago that the legitimacy of benefits founded only on the fact of citizenship was not generally accepted outside the rarefied realm of social reformers and theorists (Pinker 1971: 142). The validity of this insight can be judged most brutally in the effects of the cutbacks that started in the 1970s. In some welfare states, and nowhere more so than in the two nations of American social policy, the poorest are those whose benefits have been most harshly scaled back. Theirs are the benefits founded on no contractual legitimacy, the ones given by virtue of need alone, the ones that are therefore most vulnerable to political haggling. The benefits for insurance contributors, in contrast, the ones sanctioned by the market, the ones that the great mass of the middle class thinks it has paid for and will accordingly not relinquish, are those that have proven most resistant to erosion (Goodin and Le Grand 1987; Le Grand and Winter 1986; Hills 1991: 344–7; Pfaller *et al.* 1991). The more firmly social rights are based on market principles, the more durable they have proven to be.

BEVERIDGE IN A WORLD VIEW

Beveridge and his most important interpreters, Marshall and Titmuss, collectively anchored the notion of social citizenship as a major turning point in the evolution of western society. The Beveridgean reforms, and more generally British social policy development, did not bring this concept to its full fruition, a task probably accomplished by the Swedes sometime in the 1960s. But they may none the less be credited with posing this possibility for the first time as a comprehensive goal and for taking major steps towards it. The idea of social citizenship has been attacked for being parochially derived from British developments alone (Mann 1987; Turner 1990). Much of such reproach is certainly well merited. But much of it also builds on claims that the Anglo-Saxon route to modern forms of political community differed significantly from others, especially the German—claims that are part of an outdated reading of European history that relies on overly static notions of bourgeois revolution and a German *Sonderweg*. Such criticism also ignores the extent to which social citizenship was a goal expressly adopted by other nations as their own in the postwar period. No one has been more assiduous in claiming social citizenship as theirs than the Swedes, even to the point of denying Beveridge any influence whatsoever. Moreover, whenever European students of social policy, with the exception perhaps of the Swiss, bother to compare their systems to others, whatever differences separate the European arrangements from each other quickly tend to fade in juxtaposition to what they share in common and in contrast to the rest of the globe. Beveridge and Marshall, in other words, managed to formulate something that has had an importance far beyond Britain.

None the less, it is true that the whole concept of social policy associated with their endeavours has in recent years eroded in terms of its ability to supply an understanding of the welfare state as a phenomenon found increasingly throughout the entire world. How should we evaluate the social citizenship welfare state in the light of these newest global developments in social policy? Until recently, much literature on the welfare state took the social citizenship model as the endpoint of social policy development. Sweden under Social Democratic reign was the welfare Mecca that all other nations were either striving towards or abjuring. The road to the welfare state was seen as a simple two-way street with movement possible only towards or away from the social citizenship model. One of the many peculiarities of this view was that it subjected developments in that increasingly dominant part of the world, that may rightly be considered as consisting of welfare states in one incarnation or another, to the intellectual hegemony of the historical evolution of one unusual and idiosyncratic corner of the globe: Sweden; somewhat more broadly phrased, Scandinavia; or, in the widest formulations, western Continental Europe north of the butter/oil line. The question is why, once we look away from the normative assumptions that often colour the hopes held by many students of social policy for the welfare state, developments that are localized to so comparatively limited an area should set the standard for all other places.

Gerhard Ritter, in a major reinterpretation of the global history of the welfare state, has tried to make Germany, rather than the Anglo-Swedish, Beveridge-Möller-Myrdal approach, the historically appropriate benchmark for the evolution of the welfare state (Ritter 1991). More provocatively, Richard Rose has recently argued that, measured in terms of geopolitical clout, what he calls the American-Pacific model of the welfare state should be the dominant prism through which to observe social policy development (Rose 1991). The American-Pacific model, for whatever worth so sweeping a typology can have, includes the major Pacific rim nations and involves a welfare state where the state plays a much less pronounced role than in the social citizenship model, one in which much social provision is given over to private, family, and business interests for administration and execution. Similar attempts to identify qualitatively different kinds of welfare states, not just different approximations to the ideal type of the social citizenship model, can be found in much recent literature on the welfare state (Baldwin 1992).

To the extent that this sea change in approaches to the welfare state holds, it obviously has implications for the social citizenship model and for any attempt to evaluate Beveridge's place in history. If the welfare state based on social citizenship is but one, and not even necessarily the most important, variety of welfare states, then the grand teleology inherent in Marshall's vision must come apart. The tension and ambiguity in the concepts of social citizenship and social rights are thus brought to the foreground. The beneficiary by virtue of citizenship and the beneficiary by contributory effort are more sharply distinguished in the privatized models of the welfare state than in the social citizenship model. Certain benefits that in some systems are social rights provided by the state are, in others, social rights bought on the market. The accent in these latter systems has shifted away from the citizen to the contributor. As these privatized systems come to dominate our view of the welfare state, the romance of the social citizenship model will be over.

FROM ONE NEW WORLD ORDER TO ANOTHER

Must Beveridge's ship rise and fall with the tides of the social citizenship welfare state? To the extent that he is one of its founders, clearly it must. The crucial emphasis on universality is one of the tenets of the social citizenship faith that we owe to him—one which we must, alas, watch honoured increasingly in the breach. But there is, at the same time, the individualistic, the liberal bent to Beveridge's thought. Viewed from the perspective of the social citizenship model, these aspects of his philosophy have been attacked most stridently. It was, so the usual claim runs, Beveridge's emphasis on voluntary action, on limiting the state's role, on encouraging individuals to provide for themselves beyond the state's purview, thus creating a gulf between those with and those without, that hobbled British social policy compared to those nations in which the state was made responsible for all aspects of provision. However, if Beveridge's philosophy is to maintain its force in the era when the social citizenship welfare state becomes marginalized, then it is precisely these vilified aspects of his philosophy that will be sought out. It is the anti-statist parts of his thought, if any, that harmonize with the American-Pacific model of social policy, or whatever (if any) designation eventually sticks to describe all those welfare states that are not like Sweden in the 1960s and unlikely to become so. It is these aspects of his philosophy, if any, that are likely to appeal to reformers in Eastern Europe who face the peculiar predicament of grappling with the legacy of decades, if not centuries, of an all-assuring state, and who, at the same time and precisely for this reason, are fuelled by desires to cut back the statist undergrowth in hopes of letting civil society luxuriate.

Sometime during the First World War, Beatrice Webb remarked rather sourly that it was 'a queer result of this strange and horrible war', that Beveridge of all people should have 'risen suddenly into the limelight as an accepted designer of the New World Order' (Harris 1977: 426). Were any contemporary reformers now to take inspiration from his philosophy, it would be hard to say why Beveridge was any more peculiar a formulator than those who claim to be designing the new world order of our own age.

REFERENCES

Baldwin, P. (1990), *The Politics of Social Solidarity: Class Bases of the European Welfare State*. Cambridge: Cambridge University Press.
——(1992), 'The Welfare State for Historians: A Review Essay', *Comparative Studies in Society and History*, 34/4.
Ewald, F. (1986), *L'État providence*. Paris: Grasset.
Goodin, R. E., and Le Grand, J. (eds.) (1987), *Not Only the Poor: The Middle Classes and the Welfare State*. London: Allen and Unwin.
Griffiths, J. (1969), *Pages from Memory*. London: Dent.
Hacking, I. (1990), *The Taming of Chance*. Cambridge: Cambridge University Press.
Harris, J. (1977), *William Beveridge*. Oxford: Clarendon Press.
Hills, J. (ed.) (1991), *The State of Welfare: The Welfare State in Britain Since 1974*. Oxford: Clarendon Press.
Jordan, B. (1991), 'Want', *Social Policy and Administration*, 25/1.
Kincaid, J. C. (1973), *Poverty and Equality in Britain*. Harmondsworth: Penguin.
Le Grand, J., and Winter, D. (1986), 'The Middle Classes and the Welfare State Under Conservative and Labour Governments', *Journal of Public Policy*, 6/4.
Mann, M. (1987), 'Ruling-Class Strategies and Citizenship', *Sociology*, 21/3.
Parry, R. (1986), 'United Kingdom', in P. Flora (ed.), *Growth to Limits: The Western European Welfare States Since World War II*, ii. Berlin: de Gruyter.
Pfaller, A., Gough, I., and Therborn, G. (1991), *Can The Welfare State Compete?* Basingstoke: Macmillan.
Pinker, R. (1971), *Social Theory and Social Policy*. London: Heinemann.
Rimlinger, G. V. (1983), 'Capitalism and Human Rights', *Daedalus*, 112/4.
Ritter, G. A. (1991), *Der Sozialstaat*, 2nd edn. Munich: Oldenbourg.

Rodriguez, E. (1982), 'Den Progressiva Inkomstbeskattningens Historia', *Historisk tidskrift*, 4.

Rose, R. (1991), 'Is American Public Policy Exceptional?', in B. E. Shafer (ed.), *Is America Different? A New Look at American Exceptionalism.* Oxford: Oxford University Press.

Turner, B. S. (1990), 'Outline of a Theory of Citizenship', *Sociology*, 24/2.

5

Beveridge and his Assumptive Worlds: The Incompatibilities of a Flawed Design[1]

HOWARD GLENNERSTER AND MARTIN EVANS

THEME

No historical document is cited more frequently in postwar social policy debate than the Beveridge Report (Beveridge 1942). The last official review of the UK social security system described itself as the most fundamental 'since Beveridge'. The most thoroughgoing independent review of taxes and benefits, the Meade Committee (1978), advocated 'a new Beveridge Scheme' (pp. 269–94). Critics lay the blame for what they see as the failure of social security in the UK since the Second World War at Beveridge's door (Dilnot, Kay, and Morris 1984). Feminists (Wilson 1977; Pierce 1980; Land 1976) have attacked the gendered assumptions of women's dependency built into the resulting system.

In short, for modern policy analysts the Beveridge Report has become a mine for critical quotations or support—a unique statement of principle largely removed from its time and place.

The theme of this chapter is that the historical context is critical to understanding the assumptions imbedded in the Report. Only by under-standing that context more fully can we reflect usefully on its contemporary relevance. Seeing the report as a final tablet of stone misses the importance of the *process* of negotiating it and the constraints under which it was drafted.

This chapter re-examines Beveridge's reasoning as revealed in his own private papers deposited in the LSE Library. It also examines the internal debate within the Committee on Social Insurance and Allied Services and between the Treasury, the Economic Section of the Cabinet and Beveridge and Keynes using the files deposited at the Public Record Office.[2] The result is to give a deeper understanding of Beveridge's own internal conflicts, the

---

[1] For the original use of this term, see K. Young (1977).
[2] For a longer and more detailed examination of this material, see Evans and Glennerster (1993).

compromises he had to make during its drafting to accommodate internal criticism and external interests. His desire to produce a popular yet fundamental document led him to emphasize the vision and hide the ambiguities. It is this which helps to explain the Report's appeal and its weakness as a policy document. We are still in its thrall. Perhaps the Report's fiftieth anniversary is a good time to throw off this legacy.

THE ARGUMENT

The famous and explicit 'assumptions' Beveridge wrote into his Report— the central importance of full employment to any system of social security, the vital role of child support, and a universal free health service—all these have stood the test of time. They were, perhaps, its most far-sighted passages. In contrast, paradoxically, the assumptions he made about the principles that should underlie social security have lasted less well. They were backward-looking, sometimes unspoken, and often conflicting. They are, above all, out of tune with modern aspirations of family life and the changed labour market.

Beveridge was responding above all to three demands that had become articulated by progressive opinion and the labour movement at the time:

the establishment of a national minimum administered nationally;
a citizenship basis for entitlement to benefit;
no means test.

The origins of these demands long pre-date this period; but the 1941 Determination of Needs Act and the centralization of assistance in the early years of the war had already embodied some of these influences. The 1930s experience of the means test had sharpened the call for entitlement, and the War created irresistible pressure for higher pensions and more fundamental change. Beveridge sought to meet all three aspirations. To do so he chose to work within established mechanisms, such as the flat-rate insurance contribution, and not to adopt progressive funding, either progressive taxation or wage-related contributions. This made irreconcilable his objectives of subsistence adequacy and universal coverage. This was recognized at the time by those giving evidence and by internal government critics. Increasingly as the drafting progressed Beveridge was forced to recognize it too. The principle of subsistence fitted badly with flat-rate benefits, and the principle of contribution fitted ill with true universal citizenship. The first section examines these conflicts as they emerged at the time. In the second section we discuss the compromises that resulted: on rent, on women and other excluded groups, and on the poverty line. Today the contingencies he glossed over have become far more significant. The final section of the paper discusses the lasting implications of this ambiguous process.

1. THE CONFLICT

UNIVERSAL ENTITLEMENT OR STATUS THROUGH PAID WORK?

At the heart of Beveridge's thinking was a contradictory struggle between his deep desire to cover everything and everyone without a means test and his choice of method, contributory insurance through employment. He wished to give security to all, but to base this security, apart from family allowances, on participation in the labour market. Why did Beveridge not choose a citizenship basis for benefits?

Beveridge brought with him a lifetime of experience of insurance. He had played a large part in introducing unemployment insurance in 1911. He had written his somewhat hurried tract for the Liberals in 1924 advocating the insurance of 'all and everything' (Beveridge 1924). He had been a long-standing chairman of the Unemployment Insurance Committee, where he had encouraged the move to subsistence-level unemployment insurance. He accepted the compromise between employers, workers, and the state on a contributory principle as being immutable. To have gone back on it would have lost the support of the trade unions that would be necessary if the conservatives within government were to be defeated. The historical advantage of the contributory principle was that it had given recipients moral worth through contribution. There is some evidence that the passing of the 1934 Unemployment Act, which separated the administration of insurance benefits from means tested ones, had increased the acceptability of the contributory principle amongst working people (Harris 1986). An extension of the contributory principle to cover all eventualities meant that 'We are all, so to speak, made "deserving" by Act of Parliament' (Wootton 1943*a*: 361). Yet that was an exaggeration.

Evidence from the International Labour Office pointed out that when it came to women and other categories of recipient with poor labour market experience, the contribution principle would not work.[3] As the discussions advanced, some contingencies lost status by being either dropped or left to assistance because they would not fit the contributory principle. We elaborate on this in the next section. Moreover, his contributory logic led him to downgrade steadily the generosity and acceptability of assistance. In his original heads of a scheme he makes this clear:

An assistance scheme which does not in some way leave the person with an effective

[3] PRO CAB 87/79: SIC(42)39, International Labour Office memorandum.

motive to avoid the need for assistance, undermines the Security scheme ... an assistance scheme which makes those assisted unamenable to economic rewards or punishments while treating them as free citizens is inconsistent with the principles of a free community.[4]

At the Committee's first meeting Beveridge had set up a subcommittee to discuss assistance. The groups it was to provide for were defined as: 'Cripples and deformed, deaf and dumb, mentally deficient, and vagrants and moral weaklings'.[5] But also destined for assistance were those Beveridge was to exclude from contributing: separated or single women bringing up children, and those who fell out of the scheme because of administrative difficulty or cost: unemployed, self-employed, and domestic spinsters. Largest in numbers would be those who would need supplementation for their insurance benefits in the proposed twenty-year transitional period before pensions would be paid at flat rate, and those with 'exceptional' needs, above all those with rent above a minimum level. Despite the size of this residual group, which kept growing in significance as the discussions wore on, Beveridge stuck to his belief that insurance could cover virtually all categories of need. He was therefore led to downgrade assistance and reinforce its stigmatic nature at just the time when the Determination of Needs Act 1941, its abolition of the household means test, and the new Assistance Board were beginning to hold out the possibility of a more humane system of means-testing. Beveridge himself recognised this[6] but it did not change his basic view.

There was another element to the debate about the contributory principle, however, which worried the Treasury and the economists. Why have a separate system of collecting revenue from the ordinary tax system? Here the debate within the Treasury and the Economic Section of the Cabinet is instructive to the modern reader.

CONTRIBUTIONS OR A UNIFIED PROGRESSIVE TAX?

The Treasury's timeless view 'did not favour assigned revenues and felt it was objectionable to give a first charge on any source of revenue. Experience indicated that if such a fund showed a balance, there was a demand for increased benefits; but if it showed a deficit the Treasury was asked to provide a subsidy.'[7] The Economic Section's view of contributions was ambivalent.[8] In the main they considered contributions were an outdated, illogical, regressive tax.[9] Keynes, who held a kind of roving commission

---

[4] PRO CAB 87/76: SIC(41)20, 'Basic Problems of Social Security and Heads of a Scheme'.
[5] PRO CAB 87/77: SIC(A)(42), minutes of 1st meeting.
[6] BP 8/33: typed n., Means Tests, undated.
[7] PRO CAB 87/76: SIC(41), minutes of 4th meeting.
[8] PRO T 230/100: n. by R. C. Tress.
[9] PRO T 161/1164/S484971/2: Keynes, Sir William Beveridge's Proposals, 13 Oct. 1942.

within the Treasury, objected not to a specific social security tax but 'to the peculiar method of a poll tax and to the inevitable inadequacy of the contribution so long as it is a poll tax.'[10] James Meade commented:

The continuation of the principle of social security financed by compulsory *insurance* premiums is probably due to conservatism rather than to any logically more cogent reason. ... Why is it not proposed to add the costs of family allowances to the Social Insurance Fund? Surely it is just as logical to finance these by compulsory contributions as it is to finance old-age pensions by these means? Why is not part of the cost of education borne by the Social Insurance Fund, while the greater part of a national health service is to be so borne? The answer, of course, is that we all see the dangers and inequities of compulsory contributions; we are therefore unwilling to add to them, but are not yet ready to drop those which already exist— which in my view would be the sensible thing to do.[11]

Keynes came to realise that arguing for a progressive tax basis for social security was ahead of its time. Beveridge's aims but not his methods were important to support. Keynes summed up the pragmatic approach in his response to Meade:

I am very much in favour of something along the lines of Beveridge's proposals, as I gather you are. ... I agree in theory that employees' and employers' contributions are inferior to a charge on general taxes. On the other hand, it seems to me essential to retain them, at any rate in the first stages of the new scheme, in order that the additional charges on the Budget may not look altogether too formidable.[12]

In short, it would be a way of winning the Treasury over.

Moreover, the mechanism for collecting contributions existed and workers were used to it; although, nevertheless, Keynes thought that after the War the two systems could be merged. His new postwar system of taxation would therefore have included a special wage-related social security tax equivalent to 12.5 per cent of the total salary bill.[13] For Keynes the flat-rate contribution was a short-term administrative expedient. For Beveridge it was a matter of principle.[14] Here, as elsewhere, we see how wrong it is to lump Keynes and Beveridge together as later commentators tend to do.

INSURANCE AND A NATIONAL MINIMUM?

In 1924 Beveridge had not seen a unified insurance scheme as the vehicle for achieving a national minimum. The notion of a subsistence minimum seemed to offer a way of achieving both, especially when Beveridge read

[10] PRO T 161/1164/5484971/2: Keynes, letter to Sir R. Hopkins.
[11] PRO T 230/101: n. on SIC(41)20, James Meade, 20 Feb. 1942.
[12] PRO T 230/101: Keynes to Meade, 8 May 1942.
[13] PRO T 161/1164: Keynes, letter to Sir R. Hopkins 20/7/42.
[14] See e.g. his discussions with Keynes in Sept. 1942: PRO T 161/1164/S484971/2.

Rowntree's latest poverty study. Rowntree's study of York in 1936, *Poverty and Progress*, was published in August 1941, and provided the latest available information about living standards, apart from the Ministry of Labour household survey in 1937 and 1938, data from which became available in 1941 (Rowntree 1941).

Beveridge was convinced by Rowntree's study that the cause of poverty had changed to one that was largely amenable to solution through insurance benefits. The main reasons for economic insecurity and poverty had altered from low wages to unemployment and old age. The importance of this change is difficult to underestimate for Beveridge. His notes on Rowntree's book confirm that he took this causative model as his own and relied on it: 'the causes of poverty directly amenable to social insurance accounted for one quarter of the primary poverty in 1899 and for five sixths of the primary poverty in 1936'.[15] This finding meant that universal and comprehensive national insurance could solve poverty in the majority of cases. In addition to these findings, Rowntree also provided essential information about expenditure on existing insurance schemes, and gave data on incomes which allowed Beveridge to calculate that a redistribution of income within the working class could solve poverty for the lowest income groups within them.

But if Rowntree gave Beveridge support for his paradigm of national insurance, Beveridge did not allow benefits to meet Rowntree's paradigm of relieving poverty. Beveridge's main interest in poverty levels and its definition was as evidence to legitimate benefits, *at a flat rate*. For Rowntree, the logic of the poverty line was sacrosanct. If anyone fell below it, their income was deficient for minimum standards, and, in a benefit scheme which aimed at ending poverty, would have to be brought up to meet it. Rent was the essential need which varied so greatly that it could not be brought within a flat rate subsistence definition. Beveridge was caught between agreeing that poverty, in principle, should be met by his flat-rate benefit, and the cost and the practical disadvantage of having to vary benefit levels to meet actual rent. That would mean extensive means-testing. This fundamental conflict was never resolved.

SUBSISTENCE IN NAME ONLY?

While Beveridge was willing to sacrifice the principle of subsistence to the requirements of his other principles—flat rate of contribution and benefit and universal insurance—Rowntree was not: 'I feel that if this principle is adopted it will go far to defeat the purpose that you have in view in

---

[15] BP 8/28: draft, 'Scale of Benefit and Subsistence Scales'.

recommending different rates of benefit, namely, to get rid of poverty.'[16]
But Beveridge, after wavering, stuck to the other principles. 'There remains
the question of rent. For the purposes of benefit it will probably be
impossible to avoid taking a flat figure for rent for the whole country in
spite of the marked variations of rent in individual cases.'[17] Ironically,
Beveridge the social scientist was pragmatically altering the logic of subsistence to meet the political and administrative constraints. Rowntree wrote
to Jowitt to tell him that Beveridge was in breach of the poverty principle
on rents.[18] The problem of rent proved to be the easiest of the exploitable
weaknesses in Beveridge's scheme. When the matter was later discussed by
the Phillips Committee, the official Committee on the Beveridge Report,[19]
the problem of rent was seized upon to undermine the subsistence argument
for insurance benefits.

GENDER OR CITIZENSHIP?

The other fundamental inconsistency between the contributory principle
based on paid work and citizenship rights was, of course, the rights of
married women. Modern feminist writers tend to portray the social security
system as containing a hidden set of assumptions about the structure of the
family and gender relations. Beveridge was very clear about his, especially
in his private notes to himself. The role of the family was a consistent
feature of much of his writings, it was the pivotal focus of human life:

What matters vitally to every human being, is the handful of other human beings
to whom he is linked by birth or marriage, not the indifferent millions with whom
he shares this changing world ... Mating and birth, the fundamental processes by
which human life is arrived at, are the same for all men and women at all times.
They give rise to relations of companionship between man and woman, and mutual
support between parents and children and brothers and sisters and kindred—which
are at all times similar.[20]

War emphasized his view that the family was the most important institution
for stability and for the development of individual personality. The family
was an economic and social division of labour which best met those income-
support functions. The state provided welfare support in order to sponsor,
maintain, or alter behaviour to ensure the organic unity of the family, and
hence the greater organic good of the society and race. Beveridge's views
were very clear (Beveridge 1924: 4).

---

[16] BP 8/28: Rowntree to Beveridge, 1 Jul. 1942.
[17] BP 8/28: Beveridge, n. of the Subsistence Minimum for Unemployment and Sickness
Benefit, 20 Apr. 1942.
[18] See Evans (1992) on the whole issue of rent and assistance at this period.
[19] PRO/T 161/1129/548497/01.
[20] BP 11a: 'Notes for Changes in Family Life', broadcast, 23 Jan. 1932.

The difficulty for Beveridge was to bring together his largely unchanged view of the family with the changes which had occurred in his assumptions about women's status.

Beveridge idealized marriage and, by 1942, his earlier unhappiness from rejection on several occasions had changed as a result of his planned marriage to Janet Mair. His view of marriage was based on a companionship of different but equal partners. In this his views matched more modern 'progressive' ideas, 'the basis of what was considered an ideal marriage had changed profoundly from patriarchy to companionship' (Lewis 1984: 120). His views on equality of status within marriage were of long standing. In the early 1930s he broadcast on family issues and expounded the view of modern marriage as one that was evolving into a partnership of equals. In this thinking he was influenced by German academic Müller Lyer who was influential amongst feminist academics of the early 1930s (Müller Lyer 1931; Dyhouse, 1989: 73). In Müller Lyer's evolutionary development, British marriage was developing between the second stage—one of nuclear families dominated by the economic power of the man—and a third stage, which Beveridge, summarising, described as:

the personal stage, not yet wholly achieved anywhere, but gradually coming upon us. The development of manufacturing and trade deprives the household of many of its former functions. The state undertakes duties that were formerly those of the family such as education, or provision for old age. The personalities of wife and children claim and get independent recognition from the state. The family becomes less closely knit, less dominated by one member, perhaps less permanent.[21]

The change to companionate marriage, more prevalent in middle-class marriages, was accompanied by changes in the independent legal status of women within marriage which allowed them independent rights to property, and in 1937, greater access to divorce, especially on the grounds of desertion. Together with this growth in independence of legal status within marriage was the growing economic independence of women to earn, if only to earn unequal wages to men. The companionate view became the dominant paradigm of marriage in the 1950s (Finch and Summerfield 1991), but was progressive for its time, and influenced by feminist thinking. Thus, for Beveridge, the question of whether married women should work was a matter of freedom of choice, but that choice was made in an idealized partnership where the realities of power and discrimination were unrecognised:

It is true that most married women will not wish to go on working for pay because they will have plenty of work to do as housewives and mothers. But in a free society it ought to be left to the wife herself and her husband to decide on this.[22]

---

[21] BP 11a: Notes for broadcast, 23 Jan. 1932.
[22] BP 9a/80: typed draft, 'Looking Ahead: Leisure by Compulsion', 1945.

A TEAM?

Equality of status for Beveridge meant that man and wife were a *team*; within this team each was performing work of the same importance. Beveridge avowed that married women should never be called 'adult dependants'. But his conception of independence for women depended on the assumption of a fundamental difference in social and economic status for married women over single women and men. This difference was partly one of practice—'More than seven out of every eight married women in peace time follow no gainful occupation; provision for married women should be framed with reference to the seven rather than the one.'[23] But the legal duty of unconditional maintenance by the husband supplanted any consideration of the individual needs of the married woman because of the legally enforceable right to maintenance. Women 'acquire by marriage a new economic and social status. . . . On marriage a woman acquires a legal right to maintenance by her husband, as a first line of defence against risks which fall directly on the solitary woman.'[24] The state had no duty or right to supplant the economic relationships between man and wife, only to supplement them when it came to provision for children. Beveridge had a view of family income which, in Wootton's words, entailed a 'presumption of pooling' (Wootton 1943*b*).

These assumptions did not go unchallenged at the time. An alternative view was presented to him by the National Council of Women, who wanted all women and men to have equal benefit status:

It does not matter whether a woman is married or single, she will or will not be gainfully employed, or employed under a contract of service. The limit in the amount of benefit to a proportion of wages will automatically provide the spur to resume earning. It is in our opinion wrong and wholly irrelevant to use marriage and non-marriage as a factor governing insurance rights.[25]

Beveridge's reasoning on all this is interesting in the light of modern debate. If the married woman was not in employment, this did not mean for Beveridge that she was not engaged in vital and 'equally important' work. This depended on the performance of two duties, housework and motherhood.

Housework was women's work but married women's duty. The role of the married housewife thus differed from that of the spinster who stayed on to care for elderly parents in their home. Married housewifery was different because it was not through choice, but through a duty to the husband. This led Beveridge to speculate:

[23] PRO CAB 87/76: SIC(41)20, 'Basic Problems of Social Security with Heads of a Scheme', p. 10.
[24] Ibid. 19.
[25] PRO CAB 87/79: SIC(42)46, letter from National Council of Women.

It might be argued that a married woman, whether earning or not, should have her contribution record kept separate. The spinster engaged in unpaid domestic service would certainly need to have a contribution card and would no doubt be paid by her parents. But in the case of married women the husband assumes responsibility and pays a contribution to cover both.[26]

MOTHERHOOD AND PRO-NATALISM

Beveridge's conception of motherhood cannot be separated from his views on population and eugenics. But these assumptions are rarely made explicit in the published Report except for the famous phrase: 'In the next thirty years housewives as mothers have vital work to do in ensuring the adequate continuance of the British Race' (Beveridge 1942: 53). However, that was no throwaway remark. Underpinning it was a lifetime of concern with eugenics—not only the rate of birth but its quality.

Beveridge's assumptions about a declining birthrate were, by 1941, wrong. In the early 1940s the birthrate actually increased. In common with most other contemporary observers he mistakenly extrapolated previous demographic statistics (Mitchison 1977). The absence of a census in 1941 explains the paucity of contemporary demographic data, but the rising surge of pro-natalism, and its acceptance by most mainstream progressive thought, meant that in the 1940s Britain was perceived to have had a 'population problem' (Titmuss 1938; Titmuss and Titmuss 1942), and so did all the Western, white democracies (Myrdal 1940; Carr-Saunders 1936). Beveridge had been a long-term advocate of positive pro-natalist and eugenic policies. His involvement in eugenic debate was of long standing (Harris 1977: 341–2; Freeden 1979).

The Beveridge Report makes note of the population problem in general: 'With its present rate of reproduction, the British race cannot continue; means of reversing the recent course of the birth rate must be found' (Beveridge 1942: 154); but does not make any remarks about his long-held views on the quality of the population. In retrospect he saw his proposals as having mildly eugenic effects. His notes to himself on children's allowances are frank:

Children's allowances in the form proposed in my Report cannot well have any but a directly eugenic effect. The criticism to be made on the proposal from the eugenic point of view is not what it does but what it fails to do because it is too limited.[27]

Reflecting Reddaway (Fisher 1931 and 1943; Reddaway 1939), he goes on:

[26] PRO CAB 87/78: SIC(42), minutes of 19th meeting.
[27] BP 9a/78: draft notes, 'Children's Allowances and the Race, ii: Restoring the Need', undated.

A civilised community should be concerned with its own breed as it is concerned with the breed of animals, but it need not and should not interfere with the freedom of individual citizens in the matter of choosing mates. All that is essential is that the economic structure of the community should no longer be such as to favour those who are less successful rather than those who are more successful in rendering services to the community.[28]

Higher rewards had to be given to the professional classes. Beveridge concluded that what was needed were wage-related family allowances as part of pay *and* continued tax rebates for children. They never found their way into the Report. These fundamental ambiguities in Beveridge's assumptions and background thinking began to unravel as the discussion on his original proposals to the Committee (see Abel-Smith, Ch. 2 in this volume) progressed. Just some examples are given in the next section.

2. THE COMPROMISES

Beveridge's notion that insurance by itself would be sufficient to eliminate want, except for quite exceptional cases, was only tenable if the insured categories were indeed universal. As discussion of the detail progressed, reality proved less tidy. The idea that insurance benefits should be fixed at poverty levels conflicted with the notion of insurance as a system of security against income loss. Such a conception required income-related benefits. That conflict of principle was clearest in the case of industrial injury where the trade unions had a particular interest. Once again Beveridge compromised. He set industrial injury benefit at a higher level than other basic state benefits.

INDUSTRIAL INJURY

Beveridge himself saw that the nature of industrial compensation was different to other areas of social insurance, and as a result of this difference proposed a compromise of principle. In his original notes Beveridge agreed that the risk to be insured had developed in a way which differed from normal interruptions of earnings.

Damages under law were mainly based on lost earnings and hence were not suited to being defined as subsistence levels of benefit. The risks of accident or injury differed between workplaces so widely that some element of risk weighting was essential for employers. Beveridge's conception of industrial disability was therefore profoundly influenced by what had gone before. Whether this view was formed in anticipation of TUC demands is

[28] Ibid.

not clear; however, he was faced with a logical as well as a political dilemma. How was he to reconcile the conflict between an earnings-related benefit and a flat-rate system and to accommodate trades union views?

In fact, industrial injuries went to the heart of the conceptual difficulty posed by any attempt to combine the insurance principle with the flat-rate national minimum. Security against loss of earnings implied a wage-related scheme. The discussions pointed to the impossibility of a universal approach without a citizenship benefit based on assessed disability or an earnings-related benefit to reflect the loss of earnings. What agreement there was on Beveridge's compromise was based not on unanimous agreement to a universal solution but on sectional interest.

WOMEN'S CONTINGENCIES

Were women to be equal as workers and hence contributors, or were non-working women's needs, in particular those of married women, also to be included in an insurance scheme? Beveridge was determined to include women, both married and unmarried, within his universal insurance scheme.[29] But how was it to be done?

In the earlier notes Beveridge made on the scheme, he considered whether benefit rates for women should be equal, and on what basis married women should be included in the scheme. He only saw three alternatives for the inclusion of married women: at a special rate; after a special test; or on the basis of limited contributions from work. One of the outcomes of attempting to include married women as citizens under an employee-based contribution scheme was that married women who did not work would inevitably be dependent on husbands' contributions. Beveridge rationalized this in the following way:

Marriage should be treated as beginning a new life for the woman. She should not carry on into the first year of marriage during which she is no longer dependent on earnings (i.e. dependent on husband's earnings), claims to unemployment or disability benefit based on previous contributions. She should get the value of her contributions before marriage in other ways.[30]

The treatment of married women is one of the most troublesome problems in social insurance. The problem is approached here on a new line ... by recognition of housewives, that is married women of working age living with their husbands, as a distinct security class requiring provision for risks peculiar to themselves—the economic risks of marriage.[31]

---

[29] PRO CAB 87/77: SIC(42), minutes of 5th meeting.
[30] PRO CAB 87/80: SIC(42)60, report of Sub-Committee on Administration: n. by Chairman.
[31] PRO CAB 87/76: SIC(41)20, 'Basic Problems of Social Security with Heads of a Scheme', p. 10.

There was no international precedent for Beveridge's unequal treatment of married women.

WIDOWHOOD, SEPARATION AND DIVORCE

If women, on marriage, entered into a new insurance status, then it followed that their status must change on the end of marriage. As insurance was against economic insecurity and married women relied on their husbands' earning power for such security, then Beveridge saw the premature end of marriage as an essential contingency:

One of the economic risks of marriage to the woman lies in the possibility that the marriage may end prematurely through death of the husband, by desertion or by legal separation, bringing to an end the maintenance upon which during marriage she has relied, and for which she has given unpaid work or the opportunity of fitting herself for such work.[32]

Beveridge in his original proposals reversed his previous thinking that widows should primarily be deemed as able to return to the labour market; he proposed a pension until 60, with higher additions if widowhood began after the age of 55.

The logic of widowhood held also for separation, the only proviso being the potential abuse of such a provision and the link between the Courts, alimony and benefits. But the costs of widened provision became more difficult to defend, and widows and separated wives became marginalized as a result. The argument that such provisions 'subsidised sin' was not given any credence by Beveridge and such opposition came later.[33]

Beveridge reverted to the stipulation that widows without children should, whatever their age, return to the labour market after thirteen weeks of widows' allowance. In this he reflected the majority of evidence given to him on the subject (Beveridge 1942: 65). The only recognition of the poor employment prospects of such women was seen as covered by the promise of training benefit. The unfairness of this for women in their mid-fifties was opposed strongly within the Committee by Mary Hamilton and Muriel Cox, from the Ministry of Pensions, who wanted a lower pensionable age for childless widows at 50.

CARING

There was little discussion of caring responsibilities. The financial penalties of lower rates of assistance given to pensioners staying in relatives' homes

---

[32] Ibid.
[33] See PRO (PIN 8/137).

was remarked upon, but a demand to give the same rate of assistance in these cases to that received in the house of a stranger was damned as a 'commercialization of relations between parent and children' in evidence from the National Council of Social Service, and Beveridge agreed.[34] The role of the domestic spinster was discussed, but discussion centred around fitting this non-commercial arrangement into a contribution scheme which depended on contracts of employment or self-employment. At one stage Beveridge envisaged that the cared-for, usually elderly parents, would pay the contributions of the carer. As we have shown above, this situation was contrasted with that of the married woman who could in no way be termed as 'employed' by her husband. The impracticalities of such an arrangement show that the whole contributory system was flawed for carers who became, after some consideration, dependent on National Assistance.

3. THE CONSEQUENCES

Our review ends at the time of the publication of the Report, and we do not cover the reaction to and implementation of Beveridge's proposals. The appeal of the Report lay in its apparent simplicity and comprehensiveness as well as its Bunyanesque prose. Yet, we have argued, that simplicity was illusory.

Beveridge was trying to reconcile the demand for a national minimum without a means test with his original belief in the insurance of all and everything, and with his insistence that the flat-rate contribution and benefit was, although atypical in international terms, correct.

We have shown how this approach began to unravel during the discussions on the Report. The critics had come from the traditional Treasury selectivist position, most powerfully argued by Henderson (1955); from the moderate left, in the Fabian and PEP evidence, who argued for a more progressive form of revenue; from Keynes, who argued the long-term case for a progressive social security tax; and from women's groups. The treatment of rent showed up a basic flaw and Beveridge himself came close to accepting it.

An insurance-based scheme could not meet all contingencies. It did not do so then and came to do so less and less as contingencies that Beveridge downplayed, or assumed were solved, grew in importance: unemployment, temporary and part time employment, self employment on low pay, single parenthood. Rent grew in significance as rents rose in relation to income and became more geographically varied.

[34] PRO CAB 87/77: SIC(42), minutes of 8th meeting, evidence of the National Council of Social Service.

Beveridge's views on women's role were, we have argued, integral to the Report and even more distant from modern attitudes than a simple reading of the Report might suggest.

Gradually these defects came to be recognized in the succeeding decades. Wage related benefits and contributions came gradually. Women came in 1975 to gain, temporarily, some recognition of their non-paid work in the calculation of pension rights. The separation of rent from social security and 100 per cent rent reimbursement had to wait until the 1980s.

Assistance came to be seen as a necessary main-line service. Paradoxically, what the UK social security system owes most to this period *is* the idea of a national minimum—a poverty line which the central state sustained. Its origins lie with Rowntree, the Webbs indeed, but its popularization is Beveridge's. Yet he did little to advance it practically: that we owe to the much-despised National Assistance Board and its successors. It was a national means-tested safety net that was to mark the UK out from many of its European neighbours and from the United States; and it was what has given the UK, until recently, a good record in sustaining a low but effective safety net. Beveridge, by casting assistance as a minimalist agency, of lower moral standing, the recourse of 'cripples, the deformed ... and moral weaklings', only made that task more difficult.

The flat-rate and subsistence basis for social insurance was, however, to damn it. At the time it was seen as economically dangerous and too expensive a promise for the state to give. The contradiction between subsistence, rent, and flat-rate benefits provided the central weakness with which the Committee on the Beveridge Report, chaired by T. Phillips, undermined the Report. Later, as a flat-rate poverty-based scheme, it never had a hope of securing the support of the middle class as social security has done in the US. State pensions lost their citizenship support. In 1992, after a decade of serious erosion, the decline of the state pension was not a major issue of debate in the General Election. By then over half of pension income in the UK came from private schemes. Nor was anyone taken in by the term 'contribution' any more. Politicians of all kinds simply lumped it and income tax together as a combined tax rate, much as Keynes and Meade foresaw. A few years earlier the reality of a national minimum also disappeared when supplementary benefits became income support. Assistance benefits no longer have any baseline of adequacy in their design. Indeed, the Social Fund loans undermine any minimum level of weekly income, and the young unemployed may sink beneath a Plimsoll line of subsistence.

The assumptions Beveridge made about the relative unimportance of low wages and impermanent jobs are even less sustainable now than they were in the 1940s. So, too, are his assumptions about the family team, female responsibilities and the permanence of husband-and-wife relations.

He was very clear, as we saw, that women in the postwar world would not and should not be paid workers. He seemed to glimpse that the 'new marriage' might be impermanent but did not follow the consequences through. The idea of crediting child care or other forms of care for pension entitlement was not far from some of the suggestions presented to him, but would have contradicted the clear notion of work, marriage, and the family which he held. Here, too, the assumptive world has moved on. Beveridge was caught between the Edwardian world of social policy and the postwar world he could only partially glimpse. Yet he was only a creature of his times, a mirror, not a prophet. Few of his contemporaries, and certainly not the TUC, were any more farsighted.

Where Beveridge was surely right was in seeing that a national minimum, a necessarily ambiguous term (Atkinson 1990), depended fundamentally on the broader social policy framework—his formal explicit assumptions: a universal child benefit at a level that removed wage-earning families from the poverty line, a national health service free at the point of use, an active employment policy.

What we cannot deny Beveridge is his sense of vision, his attempt to think on a large scale despite opposition. It seems as necessary now as it was fifty years ago in a very different world.

REFERENCES

Atkinson, A. B. (1990), 'A National Minimum? A History of Ambiguity in the Determination of Benefit Scales in Britain', Welfare State Programme Discussion Paper WSP/47. London: LSE.

Beveridge, W. H. (1924), *Insurance for All and Everything*. London: Daily News.

—— (1942), *Social Insurance and Allied Services*, Cmd. 6404. London: HMSO.

—— (1943), *The Pillars of Security*. London: Allen and Unwin.

—— (1953), *Power and Influence*. London: Hodder and Stoughton.

Carr-Saunders, A. M. (1936), *World Population*. Oxford: Clarendon Press.

Crew, F. A. E. (1945), 'Biological Aspects', in J. Marchant (ed.), *Rebuilding Family Life in The Post-War World*. London: Odhams.

Cutler, T., Williams, K., and Williams, J. (1986), *Keynes, Beveridge and Beyond*. London: Routledge and Kegan Paul.

Dilnot, A. W., Kay, A., and Morris, C. N. (1984), *The Reform of Social Security*. Oxford: Oxford University Press.

Dyhouse, C. (1989), *Feminism and The Family in England 1880–1939*. Oxford: Basil Blackwell.

Evans, M. (1992), 'Making Rents Affordable? The Development and Outcomes of Housing and Social Security Policy in Britain, 1945–1986', unpublished Ph.D. thesis, London: LSE.

Evans, M. and Glennerster, H. (1993), *Squaring the Circle? The Inconsistencies and Constraints of Beveridge's Plan*, Welfare State Programme Discussion Paper WSP/85. London: LSE.

Finch, J., and Summerfield, P. (1991), 'Social Reconstruction and The Emergence of Companionate Marriage', in D. Clark (ed.), *Marriage, Domestic Life and Social Change: Writings for Jacqueline Burgoyne (1944–88)*. London: Routledge.

Fisher, R. A. (1931), 'The Biological Effects of Family Allowances', *Family Endowment Chronicle*, 1/3.

—— (1943), 'The Birthrate and Family Allowances', *Agenda*, 2/2.

Freeden, M. (1979), 'Eugenics and Progressive Thought', *Historical Journal*, 22/3.

Harris, J. (1975), 'Social Planning in War-time: Some Aspects of the Beveridge Report', in J. M. Winter (ed.), *War and Economic Development*. Cambridge: Cambridge University Press.

—— (1977), *William Beveridge: A Biography*. Oxford: Clarendon Press.

—— (1986), 'Political Ideas and The Debate on State Welfare, 1940–45', in H. L. Smith (ed.), *War and Social Change: British Society in the Second World War*. Manchester: Manchester University Press.

Henderson, H. D. (1955), 'The Principles of The Beveridge Plan', in *The Inter-War Years and Other Papers*. Oxford: Clarendon Press.

Land, H. (1976), 'Women: Supporters or Supported?', in D. L. Barker and S. Allen (eds.), *Sexual Divisions and Society: Process and Change*. London: Tavistock.

Lewis, J. (1984), *Women in England 1870–1950: Sexual Divisions and Social Change*. Brighton: Wheatsheaf.

Meade Committee (1978), *The Structure and Reform of Direct Taxation*. London: IFS/Allen and Unwin.

Mitchison, R. (1977), *British Population Change Since 1860*. London: Macmillan.

Müller Lyer, F. (1931), *The Family*, trans. F. W. Stella Browne. London: Allen and Unwin.

Myrdal, G. (1940), *Population: A Problem for Democracy*. Cambridge, Mass.: Humphry Milford.

Pierce, S. (1980), 'Single Mothers and the Concept of Female Dependency in the Development of the Welfare State in Britain', *Journal of Contemporary Family Studies*, 11/1.

Reddaway, M. A. (1939), *The Economics of Declining Population*. London: Allen and Unwin.

Rowntree, B. S. (1941), *Poverty and Progress: A Second Social Survey*. London: Longman Green.

Titmuss, R. M. (1938), *Poverty and Population*. London: Macmillan.

—— and Titmuss, K. (1942), *Parents Revolt*. London: Secker and Warburg.

Wilson, E. (1977), *Women and the Welfare State*. London: Tavistock.

Wootton, B. (1943a), 'Before and After Beveridge', *Political Quarterly*, 14/4.

—— (1943b), 'Am I My Brother's Keeper?', *Agenda*, 3/2.

Young, K. (1977), 'The Assumptive World of Policy Makers: Values in the Policy Process', *Policy and Politics*, 5/3.

6

Beveridge and Old Age

JOHN MACNICOL

INTRODUCTION

In most accounts of the making of the Beveridge Report, the saga of retirement pensions has received relatively little attention. Generally, Beveridge's task has been seen as unproblematic and essentially managerial—to merge and universalize the two existing schemes of non-contributory (1908) and contributory (1925) old age pensions into one new system, to co-ordinate this with other parts of the reorganized social security plan, and to bring pensions up to a level of notional 'subsistence'. Yet, as Beveridge himself fully realized, retirement pensions are the single most important element in modern welfare states. From the vantage-point of 1942, he could see that the spread of retirement over the course of the twentieth century was creating a large and growing class of welfare claimants at the top end of the age structure, such that state pensions would become easily the biggest item in the social security budget and a major item in total public expenditure. Provision for age was thus, for Beveridge, 'the largest single problem in social insurance' (1943: 68–9). Indeed, 'the problem of age' was to dominate the Beveridge Report such that, as this paper will show, old people were to be treated in a markedly different way from other envisaged clients of the brave new welfare state. The problem of old age income support had a long history, and by the late 1930s was reaching a crisis. Beveridge's task was to resolve this crisis. But the resolution was not an easy one to achieve, since it required a reconciliation between the essential legitimating principles of the Beveridge plan—in particular, adequacy of benefit and universality of cover—and the fiscal realities that constrained the redistributive potential of those principles.

OLD AGE PENSIONS, 1878–1942

The 1908 Old Age Pensions Act offered the aged poor in Britain very limited protection against poverty. The story of how the original pension proposals were whittled down under Treasury pressure is well known, and need not be repeated here. Essentially, in order to limit the cost to something around £7,000,000 per annum the qualifying age was raised from 65 to 70 and restrictions relating to means, nationality, status, and character were attached. (These latter proved difficult to operate and were considerably relaxed in 1911; they tend to be of interest primarily for their symbolic significance.) By these restrictions, the expected number of pension claimants was considerably reduced: in the United Kingdom in 1907 there were 2.1 million persons aged 65 and over and 1.25 million aged 70 and over; but the first payments in January 1909 went to a mere 490,000 pensioners, this figure rising to 642,000 by March 1912 because of the 1911 relaxations.

Most historians have emphasized the niggardly nature of the 1908 Act. But I would here like to suggest that it contained three elements which, *potentially* at any rate, made it probably the most radically redistributive piece of social policy ever introduced.

Firstly, the Act primarily benefited women. Although making up 58.6 per cent of the population aged 70 and over, they constituted fully 62.5 per cent of old age pensioners. The 1908 Act proved, if proof were needed, what Charles Booth and a few other thoughtful commentators had been arguing—and which, no doubt, every working-class woman knew—that poverty in old age was essentially a woman's problem. The combination of low wages when single, full-time motherhood, an almost total inability to accumulate savings over the life cycle, plus greater longevity, made old age much more economically hazardous for women than for men. Indeed, the feminization of poverty in old age has been a striking feature of the twentieth century, though somewhat neglected in social policy literature (which has tended to focus on the rather more controversial terrain of single-mother poverty).

Secondly, the Act was tax-funded and thus highly redistributive in that it targeted the poorest of the working class. This point was not lost on socialists, who henceforth began to see old age pensions as one channel through which the capitalist class could be stripped of its wealth. By 1919, for example, several labour organizations were committed to the demand for a 'citizenship' pension of £1 per week paid as of right, with no means tests, to all aged 60 or over. The magnitude of this demand can be demonstrated by the fact that such a proposal would have cost around £214,000,000 at a time when the existing pension scheme was costing £17,728,000.[1] The point was also not lost on the Treasury. Almost as soon as the 1908 Act had passed, the Treasury began its long campaign to contain the cost of pensions by shifting pension funding onto a contributory insurance basis. The publication of the Beveridge Report was the culmination of that campaign.

---

[1] This was the demand from several labour representatives (e.g. G. H. Stuart Bunning of the TUC, or Mrs E. M. Lowe of the Standing Joint Committee of the Industrial Women's Organizations) to the 1919 Ryland Adkins Committee on old age pensions.

Thirdly, there was no retirement condition. Subject to the sliding-scale means test, a pensioner could go on working and claim the pension. The 1908 Act was thus one of the few examples in modern welfare history of a guaranteed basic income paid regardless of whether or not the applicant was in work, with a tapering income disregard. In effect, it was a virtual negative income tax scheme.

Gender blind, redistributive, targeting the poor and paid to recipients by virtue of their status as citizens rather than as producers, the 1908 Old Age Pensions Act represented that now forgotten aim explicitly voiced by radical reformers in the early years of the twentieth century—to achieve the endowment of a particularly needy group in society. The term 'endowment' is an interesting one, reflecting a welfare ideal often voiced by socialists and taken up by bolder spirits such as Charles Booth (1892). (We should also note its use by feminists in the early discussions of 'motherhood endowment'.) 'Endowment' implied the establishment of the same automatic, citizenship right to income for the working class in times of need that the middle class enjoyed—without any notion of just desert—via private inheritance. The fact that a piece of social legislation with so much radical potential should have been passed by the 1906–14 Liberal Government is puzzling. To understand why, we need to examine briefly the campaign for old age pensions that led up to the 1908 Act.

The origins of old age pensions must be located in the profound changes that began to take place in the structure of the British labour market during the last two decades of the nineteenth century as the economy moved to a late-industrial stage of development. Put briefly, there began a crumbling away of job opportunities for older workers in the face of technological innovation. The Victorian labour market had been highly age stratified, with considerable fluidity of labour: whereas a minority of skilled workers might be able to stay in one trade for life, for the unskilled majority negotiation of the life-cycle necessitated frequent changes of job dictated by factors of physical strength and endurance, and hence by age. (We can see this best illustrated in the most backward sector of the economy— agriculture—where progress through the life-cycle would be marked by frequent and subtle changes of job.) Where sectors of industry were most labour intensive, so was employment most age stratified, and so, by and large, were there the highest proportions of older workers; from the 1880s onwards, these were the areas of industry that were the most likely to be in decline.

As the production base became more and more technology-intensive, so there began a slow de-skilling of older workers and, simultaneously, the notion of a 'job for life' spread down the occupational structure. What was happening was a crisis of *male* employment at the top end of the age scale. Elderly women had always been poor, but their plight attracted little attention compared with the increasing focus, voiced in euphemistic terms, on the 'worn out' worker or 'veteran of industry' who had served his time in the 'industrial army' and now needed a 'well earned rest'. Paradoxically, therefore, non-contributory state pensions originated in concerns over the elderly male worker but, once introduced, primarily benefited elderly women. The debate on old age pensions from the 1870s onwards was impelled by these long-run economic changes, which were part of broader shifts in the labour force participation rates of different groups in the population. Slowly but inexorably, the older worker was being marginalized.

The campaign for old age pensions between 1878 and 1908 has been well described by a number of historians, and does not need to be outlined here. The economic imperatives, already described, were mediated through a variety of political, social, and cultural factors: the pressure of an enlarging franchise, which caused astute politicians like Joseph Chamberlain to take up the question; the ambiguous role of the friendly societies; the empirical spadework of Charles Booth; the continuing theme of Poor Law reform; and the crucial interest of the labour movement.

Old age pensions posed enormous problems for the capitalist state. On the one hand, they were necessary in order to accelerate the steady exit of older workers from the labour force, in the name of industrial efficiency. Hence in the interwar years there were frequent calls from politicians, industrialists and trade unionists for an improved pension scheme that would speed up 'the exit from industry'. Pensions also performed a powerful legitimating function at a time when the political threat from organized labour was growing, if episodically so. Yet, on the other hand, there was a real danger that pensions could become an enormously expensive item of social policy, given the ageing of the British population: 'over generous' concessions could open the way to demands for the further 'endowment' of the working class, via highly redistributive policies. This was further exacerbated by an inherent problem peculiar to pensions: to be effective against old age poverty, they had to target the 'bad risks'—women, the low paid, the casual workers—whose industrial value was marginal, whose poverty was acute and whose ability to pay regular contributions was doubtful; the most obvious way of achieving this was via a non-contributory scheme. But all non-contributory schemes were expensive, redistributive and vulnerable to populist pressure. The political challenge was to construct a contributory scheme that would fund the de-industrialisation of older workers and, at the same time, somehow provide a modicum of cover for the 'bad risks'.

Essentially, therefore, what gave the old age pensions campaign such a powerful momentum was the fact that it was built upon an unholy and unintentional alliance between conservatives and socialists—an alliance that reflected the contradictory nature of pensions. Thus one half of the campaign contained those classic ingredients of the conservative position on nineteenth-century social questions—a tightening-up of the Poor Law so that it could focus more effectively on the able-bodied male, the remoralization of the poor, and state intervention to be contemplated only in so far as it achieved a redistribution of the working-class individual's lifetime earnings towards vulnerable points in the life-cycle. These were the essential principles of Canon Blackley's (1878) scheme.

Concern of conservatives over the liberalizing tendencies in the Poor Law was directed not so much at the more 'generous' treatment of workhouse inmates that had spread since 1834—the introduction of snuff, toys, books, and toilet paper was hardly an issue of pressing importance—but at two late-nineteenth-century tendencies. Firstly, yielding to pressure for better workhouse treatment of groups marginal to the labour market (e.g. children, widows, the elderly) made it more difficult to discipline the able bodied male, whose industrial behaviour was seen as the key to the revival of British capitalism: only if the former were removed from the orbit of the Poor Law could the latter become the focus for policy. Secondly, each advance of democracy rendered the Poor Law more vulnerable to popular control, and hence made it more likely to become a mechanism for redistributing wealth. A striking example of this can be found in the statements by several witnesses to the 1895 Aberdare Commission that an increasing number of the urban working class were holding the view that, if they had paid rates all their lives, they were automatically entitled to Poor Law relief in old age: as one of the Commission succinctly put it, 'There are some who think that it [the poor rate] is in the nature of an insurance contribution by the ratepayer against his own old age.'[2] Thus a 'back to 1834', tightened-up Poor Law would be impossible without the elderly removed. Public opinion would be outraged if Chadwickian solutions were applied to the old. As Joseph Chamberlain argued, there would be widespread opposition, and then the whole Poor Law might be in danger: 'If you turn the screw much more there will be an outbreak', he said. On the other hand, if the elderly were removed,

we should then justify an even more stringent administration of the present Poor Law, and should meet the prejudice which rightly or wrongly now exists, on the ground that the old are treated with considerable hardship.[3]

However, for all his political guile Chamberlain could never overcome the simple but devastating problem inherent in all conservative schemes of old age pensions: they had to be contributory, to accord with conservative

[2] A. C. Humphreys-Owen, *Minutes of Evidence Taken Before the Royal Commission on the Aged Poor (1895)*, ii. C 7684; 1/86.
[3] Ibid. 653, 657.

notions of fiscal responsibility, yet such insurance-based schemes would do nothing for the 'bad risks' who, in old age, needed pensions most.

Logically, Charles Booth should have favoured contributory pensions, for his political outlook was conservative. He was, after all, as fervent a supporter of a 'back to 1834' Poor Law as were Blackley and Chamberlain. But the contradictory implications of pensions were personified in Booth. For a variety of possible reasons—because he was closer to the realities of business life, because he was something of an outsider, because of his intellectual honesty, or even perhaps because of a charming, apolitical unworldliness—he realized that the utter impracticality of contributory pensions rendered them irrelevant from the start. Repeatedly, he stressed that they would do nothing for the old age poverty of the low paid and women: if these groups really were to be lifted off the Poor Law, then a tax-funded pension scheme commencing at the age of 65 would have to be introduced. Booth also seems to have possessed an astute understanding of the profound changes that were taking place in late-industrial capitalism and were shaking out older workers: large sections of the 'Industry Series' in *Life and Labour* are devoted to detailed accounts of how older workers were becoming de-industrialized. In *The Endowment of Old Age* Booth summed up the problem:

Old age fares hardly in our times. Life runs more intensely than it did, and the old tend to be thrown out. Not only does work on the whole go faster and require more perfect nerve, but it changes its character more frequently, and new men—young men—are needed to take hold of the new machines or new methods employed. The community gains by this, but the old suffer. (Booth 1892: 167)

Booth's support was gladly enlisted by the labour organizations who were voicing growing demands for state pensions in the 1890s and 1900s, and represented the other half of the campaign. Spearheaded by the National Committee of Organised Labour for the Promotion of Old Age Pensions, the labour movement built up strong political pressure for a non-contributory, tax-funded scheme. By the end of the 1890s, the rather anodyne and delaying-tactic procedures of the three official committees (Chaplin, Aberdare, and Rothschild) had passed into history. By 1908, both political pressure and welfare logic had made non-contributory pensions the only immediate option for the Liberal Government. However, both Treasury planners and political conservatives believed that a shift to contributory pensions would be possible in the long term, and set themselves this important aim.

This brief excursion into the pre-1908 history of pensions is necessary, for it shows how, from the very start, sharp political battle-lines were drawn up on the question of pension funding. These were to reappear after the First World War when, faced with irresistible evidence of substantial pensioner poverty in the pages of the 1919 Ryland Adkins Report, Lloyd George's coalition Government hurriedly doubled the pension rate to 10s. 0d. per week. However, this action did nothing to defuse what Bentley Gilbert has called the 'unexploded bomb' of the pensions issue (1970: 238). Though somewhat limited by a labour aristocrat outlook, the National Conference on Old Age Pensions (founded in 1916) acted as a vociferous pressure group on pensions, and allied itself with other labour organisations.

The demand for universal, tax-funded pensions, adequate in amount to provide an 'honourable retirement' for all who wished to leave their jobs at 60, was the spectre that stalked the corridors of Whitehall in the early 1920s, and stimulated urgent, semi-secret planning by the Anderson Committee of senior civil servants in 1923–4. The Anderson Committee's deliberations formed the basis of the Conservative Government's 1925 Widows', Orphans', and Old Age Contributory Pensions Act—a piece of legislation which was a notable triumph for Neville Chamberlain as Minister of Health, and a vitally important *coup* for the Treasury: a new contributory pension scheme, allied to National Health Insurance, was introduced for men and women aged 65–70, and was designed gradually to replace the 1908 scheme. (The Treasury had even contemplated its immediate replacement, but had drawn back from this radical and potentially controversial step.) In winning this victory, Chamberlain was handed a golden political opportunity by the 1924 minority Labour Government which had spectacularly thrown away the chance to improve the non-contributory scheme, or lower the age of eligibility—a failure of nerve which partly reflected the Labour Party leadership's growing ambivalence on the contributory principle.

The shift to contributory pensions in 1925 was an enormously important milestone in the whole of British social policy development, for it finally killed off hopes for a tax funded income support system. Reluctantly, trade unionists accepted that any future improvement in benefits would have to be achieved by juggling with higher contributions. As Ernest Bevin—ever the pragmatist—recollected in 1939, the TUC had long preferred non-contributory pensions, but had had to change their view after the 1925 Act 'in order to try to get a scheme through, in order that we should not have to run the gauntlet of party conflict'.[4] Henceforth, Treasury officials were only prepared to conduct a dialogue with those organisations, such as the TUC, who accepted that arguments for higher pensions were essentially arguments for higher contributions from working people. If working people were unwilling to pay higher contributions, then 'by sticking to the contributory principle the Treasury [was] on firm ground in refusing the

---

[4] PRO T 161/941 (S.44330): Memorandum, 'Deputation to Chancellor of the Exchequer from Trades Union Congress, 15 Feb. 1939. Note taken by Treasury Reporter'.

demands of the powerfully organized old age pensions movement', as D. N. Chester put it.[5] Thus the mechanics of contributory insurance funding effectively built a wall round the state pension scheme, insulating it from demands for 'adequate' pensions and minimizing its redistributive potential. The class nature of the 1925 Act is illustrated by the fact that it was accompanied by tax cuts for the middle classes, to the tune of £42,000,000: as Hugh Dalton pointed out at the time, this money was more than enough to make the new scheme non-contributory, with double the rate of widows' and orphans' pensions.[6] However, such alternatives were never considered.

In the 1930s, discussion on pensions centred on the possibility of introducing a new, radically improved scheme which would carry a compulsory retirement condition and would thus effect a redistribution of jobs to the young unemployed. Considered and eventually rejected by the 1929–31 Labour Government, the idea continued to have some appeal in certain quarters—notably, the research organization Political and Economic Planning (PEP 1935). But although this discussion kept alive the issue of pension adequacy (most schemes envisaging at least a doubling of the existing pension), it also bred a growing ageism: increasingly, older workers—found to be concentrated in declining, heavy industries—were viewed as a cause of industrial inefficiency. Added to this, the late 1930s 'population panic' raised alarmist fears about the social and economic consequences of an ageing population. Retirement pensions were also becoming of interest to the Trades Union Congress, for a quite different reason—that, at a time of economic recession, many older workers were experiencing wage cuts equivalent in value to the amount of the pension.

THE OUTBREAK OF WAR

Strictly speaking, the saga of Beveridge and pensions began not in 1941, nor even in 1939, but around 1935. For it was in the mid-1930s that there began a slow welling-up of protests that the pension was grossly inadequate and should be increased. The Treasury carefully monitored the various suggested schemes, classifying them according to what they would cost. The cheapest suggestion was to grant pensions at the age of 60 to wives of male old age pensioners who were unemployed, in order to ease a small area of hardship where an unemployed man with a younger wife could find himself moving at age 65 from unemployment benefit of 27s. 0d. per week (for man and wife) to a single old age pension of 10s. 0d. per week. More expensive

---

[5] PRO CAB 123/45: D. N. Chester, Memorandum, 'Financing of the Proposals in the Beveridge Report', 18 Nov. 1942.
[6] House of Commons, *Official Report* (Hansard), 20 May 1925, cols. 457–60.

was the demand for pensions at any age for wives of unemployed men, or pensions for spinsters at age 55 (the subject of a lively campaign by Florence White's National Spinsters' Pensions Association, founded in 1935). The Labour Party published *Labour's Pensions Plan* in 1937, promising an improved contributory pension (with a retirement condition), and increasingly raised the pensions issue in the House of Commons.[7]

Most important of all was the formation, just before the outbreak of war, of the National Federation of Old Age Pensions Associations (NFOAPA). Its rather earnest and cumbersome title belied considerable militancy of aims and methods. Riding on the crest of reformist 'middle opinion', the NFOAPA conducted a strident and uncompromising campaign on the adequacy of the pension. Its tone was confrontational, uncomfortably reminding politicians of all parties of their failure to raise the pension in the previous twenty years: pensioners were encouraged to put pressure on their local MPs, Federation candidates were even put up for local elections, and in 1939 a petition was presented to Parliament containing 5,000,000 signatures (Blaikie 1990). The Federation demanded pensions of £1 per week (single) and £2 (couple) for all aged 60 and over (later raised to 30s. 0d. and £3), 'freed from any means or needs test, to be given as a right and a just reward for services rendered in producing the wealth of the country'.[8] The cost of this would have been £240,000,000.

By the end of the 1930s, therefore, there was growing concern within Whitehall over the strength of the pensioners' lobby, and over the fact that an improvement in the basic pension was becoming an all-party issue. There were frequent debates in Parliament on the matter, more and more deputations were knocking on ministers' doors, and in late 1939 the TUC succeeded in forcing the Chancellor of the Exchequer, Sir John Simon, to undertake an official enquiry. As one Treasury official nervously minuted:

There are about 2,500,000 old age pensioners, and if these are organised to vote on the subject at the next election, it may well become a first class issue.[9]

At the start of the Second World War, a number of events combined to throw the poverty of old age pensioners even further into public discussion, and put more pressure on the Government than at any time since the immediate aftermath of the First World War. A variety of severe social disruptions brought great hardship to the more vulnerable of the elderly population, and forced their plight onto the attention of social work and voluntary organizations. Under the Government evacuation scheme, many

---

[7] For a monitoring of these developments, see e.g. Treasury memoranda in PRO T 161/930 (S.42179).

[8] *Memorandum of Evidence by the National Federation of Old Age Pensions Associations* (14 Apr. 1942), Cmd. 6405 1942: 238.

[9] PRO T 161/930 (S.42179/01): Frank Tribe to Sir Alan Barlow, 18 Feb. 1939.

frail old people were dispersed from their homes in the cities to rural reception areas; still largely undocumented, the disruption to their personal lives must have been considerable. The wartime Emergency Medical Service necessitated the discharge of some 140,000 patients from hospital to their own homes, where they were left to fend for themselves; many of these must have been elderly and infirm. They then had to try and find places in remaining hospital beds while EMS beds lay empty. Wartime social triage was an uncomfortable reminder of the low status accorded to old people. Again, from September 1940 old people had to contend with the night-time terrors of the Blitz, which was especially dangerous for them: their rates of civilian casualties were higher than those for the rest of the population. Many sought refuge (and companionship) by becoming permanent residents of air raid shelters. As the Blitz intensified, more and more government intervention had to be organized (such as the establishment of an 'Evacuation of the Aged Committee' in November 1940). All these events threw the problems of old people into the political arena (Means and Smith 1985, ch. 2; Titmuss 1950).

We should also note that the change of government in May 1940 (involving the participation of Labour and Liberal leaders hitherto excluded), and the arrival of full employment later that year infused the British labour movement with a new confidence and led to a welling-up of social reformist demands generally. In the short term, the National Federation gained enormously: pointing to the huge cost of the War, it declared gleefully that, 'The war has taught us that the question "where the money is to come from" need not deter us'.[10] In the longer term, however, the incorporation of the Labour Party into government removed the Federation's main constituency of support in the House of Commons, and fatally weakened it.

The first capitulation to this new pensioner militancy was the lowering of the female pensionable age to 60 and the introduction of supplementary pensions. Under attack from all sides for its incoherent domestic economic policy (particularly its failure to control inflation), Chamberlain's wartime government introduced the Old Age and Widows' Pensions Bill in January 1940, granting the right to a contributory pension to some 310,000 women aged between 60 and 65. This—the outcome of the Treasury enquiry—was little more than a holding operation against the tide of pensioner militancy. It was, in effect, one of the lines of defence drawn up by the Treasury in the late 1930s to head off demands for an across-the-board rise in the basic pension. In presenting the Bill to his War Cabinet colleagues, the Chancellor of the Exchequer, Sir John Simon, admitted that it was 'in lieu of a scheme

---

[10] *The Pensioner*, Mar. 1941.

for a flat rate increase' for all pensioners.[11] Short-term political expediency established different qualifying ages for men and women that became permanent and were to have major implications for pension funding in the future.

Under the same Act, pensioners could apply to the Assistance Board for supplementary allowances if they could prove that they were in need. In the early months of the war, high inflation eroded the value of the pension, and gave new ammunition to pensioners' organisations: between September 1939 and March 1940, for example, retail prices rose by 15 per cent. Designed to head off demands for higher pensions from the NFOAP and other groups, this innovation only served to throw a brighter illumination on old age poverty. In the late 1930s, only 275,000 pensioners had been applying for Poor Law public assistance, and the Treasury had repeatedly deployed this statistic as evidence of pensioner prosperity. Roughly 400,000 pensioners were expected to apply for supplementation, yet fully 1,275,000 applications were received in the two months after the scheme commenced in June 1940, causing the *Times* to make its famous comment about the 'remarkable discovery of secret need' that had been made.[12] For the remainder of the war, the Assistance Board took an increasing interest in the poverty of pensioners, carrying out several important surveys into their financial circumstances (Deacon and Bradshaw 1986: 37–8).

THE BEVERIDGE COMMITTEE

The growth of this new political confidence by pensioners' organizations and the discovery of proliferating needs of old people led many old age pressure groups to regard the appointment of the Beveridge Committee in June 1941 as an opportunity to conduct a wide-ranging review of the social, economic, and familial circumstances of the aged. Many of them submitted memoranda to that effect: for example, the National Council of Social Service wanted a thorough investigation of medical and nursing services, of institutional care, and of problems such as loneliness.[13]

However, they were to be disappointed. With typical single-mindedness, Beveridge confined himself solely to the question of pensions funding. On the face of it, 'the problem of age' merely involved a rationalization of the chaotic administrative structure that had grown up piecemeal: the 1908 non-contributory scheme was administered by the Customs and Excise Department, with pensions paid through the Post Office; the 1925 con-

---

[11] PRO CAB 65/5: War Cabinet 15(40)4: minutes of 16 Jan. 1940.
[12] *The Times*, 19 Aug. 1940.
[13] National Council of Social Service, *The Needs of the Aged*, 2 Apr. 1942.

tributory scheme was the responsibility of the Ministry of Health, and operated as part of the National Health Insurance system; supplementary pensions, introduced in 1940, were paid by the Assistance Board and carried a means test quite separate from the 1908 scheme.

'It is all incredibly and senselessly complicated', wrote William Robson despairingly of the various pension schemes that had grown up between 1908 and 1942 (1943: 15). But Robson was being typically ingenuous: as this paper has shown, such complexity was not the result of happenstance but reflected the fierce political controversies that had accompanied the evolution of state pensions. Thus the apparently dull, managerial questions in pensions reorganization masked three vitally important and interrelated issues that were settled by Beveridge.

The first was that pensions were made universal and their financing was shifted completely onto a contributory basis. Put crudely, the extension of the right to a pension to every citizen was the political 'sweetener' that made possible an important victory for the Treasury in its long battle to alter the basis of pension funding. Henceforth, the redistributive element in pensions would be severely curtailed: it would be predominantly an insurance-based 'pay-as-you-go' scheme with, at any one time, the young financing the old.

The second important issue was that the pension level needed considerable improvement, in accordance with the central principle of the Beveridge Report that all benefits should be at 'subsistence' level. If the new retirement pension levels were to harmonize with the levels for unemployment and sickness benefit—24*s.* 0*d.* per week (single) and 40*s.* 0*d.* (married couple)— they would have to be more than doubled from the prewar rate of 10*s.* 0*d.* per week. This was an innovation that was vital to the legitimation of the whole Beveridge Plan. The entire scheme had to be comprehensive, universal and insurance-based. It was essential to iron out the discontinuities between different benefit levels that had been a confusing feature of the pre-war income maintenance system, and set all of these benefits at a monetary level that could be justified by the concept of 'subsistence'. (This had been a particularly glaring problem before the War, with unemployment versus sickness benefit.)

There were tactical reasons too. Demands for 'adequate' pensions had been voiced repeatedly by the labour movement and pensioners' organizations in the previous two decades, such demands reaching a crescendo in 1939–42. Indeed, the whole question of minimum nutritional standards had been one of enormous political controversy in the 1930s. As has been shown, a holding operation had been conducted by the Chamberlain Government's granting of supplementary pensions and lowering of women's eligibility age in 1940. But all experts on social policy realized that, in the changed political atmosphere of wartime, subsistence pensions were an inevitability. For example, Wilson and Mackay's classic study, published in the year that the Beveridge Committee was set up, recognized this (1941: 215). The question was, therefore, this: could the Report's commitment to subsistence benefits be honoured in the case of pensioners, given the continued ageing of the British population and thus the cost of pensions in the future?

Thirdly, the new pensions carried a retirement condition. For the first time, receipt of a state pension would be conditional upon withdrawal from the labour market. The movement for retirement pensions that had begun within the labour movement in the 1920s, largely as a response to mass unemployment and fears of wage cuts, reached its logical conclusion in the postwar social security scheme. On the face of it, therefore, it would seem that the labour movement had succeeded in persuading Beveridge of the need to redistribute jobs to the young, and simultaneously to protect the wage-structure. But, in one of the oddest paradoxes of social policy history, the stated intention behind Beveridge's innovation was precisely the opposite of what previous advocates had suggested. He hoped that the retirement condition would *discourage* withdrawal from the labour market, and thus contain the cost of pensions. Interestingly, Beveridge did not share the pessimism of those who in the 1930s had argued that the drive for industrial efficiency required a faster removal of aged, 'worn-out' workers. On the contrary, he argued that all the available evidence on the health status and life expectancy of older workers supported the view that many of them were quite capable of remaining at work past the age of 65 (Beveridge 1942: para. 255). He also showed scant concern for the wage-reduction fears of trade unionists, or for their belief that postwar unemployment would be lessened by a retirement condition.

In essence, Beveridge's problem was simple: the faster the rate of retirement, the more expensive would be the cost of pensions. The first and most important task, therefore, was to ensure that the new pension scheme was contributory. Placing it in the context of a comprehensive and universal social security scheme was politically a perfect opportunity to do this, and thus to complete the long campaign that the Treasury had been waging since 1908. We should note that Beveridge had always been opposed to non-contributory pensions (1953: 55–9). In effect, the 1908 scheme was to cease, and the 1925 scheme was to be extended in coverage to replace it— exactly what had been on the Treasury agenda in 1923–4, and which the 1925 Act was gradually bringing about anyway. This essentially conservative change was made politically possible by extending pension coverage to all and placing this change in the context of a comprehensive 'cradle to grave' package. Thus universality legitimated the insurance principle, and the insurance principle legitimated inadequate pensions.

THE RETIREMENT CONDITION AND SUBSISTENCE PENSIONS

The possibility of a retirement condition was first raised by the TUC General Council representatives when they came to give oral evidence to the Beveridge Committee on 14 January 1942. Significantly, it does not seem to have figured in any of the Committee's discussions in the preceding six months, though Beveridge did include it in his series of 'some principal questions' that organizations submitting evidence should consider (Cmd. 6405 1942: 2). In part, the TUC's motive was the rather self interested one that had shadowed trade union discussion of pensions over the previous twenty years—that without such a condition (and without any legislation protecting the wage levels of older workers), employers would impose wage cuts on their employees aged 65 and over equivalent in amount to the level of the pension. But the TUC representatives were also insistent that the pension should be substantially raised, and that it should represent the 'citizenship' pension long demanded by the labour movement: 'the fact that they are retired seems to be all the more reason why they should have money to enjoy life when they have the time', said J. L. Smyth. The TUC representatives challenged Beveridge's assumption that the nutritional needs of pensioners were less than those of working-aged adults, and protested that his proposed pension level was inadequate.

In reply, Beveridge expressed the fears that were to dominate his whole outlook on pension funding: he did not want to direct resources to pensioners 'at the cost of the children, at the cost of others'; the problem was how to give pensioners fair treatment 'without ruining the country'. Smyth was much less pessimistic. He suggested that the answer could be found in improved productivity, and hence a larger tax base, via a properly-planned economy. Almost casually, he added that unemployment could also be lowered by shrinking the labour force through the imposition of a retirement condition.[14]

Beveridge initially dismissed the idea. He rejected the view that there was a natural limit to the total of employment at any one time (Henderson 1955: 198). In any case, a retirement condition would be riddled with practical difficulties. His principal civil service advisers on the matter agreed: public opinion would not tolerate pensioners being prosecuted for the 'offence' of performing paid work; an effective work test would be clumsy and expensive to operate, and a simpler declaration of unemployment (to be signed by the pensioner) was open to fraud; resentment might be felt by those who had paid contributions for fifty years and then would be told that they were ineligible for their pension; investigating officials might find it difficult to decide whether odd jobs for cash really constituted paid work.

[14] PRO CAB 87/77: SIC(42) 1st meeting, 14 Jan. 1942.

Perhaps the most perceptive objection came from P. Y. Blundun (of the Ministry of Labour), who argued that if the aim of a retirement condition really was to reduce competition in the labour market and lower unemployment, it should only target the small number of pensioners (maybe only ten per cent of them) who genuinely were industrial competitors with the young; this would be well-nigh impossible to achieve through legislation.[15]

However, a rather more positive view came from Sir George Reid, who, as the Assistance Board's representative, had first-hand experience of means testing procedures under the 1940 supplementary pensions scheme. Reid believed that the vast majority of pensioners were honest citizens, and that a signed declaration from them could be trusted. Regular home visits by the Assistance Board to check that supplementary pensioners had no other resources had confirmed this; indeed, the Board had been able to cut down on such visits. Reid also made the point that a retirement pension was irrelevant to the poorest pensioners, since they would have no work anyway: in one week in November 1941, only 684 out of 1,100,000 supplementary pensioners had earned more than the 5s. 0d. income disregard. (A very high proportion of these supplementary pensioners were, of course, women.)[16]

These civil servants had unwittingly touched upon the crux of the whole pensions paradox: if a retirement condition would make no difference to the rate of retirement, then what was the point of having it? As has been argued earlier in this paper, retirement had spread because long-run changes in the industrial infrastructure had slowly shaken out older workers. The two pension Acts may have had some effect in accelerating this trend, but that effect was secondary and probably marginal. As has been noted, Beveridge himself realized that, because of improved health status, more workers than ever were capable of staying on in employment; the fact that they were not doing so should have made him conclude that there had been a steady decline in demand for their labour. Again, even if there were some element of consumer choice in the decision to retire, no model of economic rationality could explain a decision voluntarily to live on the pitiful level of pension (10s. 0d. per week) previously offered, as the supplementary pension episode had convincingly shown. What, then, was the point of a retirement condition?

The TUC General Council's position on the matter was quite clear. They were caught on the horns of a dilemma not of their own making: they argued strenuously for higher pensions, yet realized that every shilling added

[15] PRO CAB 87/79: P. Y. Blundun, Memorandum, 'Retirement Pensions: Practicability of Enforcing Conditions', 17 Apr. 1942; ibid. E. Hale, Memorandum, 'Retirement Pensions', 24 Apr. 1942.
[16] Memorandum, 'Practicability of Enforcing a Retirement Condition. Supplementary Pensions Experience', 11 Apr. 1942, ibid.

to the pension would result in equivalent wage cuts for older workers. Firmly wedded to the Bevinite belief in free collective bargaining without legislative interference, TUC leaders never mentioned the possibility of making such wage cuts illegal. (Admittedly, this would probably have resulted in employers sacking older workers.) An improved pension carrying a retirement condition would both offer older workers the 'honourable retirement' that the labour movement had long sought, and would liberate jobs for the young: 'We want to make them play', said one delegate, in somewhat authoritarian vein: 'They have been made to work, and we want to make some of them play and have leisure at the end of their lives: and we think they ought to make way for the young people'.[17]

Other organizations took varying positions on the matter. The NFOAPA cited numerous cases of wage reductions that had been forced upon pensioners by employers as a condition of their continuing in their jobs, and in the course of a rather confrontational encounter with Beveridge, demanded pensions of £1. 10s. (single) and £3 (married couple) for all aged over 60 as the price for a retirement condition.[18] Only a pension of such adequacy, they argued, would empower older workers with the free choice of whether to retire or continue in work (Cmd. 6405 1942: 239). The British Employers Confederation had no strong feelings either way. The National Spinsters' Pensions Association wanted the qualifying age for women reduced to 55. And the Fabian Society proposed an interesting 'double-deck' scheme, whereby men of 65 and women of 60 would receive a 10s. 0d. pension if they continued in work; however, if they chose to retire they would receive a pension that was 'adequate' in amount, but not so high as to induce substantial retirement (ibid. 38–9).

It has become something of a commonplace that the vast majority of organizations that gave evidence to the Beveridge Committee were in substantial agreement with each other, and that Beveridge simply packaged together this consensus in his Report. However, it may now be time to strike a note of caution on this well-worn theme in the social history of the Second World War; quite possibly historians have allowed their judgements to become clouded by the undeniable public adulation accorded to the Report and—less forgivably—by the massive (if last minute) governmental propaganda campaign in its favour, which ensured that most media comment was uncritical. Certainly, the deeper one investigates the complicated saga of retirement pensions, the less easily does this consensual explanation fit.

In fact, there was a substantial difference between working-class bodies like the NFOAPA and the TUC, whose sanctioning of a retirement condition was predicated on the assumption that 'adequate' pensions would

<hr/>

[17] F. H. Wolstencroft, SIC(42) 9th meeting, pt. 1, 6 May 1942, ibid.
[18] SIC(42) 11th meeting, pt. 1, 20 May 1942, ibid.

be paid, and middle-class 'expert' bodies like the Fabian Society, for whom the essence of the problem was the containment of pension costs in the future. Reading through the Federation's *The Pensioner* for the War period one discovers a perspective on the 'Beveridge revolution' somewhat at variance with the conventional welfare historiography. The Federation feared—correctly—that the introduction of supplementary pensions, plus the incorporation of the Labour Party into government, had greatly weakened the pensioners' cause, and when Beveridge's proposals were published they reacted with anger. 'We shall completely disregard the Beveridge Report, which offers present day pensioners nothing', said *The Pensioner*, adding, 'It is obviously not a new world we are heading for, but merely a patched-up old one'.[19]

By contrast, the evidence of the Fabian Society is a striking example of the extent to which liberal 'middle opinion' had become thoroughly infused with a savage ageism. Crude demographic determinism was used to justify the abandonment of the subsistence principle for old people. Directly confronting the NFOAPA (but not naming them), the Fabians argued that the changing age distribution of the British population 'automatically' ruled out 'the extremely generous schemes which are being canvassed in some quarters'. Pension costs would escalate unless steps were taken to encourage deferred retirement. Against a background of all the early-war evidence of substantial poverty amongst old people, they warned of the dangers of treating pensioners 'extravagantly', via 'excessive provision', since 'it would be a fundamental error in social policy unduly to divert resources to the aged at the expense of the young': thus 'each half crown a week must be carefully weighed and calculated.... The Report strikes a reasonable balance between impractical extravagance and inadequacy of benefit' (Clarke 1943: 288–9; Cmd. 6405 1942: 38–9).

Beveridge shared these sentiments down to the last comma. Indeed, phraseology from the Fabian evidence was to reappear as text in his Report. By the middle of 1942, he was becoming very concerned about the precise meaning and economic implications of 'adequate' pensions (i.e. roughly 24s. 0d. per week for a single person, 40s. 0d. for a couple). Essentially, he had three options. The first was to grant universal pensions without a retirement condition. But if these were not to be 'an extravagance which cannot be justified' (in the sense that they would be enjoyed by workers aged 65 and over as well as by retirees without any other resources), they would have to be below subsistence. There would then have to be widespread supplementation by the Assistance Board, which had to be ruled out because it would be unpopular, 'contrary to social policy' (by which Beveridge meant the insurance principle that glued together the whole social security plan) and because 'any means test discourages thrift and saps inde-pendence'.[20] Decoding this rhetoric, one cannot help concluding that what Beveridge feared most was that if social insurance were seen by the public as inherently incapable of delivering adequate pensions, its legitimacy would then collapse—thus opening the way to demands for a highly redistributive tax-funded scheme.

The second option was to raise the minimum pension-eligibility age (especially for women). This Beveridge quickly dismissed as politically impossible, given that the age of 65 had become embedded in public consciousness, with women recently winning the victory of a lowered age. Besides, the spread of retirement in the future would render the holding of any higher age impossible.

This left the third option—to renege on the commitment to full subsistence pensions, and to introduce a retirement condition that, contrary to what the TUC wanted, would encourage the *postponement* of retirement. As Neville Chamberlain had discovered in 1925, the inherent fiscal limitations of social insurance could be used as a political buffer to hold back demands for higher pensions.

By the summer of 1942, a new factor had emerged which made it all the more imperative to Beveridge that he reduce the cost of his new pension scheme. As is well known, the Treasury had become increasingly concerned over the financial implications of the whole plan for social security, and Beveridge was under strong pressure to make substantial economies. The Government Actuary, Sir George Epps, drew up several memoranda out-lining the cost of Beveridge's proposals for 1944, and from these we can see that pensions were a major focus of concern. Working on the basis of 'subsistence' pension levels of 25*s*. 0*d*. per week (single) and 40*s*. 0*d*. per week (couple) Epps found, not surprisingly, that they would be the largest single item at a predicted gross cost (before income from contributions) of £308,000,000, compared with £104,000,000 for unemployment benefit and £163,000,000 for children's allowances at that stage; they would initially cover 1,200,000 men and 3,550,000 women pensioners. Epps warned that the only item of social security that would be likely to change in the future would be pensions, because of demographic trends. All in all, Epps's calculation was that the Beveridge proposals would result in a net increase in Treasury expenditure of £240,000,000 per annum.[21]

Even before Epps had produced these precise figures, concern over the possible cost of the Beveridge proposals had led to an intense burst of intra-Whitehall politicking. Memoranda on the financial implications circulated urgently, with most concern being expressed on pensions: Beveridge later

[20] BP 8/33: Memorandum, 'Pensions Finance', 16 July 1942.
[21] PRO CAB 87/82: SIC(42)137, *Finance of the Proposals in the First Draft of the Chairman's Report. Memorandum by the Government Actuary*, 18 Aug. 1942.

observed that, at this crucial stage, the finance of the scheme was 'coming ever more to depend on what we did about pensions for those at or near the pensionable age' (1953: 309). From March 1942 onwards, Beveridge corresponded on the matter with his old friend Maynard Keynes (now a Treasury adviser) and, in a series of meetings in July and August, the two men came up with a package of cuts that would render the Report more acceptable in official circles. Keynes agreed to obtain Treasury support provided that the additional cost of the Beveridge plan to the Exchequer was kept to £100,000,000 per annum for the first five years of its operation. The urgent priority was to cut the cost of pensions, and two proposals were agreed in order to achieve this: firstly, funding was shifted onto more of a 'pay-as-you-go' basis; and secondly, subsistence pensions were only to be introduced after a transitional period (initially sixteen years, then settled at twenty years). The other principal economy measure was the exclusion of the first child from the family allowances scheme. By the end of August these cuts had been made (Harris 1977: 407–12).

It would be wrong to see Beveridge's capitulation as anything other than willing. In their meetings, a somewhat surprised Keynes found that, far from having to persuade a reluctant Beveridge round to the Treasury's point of view, he was preaching to the converted. For example, after their first meeting, on 7 July 1942, Keynes reported that Beveridge had 'by no means closed his mind to pensions on a much lower scale, such as 15s. 0d. single and 25s. 0d. double. Indeed, he said that he had started with that sort of figure in mind himself.'[22] Again, in *Power and Influence*, Beveridge gave an accurate and candid account of his position:

I found myself able to satisfy Keynes's condition for support, provided that I spread the introduction of adequate contributory pensions over a substantial period of transition. I wanted to do this in any case ... (1953: 309)

For Beveridge, the subsistence principle was absolutely central to his plan: he was later to declare it 'the heart and soul of the Beveridge Report'.[23] But where old people were concerned, this commitment was abandoned in August 1942. Thus in the penultimate version of the section of the Report on 'the problem of age' Beveridge constructed a series of arguments to show that 'subsistence' was an arbitrary and capricious concept. There were a number of factors that made the calculation of subsistence levels in the future 'to some extent a matter of judgement', he maintained. The future cost of living was uncertain, and it could vary region-by-region. Rent levels differed greatly between households, and insurance benefits based on the flat-rate principle could not take account of this.

[22] PRO T 161/1164 (S.48497/1), Memorandum, 'Notes on Conversation with Sir William Beveridge', 7 July 1942.
[23] BP 7/6: Beveridge to Lord Amulree, 21 Jan. 1954.

Underpinning all these arguments was the need to avoid any 'unnecessary expenditure on retired persons, in view of the very large number of such persons and the resulting burden upon the working population'. Hence whereas in the early drafts of the Report the level of the pension had been set at the same level as unemployment and sickness benefit, by the summer of 1942 'the imperative need for economising' had made this 'unnecessary generosity'. To those, such as the NFOAPA and the TUC, who saw adequate pensions as an essential prerequisite of a retirement condition, Beveridge responded:

It may be argued that it is unreasonable to require retirement as a condition of pension unless and until the pension is adequate for subsistence. This might be so if the object in view was to encourage retirement. That, however, is not the policy underlying these proposals. On the other hand it is unreasonable for an individual to demand more pension than he is now receiving, or indeed any pension, as a birthday present, while announcing his intention to go on working and earning.[24]

The peculiarity of this logic must raise the question of whether Beveridge was using the retirement condition opportunistically to justify a containment of the pension level—especially as, in Appendix A to the Report (on the financial implications), Sir George Epps (the Government Actuary) argued that Beveridge's new pension proposals would probably *increase* the rate of retirement (Cmd. 6405 1942: para. 54). To confuse matters even further, at one point in the Report Beveridge argued that 'making retirement from work a condition of pension is a logical consequence of giving adequate pensions' (1942: para. 133).

Thus in the final published Report, the new retirement pension scheme commenced at only 14*s.* 0*d.* (single) and 25*s.* 0*d.* (couple) per week, rising every two years by increments of 1*s.* 0*d.* (single) and 1*s.* 6*d.* (couple), so that the full rates of 24*s.* 0*d.* and 40*s.* 0*d.* respectively would only be attained in 1965. This was what came to be known euphemistically as 'the golden staircase'. Given the rise in the cost of living between 1938 and 1942 (roughly 25 per cent), and the continued rise that was likely to take place to 1945, these new rates represented a derisory increase on the prewar rate of 10*s.* 0*d.* A significant change introduced by Beveridge was the reduction in the married couple's rate, which hitherto had always been double the single rate. Again, the increases in the basic pension in respect of each year an individual postponed retirement were less than the actuarial value of the postponement. Perhaps the most significant implication of all was the fact that, as Beveridge admitted, the Assistance Board would have to continue topping up these inadequate pensions by means-tested supplements. The Beveridge social security scheme was thus to withhold from its largest

---

[24] PRO CAB 87/82: SIC(42)136, *The Problem of Age. Memorandum by the Chairman*, 20 Aug. 1942. This appears as para. 249 of the Report, but with the last sentence toned down.

client group that principle that was most central to it—insurance based subsistence benefits as of right, without means tests. Finally, as has been noted, abandonment of the subsistence principle was logically inconsistent with the existence of a retirement condition. However, these and other internal contradictions within the Report—such as the incompatibility of the flat-rate principle with the subsistence principle—were the price paid for deference to political and economic realities.

CONCLUSION

Space does not permit a full account of what happened subsequently to the Beveridge pension proposals: this paper limits itself to an analysis of Beveridge's role. Suffice it to say that, under pressure from Ernest Bevin, the War Cabinet quickly abandoned Beveridge's transitional arrangements, and decided that the full pension rates should be paid from the commencement of the scheme, thereby immediately confirming the Treasury's prediction that the 'golden staircase' had always been politically unworkable. Thus the postwar Labour Government set pension levels at 26*s.* 0*d.* (single) and 42*s.* 0*d.* (couple) in the 1946 National Insurance Act. This represented a marked improvement, in real terms, on prewar pension levels. However, largely because of the stubborn problem of rent (which had defeated Beveridge) there still had to be considerable supplementation by the National Assistance Board, so that by 1954 twenty-seven per cent of pensioner households were in receipt of NAB grants of one kind or another. We should, of course, be wary of attributing the arrival of Rowntree-type 'subsistence' benefits to Beveridge or any subsequent government: it was the rise in real wages, pulling benefits up in their wake, that brought this about in the late 1940s. The painstaking calculations by Beveridge's Subsistence Sub-Committee should not be allowed to obscure the fact that Beveridge's benefit levels were primarily dictated by two factors that had little to do with the nutritional needs of an individual. First, there was the 'less-eligibility' requirement that they be pegged just below the bottom of the wage structure; hence a comparison of the relationship of unemployment benefit levels to wages shows no relative improvement between the 1930s and the late 1940s (Macnicol 1980: 216). The second factor was the Treasury-driven constraint of a finite and 'acceptable' amount of public expenditure available for the whole social security scheme. Essentially, Beveridge saw his task as the sharing out of this fixed sum of money between the claims of competing groups (notably, children versus the retired). These two considerations dominated all discussions of what Keynes rather cynically called 'the alleged subsistence level'.[25]

---

[25] Memorandum, 'Notes on Conversation', op. cit.

The retirement condition was introduced, but only for the first five years after pensionable age. Its effect on the rate of retirement was probably marginal, and certainly not in the direction that Beveridge had hoped. Both the earnings disregard and the level of annual pension increment for postponed retirement were too low to encourage continuance at work (Harper and Thane 1989: 47). In an operational sense, the retirement condition was a massive irrelevance. Given that it was a product of a long-run decline in the demand for older labour, retirement continued at roughly the same rate after 1946 as before—in other words, independent of any attempts to tinker with it via policy—as can be shown in Table 6.1.

Table 6.1.   Percentage of Old People Classified as Occupied in Britain

Year	Men			Women	
	65–9	70 +	65 +	65 +	60 +
1921	79.8	41.2	58.9	10.0	12.8
1931	65.4	33.4	47.9	8.2	11.0
1951	48.7	20.9	32.0	5.3	8.0
1961	39.0	14.9	24.5	5.5	9.9

Source: George (1968: 162).

This necessarily brief excursion into the complicated saga of pensions illustrates many of the points raised by past commentators on the Beveridge Report. Depending on how one wishes to unravel its ambiguities, the Report can be placed somewhere on a spectrum of interpretations between two extremes. At one end of this spectrum, it appears to be a bold, radical, and innovative plan set within the parameters of a vague liberalism, probably shared by most British citizens at the time, and the anticipated economic constraints of a postwar world, the worrying uncertainty of which no responsible economist could ignore. At the other end, it appears as a recipe for a welfare capitalism that would minimize redistribution of wealth, contain more radical demands, perpetuate the illusion of equality, and leave its most vulnerable citizens in continuing poverty. These ambiguities were very apparent in Beveridge's treatment of old age; but on closer examination one cannot help concluding that old people were accorded especially unsympathetic treatment in the Report, reflective of their continuing social and economic marginalization.

This was particularly true for women pensioners. Under the 1908 Act they had received an old age pension by virtue of citizenship and need; but Beveridge's proposals completed the trend begun in 1925, whereby the technicalities of contributory insurance required that married women be seen as members of a household, eligible by virtue of their husbands' contributions. In Beveridge's scheme, the married woman's pension was rolled up within the joint pension, which, for the first time, was less than double the single rate. Interestingly, this downgrading of the married woman's status was reflected in Beveridge's frequent assumption in the Report that the joint pension was the property of the husband: for example, 'a married man ... who reaches the age of 65 in 1949, if he then retires, will receive a basic pension of 28s. 0d. a week' (Beveridge 1942: para. 246). This was not primarily a consequence of Beveridge's patriarchal assumptions: it was the inevitable outcome of a funding mechanism that was designed to minimize redistribution. To be sure, anyone who trawls through Public Record Office files will find the private exchanges between officials overlaid by a patina of sexism and thinly-disguised contempt for women's organizations; but this pales into insignificance compared with the hostility shown to the radical, avowedly working-class National Federation of Old Age Pensions Associations.

The Report's proposal for universalizing pensions and removing all means tests appeared radical; and yet the reality was that, had Beveridge's pension levels been introduced, there would have had to be massive reliance on means-tested supplements from the National Assistance Board. Even with the improved pension levels, the extent of pensioner reliance on assistance supplementation was a major reason for the 'rediscovery of poverty' in the 1960s. Pensioners were singled out as the one group excluded from the subsistence principle so central to the Report. Looking at the pension rates actually recommended for 1945, the Report does in fact emerge as a very successful bulwark against the militant demands of the NFOAPA and other organizations at the start of the war for pensions of £1 per week for all at the age of 60. The forcefulness of Beveridge's ageist rhetoric (often toned down between penultimate draft and the published Report) was partly rooted in 'rational' concerns about the inexorable, demography-driven rise in pension claims into the future, but it may also have reflected a subconscious fear of the redistributive consequences of working-class pensioner militancy. Thus for Beveridge, containment was just as important as innovation.

REFERENCES

Beveridge, W. H. (1942), *Social Insurance and Allied Services*, Cmd. 6404. London: HMSO.
—— (1943), *The Pillars of Security*. London: Allen and Unwin.
—— (1953), *Power and Influence*. London: Hodder and Stoughton.
Blackley, W. L. (1878), 'National Insurance: a Cheap, Practical, and Popular Means of Abolishing Poor Rates', *The Nineteenth Century*, 4 (Nov.) 834–57.

Blaikie, A. (1990), 'The Emerging Political Power of the Elderly in Britain 1908–1948', *Ageing and Society*, 10: 17–39.

Booth, C. (1892), *Pauperism, a Picture; and the Endowment of Old Age, an Argument.* London: Macmillan.

Clarke, R. W. B. (1943), 'The Beveridge Report and After', in W. A. Robson (ed.), *Social Security*. London: Allen and Unwin.

Cmd. 6405 (1942), *Social Insurance and Allied Services, Appendix G: Memoranda from Organisations*. London: HMSO.

Deacon, A., and Bradshaw, J. (1986), *Reserved for the Poor: The Means Test in British Social Policy*. Oxford: Martin Robertson.

George, V. N. (1968), *Social Security: Beveridge and After*. London: Routledge and Kegan Paul.

Gilbert, B. (1970), *British Social Policy 1914–39*. London: Batsford.

Harper, S., and Thane, P. (1989), 'The Consolidation of "Old Age" as a Phase of Life, 1945–1965', in M. Jeffreys (ed.), *Growing Old in the Twentieth Century*. London: Routledge.

Harris, J. (1977), *William Beveridge: A Biography*. Oxford: Clarendon Press.

Henderson, H. D. (1955), 'The Principles of the Beveridge Plan', in H. D. Henderson (ed.), *The Inter-War Years and Other Papers*. Oxford: Clarendon Press.

Macnicol, J. (1980), *The Movement for Family Allowances, 1918–45*. London: Heinemann.

Means, R., and Smith, R. (1985), *The Development of Welfare Services for Elderly People*. London: Croom Helm.

Political and Economic Planning [PEP] (1935), *The Exit from Industry*. London: PEP.

Robson, W. A. (1943), 'Introduction: Present Principles', in W. A. Robson (ed.), *Social Security*. London: Allen and Unwin.

Titmuss, R. (1950), *Problems of Social Policy*. London: HMSO.

Wilson, A., and Mackay, G. S. (1941), *Old Age Pensions: An Historical and Critical Study*. London: Oxford University Press.

7

Condemned to Deprivation? Beveridge's Responsibility for the Invisibility of Poverty

JOHN VEIT-WILSON[1]

UK
HSS
I30

INTRODUCTION

The question this chapter asks is, how far can the Beveridge Committee's adoption of the concept of 'minimum subsistence' to justify the recommendations in its Report (Beveridge 1942, which I shall refer to as SIAS) for the levels of adequate social security benefits, be seen as responsible for condemning the poor in Britain to blame for their deprivation? The Report, which was largely written by William Beveridge himself, stated:

The fourth fundamental principle is *adequacy of benefit in amount and time*. The flat rate of benefit proposed is intended in itself to be *sufficient without further resources to provide the minimum income needed* for subsistence *in all normal cases*. It gives room and a basis for additional voluntary provision, but does not assume that in any case. (Beveridge 1942, para. 307: 122; emphasis added)

The italicized words suggested that if subsistence benefits were adequate, enough to live on without supplementation, then failure to live a conforming and participatory social life on incomes at or close to subsistence was caused by the inadequacy of the recipients and not of the incomes. As a result, when National Assistance (NA: 1948–66) was claimed to provide a subsistence floor, poverty as low income was described as invisible (a former Secretary of State for Social Security claimed that there was not a single

[1] This chapter draws on material from a longer study of concepts of poverty and need in the British national means-tested social security scales (focusing primarily on the 'Assistance' schemes which ran from 1934 to 1966). I want to express my gratitude to former and present government officials and to a great many colleagues for the help which they have given me with various aspects of it; I am sorry not to be able to name more than those quoted in this text: Geoffrey Beltram, Jose Harris, Tony Lynes. The Leverhulme Trust generously awarded a research grant to give me time to write. I thank Tony Atkinson and Alan Deacon for their suggestions about Beveridge, and Adrian Sinfield and Michael Hill for advice on this chapter. I am grateful for the help given by the staffs of the Department of Social Security's archives, the Public Records Office, and libraries in London and York holding the papers of William Beveridge, Violet Markham, and Seebohm Rowntree.

mention of the word 'poverty' in the Hansard index from 1948 to 1965/66
(Moore 1989: 7)). There is a widespread view that continuing poverty was
then 'rediscovered' through the work of such researchers as Peter Townsend
and his colleagues (Sinfield 1968).

In the history of changing ideas about poverty, three strands are relevant
here. First is the *class-cultural stratification* of conventional assumptions
about standards of adequacy. The degree of perceived social stratification
of the lifestyles which are conventionally taken by the non-poor as the
participatory norm continues as a kind of unremarked obbligato within the
British discussion, changing in theme and volume. For Seebohm Rowntree
in 1901, the assumed stratification of lifestyle between middle and working
class was so unproblematic that he could simply take the respectable
working class as the comparator baseline for measuring deprivation. The
public issue of whether the level and tone (Veit-Wilson 1987: 207) of social
· security was adequate if it was not good enough for the middle classes
seems to have been increasingly articulated after the Second World War as
more and more of the elderly middle classes became potential beneficiaries
and the increasing homogenization of aspirational lifestyle among younger
people made the class-stratified comparison unacceptable.

The second strand is the way in which the British discussion of poverty
changed its dominant paradigm in the first third of the century, from
poverty as deprived *lifestyle* to poverty as subsistence *income*. Critiques of
these prescriptive paradigms were developed in the second half of the
century, such as the empirically-based behavioural, attitudinal, or deprivation indicator approaches, which define poverty as exclusion from, or
lack of resources of money or other kinds sufficient for, a socially-defined
participatory lifestyle (Veit-Wilson 1987).

Parallel with this changing practical application of a concept, the third
strand is the concept of minimum subsistence itself. This is often expressed
in terms of 'absolute' poverty, as it is based on the calculation of the cost
of providing for four physiological needs: food, clothing, heating/hygiene,
and shelter. Although all of these are inevitably experienced in culturally
relative ways, the minimum subsistence approach excludes all expenditures
to meet social and psychological needs: it is inherently asocial. The essential
qualifying adjective 'minimum' was often dropped in this historical discussion, but the term 'subsistence' was used to mean 'at the physiological
minimum'; it did not include subsisting at higher living standards.

To understand Beveridge's own use of the concept of minimum subsistence, we have to note the three changes in its meaning and use which
took place early in the century. This chapter outlines them first, before
suggesting how and why the Beveridge Committee arrived at its recommendations for the basis of social security benefits, and how the concept of
subsistence was adopted almost without reservation as the British official

definition of poverty. Finally, it refers to some aspects of 'invisibility', the way in which the poor were then perceived, and how this changed in the 1960s. The issue is even more topical when, fifty years after Beveridge, there is still demonstrable deprivation in Britain but 'now no universally agreed standard of poverty' (DHSS 1985: 12).

THE CHANGING USES OF THE IDEA OF SUBSISTENCE, 1899–1940

Poverty measures have been used to count the poor, to explain why they are poor, and to prescribe the least amount of money on which they ought to manage not to be poor. There are also other purposes for poverty measures (see Veit-Wilson 1989), but confusions between these three are part of this history, and the last has also been confused with the different question of the most that governments should pay in social security benefits.

At the end of the nineteenth century, Booth counted the poor in London using a visibly deprived lifestyle as the criterion of poverty, and Rowntree replicated his study in York (Rowntree 1901: 115–16, 300; 1903: 19–20; see also Hennock 1987; 1991; on Rowntree, see Veit-Wilson 1986*a*; 1986*b*). But counting the poor by the appearance of their lifestyle did not answer Rowntree's additional question, *why* were they poor: was their deprived lifestyle the result of their 'improvidence' or imposed on them by 'insufficiency of income'? (Rowntree 1901: vii). To provide an *explanation*, Rowntree developed the methodological tool of 'primary' poverty (P1: Rowntree 1901, ch. 4). Rowntree repeatedly emphasized that the P1 measure was not a level of income on which even a member of the working class could live. But he chose the criterion of 'merely physical efficiency' as its basis to pre-empt any middle class criticism of its generosity (see Veit-Wilson 1986*a*; 1986*b*). The P1 measure used the respected methods of science (nutrition and social research) to find the lowest cost of the four standard components of physiological subsistence. Rowntree himself was perfectly aware from the outset that the P1 measure was relativistic in composition and in no sense 'scientifically absolute', and he emphasized the arbitrary nature of the level he chose (1901: 141). In addition to physiological needs he realized that human social life required 'expenditure needful for the development of the mental, moral, and social sides of human nature', as well as functional 'expenditure for sick clubs or insurance' and the like, and that there is expenditure which 'may be in the truest sense "useful" which is not necessary for the maintenance of *merely physical efficiency*' (Rowntree 1901: 86–7; original emphasis). When, later, Rowntree wanted a minimum income which people could actually live on, he calculated the

Human Needs of Labour (HNOL) scales, considerably higher than P1 (Rowntree 1918; 1937).

However, its appearance of objectivity also made Rowntree's P1 tool for explaining the inadequacy of incomes into a convenient tool for *counting* the poor, defined as those having incomes sufficient only for physical subsistence. The tool avoided the subjective assessments of 'obvious want and squalor' (Rowntree 1903: 19), which failed to deal with the problem of hidden deprivations. The statistician Arthur Bowley and his colleagues used the P1 measure in a number of studies of urban poverty during and after the First World War (Bowley and Burnett-Hurst 1915; Bowley and Hogg 1925; see also Hennock 1991). Hennock has shown (1991) that Bowley was interested solely in having a research tool for the purpose of making reliable comparisons, not in the social meanings of the P1 income level he adopted from Rowntree, and he criticized 'Bowley's highly questionable adaptation of the concept of primary poverty to purposes quite different from those for which Rowntree had originally designed it' (Hennock 1987: 222). However, like Rowntree, Bowley was himself quite clear that the scientific basis of the subsistence measure was questionable and that subsistence was too low for participatory social life (Bowley and Hogg 1925: 13–14). Many more social surveys using versions of the P1 measure were carried out in the interwar period (for details see Townsend 1952; Stevenson 1977; Kent 1985; Beveridge also used and cited several of them in 1942,[2] not all correctly).

Nevertheless, Bowley's national eminence as a social statistician seems to have given weighty methodological approval to the use of the unqualified term 'poverty' for the P1 subsistence measure. Thus, by the 1930s, the common concept of poverty used in both poverty research and the discussion of policy consisted simply of the assumed cost of the four subsistence components. Widespread anxieties about malnutrition led experts such as the BMA and the League of Nations' technical advisers to propose minimum dietary standards: science defined the problem and the cost of curing it (Boyd Orr 1936; 1937). These standards affected the food element of influential new subsistence calculations such as those of R. F. George.[3]

The third change was the translation of the subsistence measure to a *prescription for social security benefits* (or in fact to a *post hoc* rationalisation of their adequacy). The first example in British government policy-making was the setting of benefit rates by the newly-founded Unemployment Assistance Board in 1934 (Lynes 1977). In spite of government claims that the scales were to be based on minimum needs, the issue of scientific

---

[2] SIC[42]3, CAB 87/79.
[3] George (1937); see also Beveridge SIC[42]3, 16.1.42 p. 2, CAB 87/79.

calculations was robustly rejected.[4] The UAB minuted that instead it '. . . had therefore proceeded on the principle of less-eligibility . . .'[5]

While knowing that its benefits scarcely covered even the cost of minimum subsistence, in public the UAB claimed that the weekly allowances were enough for all normal foreseeable needs, not only food and rent but 'renewals of clothing and household equipment', long-term as well as short-term.[6] In this contradiction between the private admission that the Assistance scales were asocial (scarcely enough for merely physiological needs) and the public claim that they were adequate for social life, we have the clear precedent for the problematic assertion by Beveridge which is the focus of this chapter.

BEVERIDGE AND HIS COMMITTEE

Beveridge had a lifelong interest in poverty. In the opening paragraph of his autobiography he quotes the advice he was given on leaving university by the Master of Balliol: 'go and discover why, with so much wealth in Britain, there continues to be so much poverty and how poverty can be cured' (Edward Caird, quoted by Beveridge 1953: 9).

Beveridge spoke and wrote a great deal about overcoming the Giant of Want by means of benefits adequate for subsistence, but the words 'want' and 'subsistence' seem to have been too commonplace and familiar for him to have given them pedantically distinct definitions, and at times he used them interchangeably. My reading is that he used the word *want* not only in a physiological sense to 'lack the means of healthy subsistence' (Beveridge 1942: 7; 1944: 17) but also for the psychological sufferings of deprivation: he argued that overcoming want meant everyone having at all times their own income at the minimum level 'necessary to meet his responsibilities', as of right and not subject to the state's demeaning means tests (1943: 83, 132). When he used it separately, *subsistence* was a different category: it meant the calculation, averaged over population groups and minor price changes if necessary (1943: 130), of the cost of 'all essentials' (1943: 55), described as the four components of physiological requirements in Rowntree's P1 measure.

In view of the later arguments about whether or not the social security scales were at subsistence level, it is important to be clear from the outset that Beveridge did not share the common assumption that subsistence

---

[4] 'There is no absolute criterion or scientific basis of need' (UAB Memorandum 9, para. 11, 19.7.34, AST12/2); similar wording in the Beveridge Report (Beveridge 1942: 14) was probably drafted by the same official, George Reid (Lynes 1977).

[5] UAB minutes, 6th meeting: 3, 13.9.34, VM6/1.

[6] Memorandum to all offices on Exceptional Needs, 19.8.35, AST7/206.

meant fanatically precise calculations of costs varying between individuals on the basis of differences in rents, in rural and urban working-class costs of living, or by their age or sex. As in the UAB before, the variables gave rise to lengthy and heated argument in the Social Insurance Committee (SIC)[7] and for years afterwards. Beveridge admitted that the components of subsistence were matters of judgement and subject to cultural change over time (Beveridge 1942: 14). The principle of minimum subsistence was more important to Beveridge than the variability of the precise figures (Beveridge 1942: 14, 103; and see Harris 1975: 239 ff.; 1977: 397; Judge 1980: 175).

Beveridge's thoughts on poverty had, of course, developed over the years (see Harris 1977; 1982; also Veit-Wilson 1992). On the question of the class stratification of lifestyle comparisons, Harris suggested that Beveridge had a 'peculiar tone-deafness or colour-blindness to questions of social class' (Harris 1982: 14). However, he was clear enough about class stratification when it came to the discussion of the resources available for redistribution within the working class to pay for the elimination of want.[8] The financial calculation of the scope for redistribution might have been very different if he had taken a more middle-class conception of minimum needs than the subsistence definition cost.

Like some others, Beveridge also had long-standing difficulty in understanding the conceptual difference between Rowntree's P1 and HNOL measures of poverty. When in 1925 Eleanor Rathbone recommended that both family allowances and minimum wages should be based on Rowntree's social HNOL scales, Beveridge instead 'proposed that both family allowances and minimum wages should be based on the mean between the two Rowntree scales' (Harris 1977: 344). The evidence from 1941 (below) suggests that he thought P1 was adequate for social life and the HNOL calculations were not really minima: one could go below them and still prescribe realistic minimum incomes on which people could be expected to live. Harris reported that his proposals for state income maintenance in his 1924 pamphlet, *Insurance for All and Everything*, suggested that the nature of subsistence was for him a statistic and not a state of living. She also noted the several similarities between this pamphlet and his 1942 report; in particular, that Beveridge proposed benefits on a similar basis to those of the 1911 insurance acts, 'not to meet subsistence needs but merely to act as a threshold for voluntary private saving' (Harris 1977: 350). Although he had changed the phrasing by 1942, his flexible approach to defining subsistence still suggested an incomplete understanding of the real costs of social life: subsistence was a standard—but individuals' needs varied; the

---

[7] e.g. 'Memorandum on Rural Differentiation'; SIC[42]115; and 'Observations on SIC[42]115'; all in BP 8/28; SIAS 1942: 77.

[8] BP 8/28: Beveridge SIC[42]3 paras. 12–13; 1942: 165–6; Harris 1977: 393.

administrative definition should take account of social perceptions of need—but benefits should be so low as to 'encourage voluntary thrift' (Harris 1977: 397).

When he started work as chairman of SIC, he was still confused: his first detailed paper on 'Subsistence standards for social security benefits' wrongly described Rowntree's 'two standards of minimum requirements' as if they were equally valid prescriptions for minimum-living incomes, one of which simply had more generous components. P1 was therefore the lowest which could be taken for social security purposes; he discussed its adequacy simply in terms of improved nutritional knowledge.[9] After comparing the P1 measure with existing insurance benefits (which paid slightly more for families with up to two children), he then set out to find support for the approach he seemed to prefer. Rowntree's initial response did not confirm Beveridge's inclinations:

We do not think that it would be wise to take the primary poverty standard as giving a minimum for social insurance benefits, but to make adjustments in my human needs figure.[10]

In spite of this, Rowntree went on to make such adjustments that the figures in the end looked more like P1 than HNOL. He and his colleague, F. D. Stuart, had cut down the clothing needs by a third and reduced the sundries element from 10s. 8d. to 2s. 4d. for a family with three children. This gave a total figure (excluding rent) at 1936 prices of 32s. 7d., which compared with a P1 level of 30s. 7d. and an HNOL level of 43s. 6d.[11] Rowntree and Stuart concluded that 'We think that 32s. 7d. is the very lowest minimum that can possibly be defended'. The exclusion of almost all of the HNOL social expenditures left little more than the asocial P1 subsistence measure, which even Beveridge had denied was a 'living standard'.[12] Rowntree himself emphasized the distinction between P1 and HNOL very clearly in a memorandum on 'Calculation of the Poverty Line'. He drew out the essential differences of purpose and therefore measures between his task of designing irreducible poverty lines to live on, and Beveridge's task of designing social security scales which had to be lower because of less-eligibility.[13]

The concept of subsistence was never again contested as the justification for the social security scales proposed in all the subsequent discussions within SIC or its Subsistence Sub-Committee (SSC), which was set up in January 1942 and included Rowntree, Bowley, and R. F. George among

[9] BP 8/28: 29.12.41.
[10] SR/B1: 3.1.42.
[11] SR/B1: 3.1.42; see also Rowntree 1941: 102.
[12] BP 8/28: 29.12.41.
[13] BP 8/28: Rowntree n.d. March 1942.

its members (Veit-Wilson 1992). Six months of argument about the precise costings of detailed components made no difference to the initial presupposition that the four subsistence components were sufficient to justify the assertions of adequacy in amount and time. Even the very small margin of two shillings for a couple, which Beveridge included for 'inefficiency in purchasing', was not costed to cover other socially necessary expenditures such as Rowntree explicitly included in the HNOL measure and excluded from P1, even if Beveridge accepted that real people might spend it on 'things not absolutely necessary' for subsistence.[14]

The SSC dealt with questions from SIC such as which nutritional standards to adopt, working-class budgets, regional differences, and whether the social security benefits should 'seek to provide a subsistence minimum or ... aim at providing part only, leaving the balance to be provided by voluntary insurance or from other sources'.[15] It agreed that the expert members were to 'prepare statements on a standard of subsistence on the following basis.... the standard should be a Spartan minimum, making no allowance for human imperfection'.[16] The SIC Secretary (Norman Chester) emphasized to Beveridge's biographer 'how limited the definition of poverty was deliberately meant to be',[17] and Rowntree noted that Beveridge's aim was no more than to provide for 'the minimum needs of physical efficiency for everyone'.[18]

Sir George Reid, now Secretary of the Assistance Board and a member of the SIC and SSC, presented a paper on 'The Subsistence Level' which reiterated his earlier advice to the UAB that 'the matter was one of social convention and expediency',[19] and concluded that all that could be done was to see if the expert proposals were 'appropriate to the purpose immediately in view'.[20] That purpose was, as before in the UAB, the justification of a lesseligible social security scale. He quoted the Ministry of Labour Household Budget Enquiry of 1937–38 to show that the proportion of total expenditure on 'miscellaneous' items (those not included among subsistence component 'necessities', including the replacement of household equipment) was 30 per cent among urban working-class households (average expenditure 86s. 3d.), and 25 per cent in rural households (average expenditure with a marginally higher average household size, 57s. 11d.).[21] This puts the figure of under 7 per cent for Beveridge's recommended 'margin' (two shillings in 32 shillings;

---

[14] SR/B5b: Beveridge 16.7.42:5.
[15] T 230/104: 'Some Principal Questions'.
[16] BP 8/28: 13.3.42.
[17] Harris, personal letter, 1.6.88.
[18] SR/B5a: 1.7.42.
[19] VM6/1: UAB minutes, 6th meeting: 3, 13.9.34.
[20] BP 8/37: Reid 20.2.42, para. 3.
[21] BP 8/37: Reid 20.2.42.

Beveridge 1942: 87) into perspective as a measure of how far from a living minimum the subsistence proposals were.

The averaging of the rent component of SIAS's social insurance scales was among the chief reasons why many people later asserted that the scales were not subsistence,[22] or rejected Beveridge's version of subsistence because the scales gave, in effect, a few pence too much to some households and too little to others (Harris 1977: 399, 422). These arguments are not, however, pertinent to the questions posed by this chapter.

THE BEVERIDGE REPORT AND REACTIONS

Many people familiar with prewar poverty, Poor Law, and means tests, welcomed Beveridge's promise of categorical benefits adequate 'in amount and in time', not requiring supplementation. These words were taken as implying that the benefits were enough for social life: there was no widely accepted alternative criterion of adequacy. The novelty of universal entitlement by contribution met social and psychological needs and gave good tone by contrast with means tests. This 'feelgood factor' may have overshadowed closer examination of benefit levels.

In many talks and articles Beveridge himself continued to convey his view that subsistence was equivalent to minimal social adequacy. He made the deliberate social inadequacy of the 'margin' (for inefficient purchasing) seem merely a matter of individual choices: it would have to cover 'any diversion from things which are necessary to things which, though not necessary, may appear preferable to the individual' (Beveridge 1943: 217 and *passim*). As late as 1961 he could still write with apparent sincerity that his plan was 'designed to combine basic security (*enough to live on at all times*) with freedom of the citizen to manage his own life and that of his dependants, and responsibility for doing so'.[23] No one who understood Rowntree's definition of primary poverty could have written that.

To consider reactions to this notion of subsistence, we must start before the Report was published. There does seem to have been a widespread view that adequacy required benefits at an HNOL and not subsistence level.[24] Beveridge had also commissioned the Nuffield College Social Reconstruction Survey (see Harris 1977: 380–1, 421–2) to study the statutory social services relating to low income.[25] It reported that the old age pensions, even with

[22] e.g. SR/B6: Rowntree 20.8.42; SR/B9: 1.1.43; 1943: 76–9.
[23] BP 8/60: Beveridge to Bremme, n.d. 4; emphasis added.
[24] PREM4/89/2: Political and Economic Planning and Fabian Society, papers 7 and 8; see also the report from Reid's group of 'Hampstead professionals', Reid to Beveridge, 18.5.42, BP8/27.
[25] CAB 87/80: SIC[42]81–3.

the supplementary pension, were considered inadequate for anything more than the relief of destitution. The Assistance Board officers simply tried to keep their costs down, and the wage stop operated by both the A B and local authorities caused considerable hardship to those of working age.[26] While the S I C thus had reliable contemporary evidence of the inadequacy for living of the comparators officials were using, existing benefits and low wages, Harris noted that the information came too late to affect the Report (Harris 1977: 422).

Once the Report was written, how did others react to the use of the subsistence measure? The officials who examined it were not interested in the issue of adequacy as such, since the main official concerns were the total costs and the effect on Treasury control of the economy.[27] On delivery by Beveridge, the War Cabinet Committee on Reconstruction Problems sent S I A S for scrutiny by a committee of officials under the chairmanship of Sir Thomas Phillips, who was already prejudiced against Beveridge (Harris 1977: 422). First, there was discussion on the questions which the committee should answer. Although this included a query on how far the suggested benefit rates should be accepted as an adequate social minimum,[28] it was not answered directly. Instead, a briefing paper by G. Stuart King (Assistance Board) stated that the benefit rates suggested in S I A S 'have the authority of Rowntree and other well-known experts, and they are not, therefore, likely to be challenged as insufficient for subsistence'.[29] King's comments give a flavour of the official notion of subsistence:

Benefit rates which are not adjustable for rent cannot therefore be regarded as anything but amounts empirically determined. Within the limits fixed by the financial possibilities of the scheme they should be as high as possible. In particular they should be such that the majority of the beneficiaries will be able to manage on them without suffering hardship and without having recourse to Assistance.[30]

Harris has suggested that the Phillips Committee fundamentally rejected the principle of 'subsistence' because flat-rate benefits could not reflect the variations in personal needs and rents (Harris 1977: 422). This explanation elides the distinction the Committee in fact made, between the principle of subsistence, which might be theoretically justifiable, and the practical impossibility of implementing it in a flat-rate scheme of benefits.[31] Baldwin reviewed the conclusions of the Committee as largely accepting Beveridge's 'proposals in practice while rejecting their theoretical justification' (Baldwin

[26] SIC(42)81: 1–4, 18–19.
[27] PIN8/87: 22.7.42; T 273/57: Henderson 4.8.42 (rept. in Henderson 1955: 195); T 273/57: Eady 22.10.42 and *passim*; see also Harris (1977: 423).
[28] PIN 8/115.
[29] AST7/607: 15.12.42.
[30] PIN8/116: 15.12.42.
[31] AST7/607: RP(43)6.

1990: 128). The Committee had, however, explicitly stated that, as it regarded it as inappropriate to take decisions on levels of benefit (apart from family allowances), it therefore made no comment on the principle of subsistence as such, but stated only that flat-rate benefits were inconsistent with variable subsistence needs.[32] Similarly, Jowitt told the T U C that the Government had not challenged the basis of subsistence, but only the impracticability of implementing it.[33]

The Phillips Committee thus did not deal with the issues of what subsistence meant or whether it was justifiable as an adequate living income. Preoccupied with costs, it implied that benefits at subsistence level were wasted on those whose rents were less than the standard flat rate.[34] King's further comments suggested other anxieties:

Public opinion may, however, demand something more than mere subsistence and such a demand is not easy to rebut by logical argument. In particular, the argument that if rates of benefit are raised above subsistence they will approximate too closely to rates of wages will lose its force if children's allowances are introduced. The issue in the last resort will depend on generally accepted views about the standards of living.[35]

But he added no evidence on what those views were or who was to hold them. What is intriguing is that King and another official supported the idea of setting the family allowance at only five shillings because 'it had the virtue of *not* pretending to be a subsistence rate', subject to fluctuation with prices and changing medical views.[36]

Why was the subsistence issue so important? The Secretary of the Beveridge Committee, D. N. Chester, gave Cabinet a revealing explanation. Expert support for the adequacy of subsistence pre-empted argument about what the level of the scales should otherwise be, higher or lower. If subsistence as the basis of comparison were rejected, it 'might make it difficult to withstand demands for higher levels of benefit'. He also justified subsistence as a 'national minimum' which should be a first charge on the nation's resources, setting a floor and abolishing want 'in this narrow sense'. If variable rents were Phillips's reasons for rejecting subsistence, then the answer was to vary the rent factor individually.[37]

At the same time, the Government also canvassed political opinion. A secret Conservative Party committee under the chairmanship of Ralph Assheton MP was appointed in December 1942 to report to the Prime Minister on MPs' attitudes to SIAS (Kopsch 1970). Its report 'decisively

---

[32] A S T 7/607: P R (43)13/W P (43)58.
[33] PIN8/7: 8.4.43.
[34] PIN8/115: final draft of report, para. 29.
[35] PIN8/116: 15.12.42.
[36] PIN8/115: minutes of the 5th meeting, 29.12.42, para. 14; underlining in original.
[37] C A B 123/45: Chester 21.1.43, paras. 10–11.

rejected' the principle of state-guaranteed subsistence; means-tested benefits should continue to play the major, not residual, role. Less-eligibility should be emphasized because the 'removal of economic insecurity would impoverish the quality of life' (quoted by Kopsch 1970: 122). Baldwin concluded that the committee viewed subsistence with alarm as an unachievable goal because of the variability of individual needs (Baldwin 1990: 130), but it seems clear that it was primarily seen as unwanted even if it were attainable.

When the Beveridge Report was debated in Parliament, the government response was to reject the implementation of the principle of subsistence on the simultaneous grounds that the concept was too imprecise and the practice was too precise, requiring frequent impracticable variations.[38] Herbert Morrison tempered this somewhat by adding that even if the Government could not accept implementation of the principle, it aimed to fix the unemployment and sickness benefit rates 'as nearly as possible' on the same basis as subsistence.[39] A Conservative member remarked that the contentious issue was the redistribution of income which Beveridge's goal of abolishing want would demand. This would place an intolerable financial burden on the middle class who were already cruelly suffering from high taxes but who were 'quite unorganized and therefore completely inarticulate'.[40]

Wider public opinion on the Beveridge report was recorded by Mass Observation (MO) and the British Institute of Public Opinion (BIPO). It was not so reactionary. MO's report stressed that 'it was freedom from want which the great majority of people considered the most important', and pointed to the altruism shown by the 'middle class people, least likely to benefit, (who) regarded it as dramatic and exciting to a far greater extent than the artisan and working class' (Mass Observation 1943: 249, 254). Nor did most people consider the cost prohibitive; if they could pay wartime taxation, they could afford contributions. It was the costs to the state and not to the individual which concerned some middle-class people. BIPO's survey of public responses did not ask about attitudes to subsistence but specifically about the proposed rates of benefit. While 55 per cent of the population said that the proposed benefit for a couple was about right, 42 per cent said it was too little and only three per cent said it was too much.[41] Addison reported the survey as finding that nearly three out of five people saw the pension rates as too low (1977: 218). Even the Nazi government's record of British reactions reported that Beveridge's poverty line was little higher than Rowntree's P1 level (Beveridge 1954: 196).

[38] *Official Report* (Hansard) 386, 16–18 Feb. 1943; Sir John Anderson, cols. 1668–9.
[39] Ibid., cols. 2037–8.
[40] Ibid., Gridley, cols. 1630–1.
[41] PREM 4/89/2: Durant, BIPO: 13.

The full effect of popular acceptance of SIAS, which included Beveridge's equation of subsistence with adequacy, was to close the public debate on adequacy for two decades. The denial that less-eligible benefits could be subsistence (since they were not individually precise) gradually merged into referring to these less-eligible benefit levels as 'subsistence' and even as poverty. The 1944 White Paper on Social Insurance dismissed the precision of subsistence. In it, Beveridge's remark about voluntary supplementation above subsistence reappeared in reverse as social insurance benefits which, if below subsistence, could be supplemented by personal savings or by National Assistance for those who had no further resources to meet their individual needs.[42] The issue of the adequacy of the social security scales was thus returned from the levels of Beveridge's proposals for categorical insurance benefits to those of the individually means-tested benefits: Assistance until 1948 and National Assistance (NA) to 1966.

Was NA adequate? The changes made in the level of the scales in 1944 and in 1948 have led scholars to differing judgements about their relation to the spurious precision of Beveridge's subsistence calculations. Deacon saw the uprating of Assistance scales in 1944 by amounts more than changes in the cost of living index, and to levels higher than recommended in SIAS, as implying that 'the assistance scale was something more than subsistence, with the corollary that someone living on less than the scale would not necessarily be regarded as living in poverty' (1982: 296), poverty being unproblematically synonymous with subsistence. He also described the insurance rates proposed by the new Labour Government in 1945 as being comparable with the real value of the SIAS proposals, although the index used was hopelessly out of date. Nevertheless, while the Minister for National Insurance, James Griffiths, was criticized for his expression that the Government had tried 'to give a broad subsistence basis to the leading rates',[43] Griffiths was indeed broadly correct—in so far as subsistence was imprecise. Two Labour MPs (Barbara Castle and Sidney Silverman) pointed out that the NI rates were well below subsistence as defined by Beveridge, the Assistance Board, and 'the more enlightened Poor Law authorities'.[44]

Griffiths's view two decades later was that the major social security benefits did embody Beveridge's recommendation of subsistence to meet basic needs (Griffiths 1969: 85; see also Hess 1981: 305). Others were less sanguine. The Assistance Board had admitted (only to itself) that some of

---

[42] Minister of Reconstruction (1944: 7); Leaper (1991: 20); among contemporary authors to emphasize the inadequacy of the social insurance scales see Robson *et al.*'s (1945) collection of Fabian Society essays, and Clarke (1945).

[43] *Official Report* (Hansard) 418, 6.2.46, col. 1742; Abel-Smith called it a 'historic fluff sentence' (1963: 9).

[44] *Official Report* (Hansard) 423, 30.5.46, Castle: col. 1411; Silverman: col. 1423.

its scales were inadequate for subsistence, both in 1946[45] and in 1948.[46] But it calculated that the new NA scales were up to a third higher in July 1948.[47] Deacon referred to the assumption that the NA scales were then above the subsistence poverty line (1982: 303), but both contemporary and subsequent authors have questioned this. An official who worked in the NAB from 1951 wrote that 'there are strong grounds for suggesting that the levels set for insurance benefits in 1948 were below any reasonable measure of subsistence at the time', redeemed in NA only by the payment of actual rents (Beltram 1984: 14–15 n. 5). Hess, too, questioned the adequacy of the NI scales for subsistence (Hess 1981: 306, 309), and quoted the opinions of Labour MPs at the time that the NA scales were too low to prevent malnutrition (a deputation of a hundred called on the NAB on 7 December 1949). The NAB was sensitive on this topic; its experts had grave (but secret) reservations on the nutritional adequacy of the scales at the time.[48] Dr Magee, Ministry of Health member of Beveridge's subsistence working party, alluded to upturns in deficiency diseases among children as recently as 1947.[49] Field noted that the revision of Beveridge's benefit rates at 1938 prices had not taken the real level of wartime inflation into account (Field 1985: 19–20); they must therefore have been below his measures of subsistence. Berthoud's examination concluded that the scales were (as usual) designed on the basis of less-eligibility (Berthoud 1985: 90) and that the 'Beveridge concept of benefits adequate for subsistence needs was not realised' (Berthoud *et al.* 1981: 138).

Subsistence, poverty, and the NA scales thus became more or less synonymous in common discourse, since the rates were a bit above or below Beveridge's subsistence measures, but not in a different category. Deacon concluded that the NA scale 'came to be seen more and more as a measure of poverty rather than as something which lifted people out of it' (Deacon 1982: 303). In spite of Beveridge's attempts, the official position that there was no necessary (let alone desirable) link between subsistence and income maintenance levels (Burns 1943: 521) was restored. Exceptionally, Ferdynand Zweig's perceptive little study of 'Labour, Life and Poverty', with its preface by Beveridge and foreword by Rowntree, offered a more sophisticated analysis than usual, by drawing attention to the asociality of prescriptive subsistence budgets designed for *homo economicus* and not for real people (Zweig 1948: 101). But Rowntree's concern for a HNOL

[45] AST12/52: Memorandum 447 paras. 20–1; see also AB minutes 6.2.46, AST7/759.
[46] AST12/53: AB Memorandum 499 para. 7.
[47] AST7/1615: NAB Memorandum 978, 19.7.57.
[48] AST7/1199: survey, n.d.
[49] MH57/221: Memorandum to Ministry of National Insurance about health implications of increases in the NI rates, 16.8.52.

minimum adequate for social life was not implemented in the income maintenance systems.

'INVISIBILITY AND REDISCOVERY': TO AND BY THE NON-POOR

The decade of the 1950s was the period of the 'invisibility' of poverty. Rowntree and Lavers's survey of poverty in York found it reduced to under two per cent by the HNOL measure (Rowntree and Lavers 1951: 31), which was around a third higher than the corresponding NA scales (Atkinson *et al.* 1981*b*: 25). George commented in 1973 that 'Rowntree's findings helped to increase the feeling of complacency in the country that poverty had been abolished' (George 1973: 53; but see Atkinson *et al.* 1981*a*: 69–70 on Rowntree's underestimate). The comparatively low rates of unemployment after the War meant that most people of working age depended on earnings. In terms of prevalence, therefore, the poverty of prewar mass unemployment became virtually invisible, and there were relatively few NA claimants other than pensioners. However, our concern is not with the prevalence of poverty but with how far Beveridge was responsible for obscuring non-poor perception of its intensity.

The concept of minimum subsistence remained the ostensible basis of National Insurance until 1954 (Abel-Smith 1963: 10) and of National Assistance until 1959. For most of the 1950s, NA attracted little attention (Silburn 1983: 135). Arguments about the NA scales were not in terms of their fundamental asocial inadequacy but the need to uprate them to maintain constant real subsistence values. MPs such as Ian Mikardo claimed that the cost-of-living index used at the time did not fairly represent the consumption patterns of low income households, particularly pensioners.[50] Lynes concluded that the periodic decisions on uprating NA were largely political (Lynes 1985: 1–2) and concerned with preventing the rates from falling below the 1948 levels (Lynes 1962: 46). The NA standards in 1959 were broadly those of 1948, as the NAB Chairman admitted to the Cabinet in asking for real increases.[51] The Government justified the increases it then gave in terms no more precise than the rhetoric of 'giving them (NA claimants) a share in increasing national prosperity' (MPNI 1959: para. 1). The increases may have been facilitated politically by rising ceilings of less-eligibility, but they were not based on an alternative criterion of adequacy, such as Rowntree's HNOL. There was no evidence that the benefits became adequate for relative social life; the contemporary impressions from research and social work suggested that they remained

[50] AST7/861 and AST7/1615 *passim*.
[51] AST7/1624: 4.5.59.

adequate for only a non-participating level of living, and thus remained versions of minimum subsistence.

In the 1950s and 1960s the setting of social security scales was a mixture of Treasury concerns about what could be afforded and political expediency. Social-security scales continued to be held below low wage rates (for a frank admission of the postwar dynamics, see DHSS 1979: 89). My interviews with retired senior NAB officials in 1988 revealed no evidence that any government department, least of all the Treasury, had any conception of poverty as a specified level of living, nor that the increases in 1959 or subsequently were influenced by any new conception of 'adequacy'. The chief perceived problem was not the adequacy of the rates but the decent treatment of pensioners (Webb 1975: 412).

It is part of received wisdom that there was a 'rediscovery' of real poverty by social research in the late 1950s and early 1960s (an idea mentioned by, for instance, Atkinson *et al.* 1981*b*: 19; Banting 1979: 68 ff.; Bull 1971; McCarthy 1986; Morgan 1984: 184–5; Sinfield 1968: 202; Webb 1975: 429). What was it that had been lost? Renewed non-poor public awareness of the persistence of the intensity of poverty in spite of subsistence benefits came from three main sources. One was the studies of the condition of old people (such as those by Townsend 1957; Cole (-Wedderburn) with Utting 1962; Townsend and (Cole-) Wedderburn 1965). Another was the statistical calculations of Abel-Smith and Townsend (Abel-Smith 1962; Townsend 1962; Abel-Smith and Townsend 1965). A major finding of both sets of studies was that significant numbers of old people were not claiming the NA to which they appeared *prima facie* to be entitled, and had incomes which fell below the incomes on average received by NA claimants. This was not thus a critique of the level of NA as such, but of its tone (mainly for old people), though the studies also found poverty amongst the low paid and large families, the unemployed, and the sick and disabled.

A third source was the increasing number of reports by social workers and sociologists on the intense poverty of families in social difficulty. This had not been readily seen in the 1950s, when earnings, family allowances, and subsistence-level social security were assumed to be adequate, and when those social workers using psychological and cultural paradigms of explanation ascribed deprivation problems more to the inadequacy of personalities than incomes. They believed that the cure was not higher incomes but better personal adjustment. It was not until this view was contested by critiques such as those of Wootton (1959; 1960) and tested by the studies of, for instance, Philp and Timms (1957), Wilson (1962), or Sinfield (1968), that the inadequate incomes of such families were more openly discussed as a cause.

The fact that Abel-Smith and Townsend (1965) used the average income levels of NA claimants as a poverty measure was not intended to validate it. Their aim was only to discover the prevalence and intensity of poverty by that official definition. Banting went as far as to suggest that it was these followers of Richard Titmuss who were themselves responsible for the widespread adoption of the social security scales as the basis of an arbitrary relative standard of poverty to set against subsistence (Banting 1979: 70). But I believe this misunderstands the difference between their expedient choice of a politically-credible line to show that people fell below it, and the longer, principled, search for the empirically-based level of minimal participatory adequacy which should supersede it (Townsend 1979; Townsend and Gordon 1989). That search approaches empirically the question which Rowntree approached prescriptively as early as 1918.

How far was Beveridge's promotion of the adequacy of subsistence responsible for the invisibility of poverty and 'blaming the poor'? One criticism must be of Beveridge's adoption as 'adequate' of the very subsistence measure which Rowntree had devised to demonstrate the inadequacy of incomes and to exculpate the poor. One wonders if Beveridge ever made the imaginative leap from his recognition of the social meanings of the freedom of having one's own income to spend,[52] to the need to have more than subsistence if social needs were to be met by those who had no surplus for the voluntary savings he presupposed. Whatever the evidence (and I have not found it), some later commentators have had little patience with such attempts to understand Beveridge's beliefs. Melling asserted that 'the important issue is not his intentions but the practical implications of his proposals' (1991: 78), and Cutler *et al.* condemned more strongly Beveridge's failure to implement his admission of the relative and dynamic nature of subsistence (1986: 11).

The poverty debate in Britain during the twentieth century has been heavily influenced by two confusions, between asocial and social minimum income prescriptions, and between minimum incomes required to avoid deprivation and maximum social security scales. Beveridge was not responsible for creating the confusion between Rowntree's P1 and HNOL scales, but he was himself either confused or devious in promoting it. A good publicist, he allied scientific expertise with powerful charismatic rhetoric to promote asocial minimum subsistence as adequate without supplementation for social security. He knew the hidden constraints were government budgets and less-eligibility, and his experts colluded with him in this. While he was not responsible for the poor tone of NA leading to low uptake, his assertions were responsible for condemning to deprivation people with incomes at, or even somewhat above, the asocial subsistence level of the scales he had validated, whose poverty was not therefore recognized as such. It is arguable that the authoritative reputation of his report curtailed

---

[52] SR/B6: 18.8.42.

the discussion of the real meaning of poverty for at least a generation, if it is not still stunting it today.

REFERENCES

PRIMARY SOURCES: THE LOCATION OF GOVERNMENT AND LIBRARY FILE REFERENCES

Files in the Public Record Office, Kew, London

Assistance Board [UAB to NAB]	AST files
Cabinet	CAB files
Ministry of Health	MH files
Ministry of Pensions	PIN files
Prime Minister's Office	PREM files
Treasury	T files

Files in the British Library of Political and Economic Science, London

BP8/   The papers of William H. Beveridge (box 8, numbered files)
VM6/   The papers of Violet Markham (box 6, numbered files)

Files in the Joseph Rowntree Foundation's Library, York

SR/B   The papers of Benjamin Seebohm Rowntree (section 'Rowntree and Beveridge'; numbered items)

PRINTED SOURCES

Abel-Smith, B. (1962), 'Social Security Since the War'. Paper presented to the British Sociological Association Annual Conference, section on 'Poverty in Britain Today'.
——(1963), 'Beveridge II: Another Viewpoint', *New Society*, 1/22.
——and Townsend, P. (1965), *The Poor and the Poorest*. London: Bell.
Addison, P. (1977), *The Road to 1945*. London: Quartet Books.
Atkinson, A. B., Corlyon, J., Maynard, A. K., Sutherland, H., and Trinder, C. (1981a), 'Poverty in York: A Reanalysis of Rowntree's 1950 Survey', *Bulletin of Economic Research*, 33.
Atkinson, A. B., Maynard, A. K. and Trinder, C. G. (1981b), 'National Assistance and Low Incomes in 1950', *Social Policy and Administration*, 15/1.
Baldwin, P. (1990), *The Politics of Social Solidarity: Class Bases of the European Welfare State 1875–1975*. Cambridge: Cambridge University Press.
Banting, K. (1979), *Poverty, Politics and Policy*. London: Macmillan.
Beltram, G. (1984), *Testing the Safety Net*. London: Bedford Square Press.
Berthoud, R. (1985), *The Examination of Social Security*. London: Policy Studies Institute.

—— Brown, J. C., and Cooper, S. (1981), *Poverty and the Development of Anti-Poverty Policy in the United Kingdom*. London: Heinemann.

Beveridge, J. (1954), *Beveridge and his Plan*. London: Hodder and Stoughton.

Beveridge, W. H. (1942), *Social Insurance and Allied Services*, Cmd. 6404. London: HMSO.

—— (1943), *Pillars of Security*. London: Allen and Unwin.

—— (1944), *Full Employment in a Free Society*. London: Allen and Unwin.

—— (1953), *Power and Influence*. London: Hodder and Stoughton.

Bowley, A. L., and Burnett-Hurst, A. R. (1915), *Livelihood and Poverty: A Study in the Economic and Social Conditions of Working-Class Households*. London: King.

—— and Hogg, M. H. (1925), *Has Poverty Diminished?* London: King.

Boyd Orr, J. (1936), *Food, Health and Income: Report on A Survey of Adequacy of Diet in Relation to Income*. London: Macmillan.

—— (1937), *Not Enough Food for Fitness*. London: The Children's Minimum Council.

Bull, D. (1971), *Family Poverty: Programme for the Seventies*. London: Gerald Duckworth and Child Poverty Action Group.

Burns, E. M. (1943), 'The Beveridge Report', *American Economic Review*, 33/3.

Clarke, J. S. (1945), 'Social Insecurity', *Political Quarterly*, 16/1.

Cole, D., and Utting, J. (1962), *The Economic Circumstances of Old People*. Welwyn: Codicote Press.

Cutler, T., Williams, K., and Williams, J. (1986), *Keynes, Beveridge and Beyond*. London: Routledge.

Deacon, A. (1982), 'An End to the Means Test? Social Security and the Attlee Government', *Journal of Social Policy*, 11/3.

DHSS [Department of Health and Social Security] (1979), *Social Security Research: The Definition and Measurement of Poverty*. London: HMSO.

—— (1985), *Reform of Social Security*, Cmnd. 9517. London: HMSO.

Field, F. (1985), *What Price a Child? A Historical Review of the Relative Costs of Dependants*. London: Policy Studies Institute.

George, R. F. (1937), 'A New Calculation of the Poverty Line', *Journal of the Royal Statistical Society*, 1.

George, V. (1973), *Social Security and Society*. London: Routledge.

Griffiths, J. (1969), *Pages from Memory*. London: Dent.

Harris, J. (1975), 'Social Planning in War-Time: Some Aspects of the Beveridge Report', in M. Winter (ed.), *War and Economic Development*. Cambridge: Cambridge University Press.

—— (1977), *William Beveridge: A Biography*. Oxford: Clarendon Press.

—— (1982), 'The Social Thought of William Beveridge'. Paper presented to the University of Edinburgh conference on 'The Beveridge Report Forty Years On'.

Henderson, H. D. (1955), *The Interwar Years and Other Papers*. Oxford: Clarendon Press.

Hennock, E. P. (1987), 'The Measurement of Urban Poverty: From the Metropolis to the Nation, 1880–1920', *Economic History Review*, 40/2.

Hennock, E. P. (1991), 'Concepts of Poverty in the British Social Surveys From Charles Booth to Arthur Bowley', in M. Bulmer, K. Bales, and K. K. Sklar (eds.), *The Social Survey in Historical Perspective, 1880–1940*. Cambridge: Cambridge University Press.

Hess, J. (1981), 'The Social Policy of the Attlee Government', in W. J. Mommsen (ed.), *The Emergence of the Welfare State in Britain and Germany 1850–1950*. London: Croom Helm.

Judge, K. (1980), 'Beveridge: Past, Present and Future', in C. Sandford, C. Pond, and R. Walker (eds.), *Taxation and Social Policy*. London: Heinemann.

Kent, R. (1985), 'The Emergence of the Sociological Survey, 1887–1939', in M. Bulmer (ed.), *Essays on the History of British Sociological Research*. Cambridge: Cambridge University Press.

Kopsch, H. (1970), 'The Approach of the Conservative Party to Social Policy during World War II', Ph.D. thesis, University of London.

Leaper, R. (1991), 'Introduction to the Beveridge Report', *Social Policy and Administration*, 25/1.

Lynes, T. (1962), *National Assistance and National Prosperity*. Welwyn: Codicote Press.

—— (1977), 'The Making of the Unemployment Assistance Scale', in Supplementary Benefits Commission (ed.), *Low Incomes: Evidence to the Royal Commission on the Distribution of Income and Wealth*. London: HMSO.

—— (1985), *Maintaining the Value of Benefits*. London: Policy Studies Institute.

Mass Observation (1943), 'Social Security and Parliament', *Political Quarterly*, 14/3.

McCarthy, M. (1986), *Campaigning for the Poor: CPAG and the Politics of Welfare*. London: Croom Helm.

Melling, J. (1991), 'Reading Beveridge: Recent Research on Pre-War Social Policy', *Social Policy and Administration*, 25/1.

Minister of Reconstruction (1944), *Social Insurance, Part I*, Cmd. 6550. London: HMSO.

Moore, J. (1989), 'The End of the Line for Poverty'. A speech delivered by the Rt. Hon. John Moore MP, Secretary of State for Social Security, to the Greater London Area CPC on 11 May.

Morgan, K. O. (1984), *Labour in Power 1945–1951*. Oxford: Clarendon Press.

MPNI [Ministry of Pensions and National Insurance] (1959), *Improvements in National Assistance*. London: HMSO.

Philp, A. F., and Timms, N. (1957), *The Problem of 'The Problem Family': A Critical Review of the Literature Concerning the 'Problem Family' and its Treatment*. London: Family Service Units.

Robson, W. A. (1945) (ed.), *Social Security*. London: Allen and Unwin.

Rowntree, B. S. (1901), *Poverty: A Study of Town Life*. London: Macmillan.

—— (1903), *The 'Poverty Line': A Reply*. London: Henry Good.

—— (1918), *The Human Needs of Labour*. London: Longmans Green.

—— (1937), *The Human Needs of Labour* (New Edition). London: Longmans Green.

—— (1941), *Poverty and Progress*. London: Longmans Green.

—— and Lavers, G. R. (1951), *Poverty and the Welfare State*. London: Longmans.

Silburn, R. (1983), 'Social Assistance and Social Welfare: The Legacy of the Poor

Law', in P. Bean and S. MacPherson (eds.), *Approaches to Welfare*, London: Routledge.

Sinfield, A. (1968), 'Poverty Rediscovered', *Race*, 10/2.

Stevenson, J. (1977), *Social Conditions in Britain between the Wars*. Harmondsworth: Penguin.

Townsend, P. (1952), 'Poverty: Ten Years after Beveridge', *Planning [PEP]*, 19/344.

—— (1957), *The Family Life of Old People*. London: Routledge.

—— (1962), 'The Meaning of Poverty'. *British Journal of Sociology*, 18/3.

—— (1979), *Poverty in the United Kingdom*. Harmondsworth: Penguin.

—— and Gordon, D. (1989), 'What is Enough?', in House of Commons Social Services Committee (ed.), *Minimum Income: Memoranda Laid before the Committee*. London: HMSO.

—— and Wedderburn, D. (1965), *The Aged in the Welfare State*. London: Bell.

Veit-Wilson, J. H. (1986a), 'Paradigms of Poverty: A Rehabilitation of B. S. Rowntree', *Journal of Social Policy*, 15/1.

—— (1986b), 'Paradigms of Poverty: A Reply to Peter Townsend and Hugh McLachlan', *Journal of Social Policy*, 15/4.

—— (1987), 'Consensual Approaches to Poverty Lines and Social Security', *Journal of Social Policy*, 16/2.

—— (1989), 'The Concept of Minimum Income and the Basis of Income Support', in House of Commons Social Services Committee (ed.), *Minimum Income: Memoranda Laid before the Committee*. London: HMSO.

—— (1992), 'Muddle or Mendacity? The Beveridge Committee and the Poverty Line', *Journal of Social Policy*, 21/3.

Webb, A. (1975), 'The Abolition of National Assistance: Policy Changes in the Administration of Assistance Benefits', in P. Hall, H. Land, R. Parker and A. Webb (eds.), *Change, Choice and Conflict in Social Policy*. London: Heinemann.

Wilson, H. C. (1962), *Delinquency and Child Neglect*. London: Allen and Unwin.

Wootton, B. (1959), 'Daddy Knows Best', *The Twentieth Century*, 992.

—— (1960), 'The Image of the Social Worker', *The British Journal of Sociology*, 11/4.

Zweig, F. (1948), *Labour, Life and Poverty*. London: Gollancz.

8

A Prophet Dishonoured in his Own Country? The Rejection of Beveridge in Britain, 1945–1970

RODNEY LOWE

In the 1940s, Beveridge self-consciously sought to establish not just a universalist but a universal set of principles for social security. 'In seeking security not merely against physical want, but against all these evils [Disease, Ignorance, Squalor, Idleness]', he asserted in his 1942 Report, 'the British community and those who in other lands have inherited the British tradition have a vital service to render human progress' (1942: para. 456). In the short term he met with considerable success. Not only were there the well-known queues outside the government bookshop in London on the day of publication, but the Report also had a major impact on Resistance movements within occupied Europe and drew a concerned reaction from the Nazi Government. With scarce-contained glee, Beveridge's wife was later to recount how copies of the Nazi response to the Report had been recovered in 1945, if not exactly from Hitler's own hand then at least from his bunker (Beveridge 1954: 195; see also Chapter 9).

The Report's success was, however, only short-lived. Within Europe this was understandable. Each country had its own traditions and culture by which, ultimately, its social security system would be uniquely shaped; and, both before and after 1948, it was well-recognized that in Britain both popular and legal assumptions about the relationship between the state and the individual were atypical. Indeed, this was admitted in the Appendix to the Report in which Beveridge sought to defend his idiosyncratic retention of the principle of flat-rate, rather than earnings-related, contributions and benefits. 'In planning social security', he reasoned, somewhat at variance with his earlier search for universal principles, 'each country ... needs a scheme adapted to its special conditions and its dominant political ideas'. Earnings-related benefits might be appropriate for 'most other countries' but they were inappropriate for Britain. 'A flat rate of benefit up to subsistence level leaves untouched the freedom and responsibility of the individual citizen in making supplementary provision for himself above that level', and this accorded better 'both with the conditions of Britain, where voluntary insurance, particularly against sickness, is highly developed and with British sentiment' (1942: 293).

More surprising was the fate of the Report in Britain. The basis of its immediate success was its vision and the apparent ease with which its recommendations could achieve what ordinary people had long wanted: freedom from poverty, guaranteed as of right without recourse to a means test. The immediate and continuing power of its vision is unquestionable. In the wartime transformation of the relatively generous, but highly anomalous, system of social insurance into a comprehensive system of universal social security, for example, one Labour minister admitted that the Report provided the vital stimulus which ministers and officials alike needed 'to quicken our steps and leap over obstacles placed in our path by timid, short-sighted or sinister persons' (Pimlott 1985: 393). After the War, it continued to inspire reformers—not least in the 1960s, when the battle between selectivity and universalism was rejoined, and a 'back to Beveridge' campaign was mounted. What is more questionable, however, is the practical success of the Report. Did it provide the blueprint for the postwar social security system?

To many commentators, the answer to this question is self-evident. The conventional wisdom of political historians remains that 'Labour's social reforms mirrored the principles of the Beveridge Report quite faithfully' (Cronin 1991: 152), and a recent social policy textbook has concluded that 'it is really quite remarkable to be able to record that Beveridge's recommendations were adopted almost in their entirety' (Hill 1990: 31). Nevertheless, it is often simultaneously acknowledged that, just as the popularity of the Report was quickly usurped by the NHS, so several of its key recommendations were never implemented (PEP 1961: 39, 192). Moreover, of those that were, many were soon either abandoned or heavily qualified. It seems, therefore, that the conclusion of the Fowler review of social security in 1985 rings more true: 'Beveridge's plan for social security was radically changed at the outset and has carried on being changed since' (DHSS 1985: 6). The purpose of this chapter is to examine the gulf between the success of the Report as an expression of an ideal and as a practical blueprint, and thus between conventional wisdom and the conclusion of the Fowler review. First it will look, in a rather less partial way than Fowler, at the rejection of Beveridge, and then at the reasons for this rejection.

THE REJECTION OF BEVERIDGE

Beveridge, as his biographer has argued, sought to produce in his Report 'not merely technical proposals' for a system of social security, but also a 'blueprint for national life' (Harris 1986: 246). The technical proposals were summarized in paragraph 17 of the Report:

The scheme embodies six fundamental principles: flat rate of subsistence benefit; flat rate of contributions; unification of administrative responsibility; adequacy of benefit; comprehensiveness and classification.... Based on them and in combination with national assistance and voluntary insurance as subsidiary methods, the aim of the Plan for Social Security is to make want under any circumstances unnecessary.

The fate of each of these principles will be examined individually before attention is turned to the rejection of Beveridge's wider 'blueprint'.

The two principles which were never implemented by the British Government were 'adequacy' and 'the unification of administrative responsibility'. The former was the more significant, especially in the light of the original intention that benefit should be adequate both 'in amount and in time' (1942: para. 307). Neither of these objectives was achieved. In relation to 'adequacy in time', for example, Beveridge's particular concern after the depression of the 1930s was that unemployment pay (subject to a requirement to accept training) should be limitless. From the start, however, it was restricted to thirty weeks—with the consequence that it was no longer 'adequate' for the long-term unemployed, who had accordingly to resort to means-tested benefit. Before 1965, admittedly, the number of such claimants were few, in part as a result of the Government's honouring one of the Report's three basic assumptions: the maintenance of employment. Nevertheless, as an indication of official reservation about the Report, it is significant that even in the mid-1940s (when the practicality of the Government's economic commitment was seriously doubted) the principle of 'adequacy in time' was rejected for fear that it might compromise the 'work ethic'.

Far more serious was the rejection by successive governments of the principle of 'adequacy in amount', because this, as Beveridge himself realized, struck at the heart of his proposals and of their popular appeal: the guarantee that all would be entitled to a subsistence income as of right without a means test. There were two genuine impediments to the realization of this ideal. First, there could be—as Beveridge himself acknowledged— no agreed, let alone permanent, definition of 'adequacy'. 'Determination of what is required for reasonable human subsistence', the Report conceded, 'is to some extent a matter of judgment; estimates on this point change with time, and generally, in a progressive community, change upwards' (1942: para. 27). Secondly, as civil servants were quick to point out, it was both illogical and impractical to try to provide a subsistence benefit through a flat-rate cash benefit. Subsistence requirements—however defined—clearly varied between regions and according to individual circumstance, such as the extent of claimants' savings or family support.[1]

Beveridge's own solutions to these genuine problems were disingenuous. As Veit-Wilson has convincingly demonstrated in this volume, he deliberately evaded a definition of adequacy and based his proposed level of benefit on a level of income just below that of the lowest paid regular manual worker. The objective, once again, was to safeguard the work ethic. He then rejected the advice of Rowntree to inject a degree of flexibility into his benefit levels by paying each claimant a fixed sum plus the actual cost of rent—rent traditionally being the most variable item in household budgets (1942: para. 213). In defence of his flat-rate principle, he persisted instead with a fixed notional sum for rent—a decision that would have condemned many claimants with high housing costs to an inadequate rate of benefit.

Successive governments could not be so disingenuous, and they responded in two different, albeit contradictory, ways. In 1944 it was officially acknowledged that flat-rate benefit and adequacy were incompatible, and so the pretence was dropped that, even on Beveridge's terms, insurance benefit should be adequate for everyone. The postwar Labour Government, for instance, agreed that benefit should provide only 'a *reasonable* insurance against want'. For the minority for whom it was inadequate, resort would have to be made to the means-tested but humane system of National Assistance (Minister of Reconstruction 1944: para. 13; Deacon and Bradshaw 1983: 45). Then in 1959, the Conservative government sought to sidestep the question of adequacy altogether. First it started to introduce earnings-related benefit so that attention would become focused instead, as on the Continent, on the maintenance of claimants' accustomed standard of living. Secondly, it began to base calculations of National Assistance and, later, insurance benefit, on the concept not of 'absolute' poverty, as favoured by Beveridge, but of 'relative' poverty—that is, not on an estimate of subsistence, but on rising average living standards.

These responses not only rejected Beveridge's own imperfect solutions but also directly contradicted a key passage in his Report. This read:

A permanent scale of benefit below subsistence, assuming supplementation on a means test as a normal feature, cannot be defended. On the other hand, to give by compulsory insurance more than is needed for subsistence is an unnecessary interference with individual responsibilities. (1942: para. 294).

The decision in 1944 obliged as many as 675,000 insurance claimants to seek an additional means-tested 'top-up' as soon as the new insurance and assistance systems became operational in 1948. Thereafter the total number

---

[1] PRO T 273/57: W. Eady, 'The Beveridge Report', 22 Oct., para. 4.

of claimants on National Assistance, rather than declining, rose to 1.8 million in 1954 and 2 million in 1966. Similarly, the introduction of earnings-related benefit in 1959 started to erode the principle that voluntary insurance alone should provide benefit above the subsistence level.

It might have been expected, given Beveridge's experience as an administrator, that the principle of 'unification of administrative responsibility' would have been more easily realized; and indeed it has been noted of the postwar period that:

one respect in which the British system is indubitably 'Beveridgean' ... is that it is nationally uniform, centralized and bureaucratic, whereas most continental systems allow much more scope for pluralism, localism and democratic self-government. (Harris 1990: 194)

The exclusion of non-governmental agencies from the provision of basic social security represented a major break with the past, with both the Victorian tradition of mutual self-help and the interwar practice of 'approved' societies within health insurance. The justification was the enhanced role of voluntary insurance *outside* the state scheme. Nevertheless the principle of administrative unity was still not realized. The consolidated Ministry of Social Security, for which Beveridge had called, was not established until 1966, and even then, the objectives of 'coordination, simplicity and economy' were far from achieved (1942: para. 29).

Lack of co-ordination was most notorious in the relationship (or rather the absence of a relationship) between the tax and benefits systems. By the mid-1960s, a combination of direct and indirect taxation (including National Insurance contributions) was actually dragging an increasing number of low paid workers below the official poverty line. Conversely, an increasing number of claimants were being discouraged by taxation from finding work: the reward for self-sufficiency could be a drop in real income as a loss of means-tested benefits coincided with the need to pay both income tax and insurance contributions (the 'unemployment' or 'poverty' traps). Such anomalies encouraged government in the 1960s increasingly to rely on means-testing to target need; and this, in turn, removed any hope of achieving simplicity. By the early 1970s there were some 45 means-tested benefits administered by central government, local authorities and the NHS on differing criteria; and central government's benefits alone had become so complex that in order to make their workloads manageable, officials had to discourage claimants from applying (Deacon and Bradshaw 1983: 111; Donnison 1982: 44). Rather than making 'want under any circumstances unnecessary', as Beveridge had hoped, the postwar social security system was actually making it inevitable.

The system was, moreover, uneconomic (Lowe 1993: ch. 6.3). Not only was the administrative cost of means-tested benefits three times as great as that of insurance benefits, but the insurance system itself had become a costly fiction. Between the late 1950s and the early 1970s, the Treasury steadily reduced its contribution to the income of the Insurance Fund from 33 to 14 per cent, with the result that the system became based no longer on actuarial principles (by which present contributions covered future risks) but on the expedient of pay-as-you-go (by which present contributions paid for current liabilities). Beveridge had sought a properly-funded insurance scheme to encourage individual responsibility and prudence, but the system quickly descended into one in which—on the Treasury's own admission— contributions were no more than a 'regressive poll tax' whose level was determined by an 'arbitrary guess by the Actuary as to what is affordable'.[2] Just as the postwar social security system failed to resolve the problem of adequacy, therefore, it also signally failed to remove the indefensible 'anomalies and overlapping, the multiplicity of agencies and the needless administrative cost' which Beveridge had condemned in the prewar system (1942: para. 29).

The Report's four other principles were implemented, but they were soon either abandoned or heavily qualified. Flat-rate contributions and benefits were abandoned, as has been seen, in relation to pensions in 1959, and in relation to all the other major insurance benefits in 1966. In 1971, higher rates of benefit were also paid to long-term claimants, such as the disabled. The 1959 pensions legislation also breached the principle of com- prehensiveness (which paragraph 308 of the Report had recommended should be 'in respect both of persons covered and their needs') by permitting—and indeed encouraging—individuals to 'contract out' of the state occupational pension scheme. By 1964 over half the workforce, some 12.2 million individuals, had done so. Thus it was only the principle of 'classification' which remained unscathed in 1970—and even this was to be eroded in 1975 when class 4 ('other people of working age, not gainfully employed') was disbanded.

Given the widespread rejection of Beveridge's technical proposals for social security, his 'blueprint for national life' stood little chance of implementation. This blueprint rested on two key principles: the elimination of commercial exploitation in the provision of security, and a determination to ensure that security should not 'impair freedom and enterprise and responsibility of the individual for his own life' (1942: para. 456). Neither was realized.

The first required, above all, a dramatic change in the most traditional form of working-class savings—the setting-aside each week of a small sum of money to cover, in particular, funeral expenses. The collection of these

[2] PRO T 227/415: Miss Whalley, 'NHS and National Insurance Contributions', 1 May 1956; see also Ch. 5.

savings, technically known as industrial assurance, was dominated by nine large life assurance companies and was, in Beveridge's opinion, the foremost example of the inefficiency and exploitative nature of unregulated capitalism. Administrative costs (at 37 per cent of premiums) were excessively high, as were the number of policies which never matured (32 per cent). The root cause of the problem, so Beveridge concluded, was 'excessive competition' between the companies, and the consequent 'feverish pressure' under which their collectors worked—especially as their salaries depended on the number of new policies sold (1942: para. 187).

Beveridge's solution was the nationalization of industrial assurance so that its administration might be rationalized and the role of its collectors transformed. As he concluded, again rather contradictorily:

The collectors now visiting at short intervals most of the houses in Britain have become in thousands of cases the friends and advisers of the families with whom they deal. Many of them are in effect travelling Citizens' Advice Bureaux; they regard themselves as servants of the public. They can find in a new relation a better opportunity and not a worse opportunity of living up to that ideal. (1942: para. 191).

Nationalization would, therefore, simultaneously end exploitation and humanize the state's social security system (thereby helping to minimize the abuse which impersonality might encourage).

His recommendations, however, were rejected. Admittedly, state provision after 1948 of a funeral grant did undercut industrial assurance; but the large insurance companies turned this to their advantage by concentrating instead on the provision of private occupational pensions, which government was encouraging through tax exemption and the contracting-out clauses in pensions legislation. This represented a double defeat for Beveridge, because he had desired the growth of small, participatory friendly societies and the control of industrial investment by the state in the long-term national interest, not by the old financial élite through its new vehicle of pension funds (Beveridge 1948: 297–301; 1944: 177–8). Furthermore, the failure to incorporate the insurance sales force within the state system—in conjunction with the rejection of Beveridge's parallel recommendation to make friendly societies and trade unions agencies for the payment of relief (1942: paras. 66–9), jeopardized the chances of state benefits becoming a vehicle for the encouragement of individual responsibility. Rather, as its traditional critics had feared, it quickly became a target for what many considered to be 'legitimate' abuse.

This latter development was particularly damaging to Beveridge because, as has been seen, his second major aim had been to ensure that social security did not demoralize the workforce. Hence, for example, his requirement that the payment of National Assistance should 'be subject to any conditions as to behaviour which may seem likely to hasten restoration of earning capacity' (1942: para. 369), that training should become obligatory after six months' unemployment, and that widows without dependants should seek work after only thirteen weeks. Beveridge's overriding fear in this respect, however, was demographic: the fear that an 'ageing population' might impair productive efficiency and individual initiative by, first, creating a labour shortage, and then placing too heavy a financial burden on the depleted workforce.

His solution to this problem was characteristically simple: the elderly should be encouraged to remain at work after the conventional age of retirement. This was both logical and practical. The average health of the elderly, for example, was far better than ever before. Why, therefore, should the effective age of retirement not go up? It could also be easily encouraged by providing, on eventual retirement, an enhanced pension in line with the extra number of years worked—although, of course, this would breach the flat-rate principle (1942: paras. 244–9). Once again, however, Beveridge's solution was rejected—although it did attract the continuing support of postwar governments (see, for example, Phillips Committee 1954: paras. 191–3). Its main opponents this time were the trade unions and employers. The former, *inter alia*, found it hard to reverse their traditional policy of championing a reduction in the age of retirement as an antidote to unemployment. The latter doubted the adaptability of the elderly to new technology, and, above all, found in part-time women workers and immigrants an alternative supply of labour. Consequently, the elderly themselves bowed to peer pressure and started to welcome greater opportunities for leisure. As a result, and again in complete contradiction to Beveridge's hopes, the proportion of people aged between 65 and 69 who were retired soared from 32 per cent in 1931 to 63 per cent in 1961 (Harper and Thane 1989; see also Chapter 6).

As a practical guide to postwar social security, therefore, the Beveridge Report was largely rejected in relation both to its technical proposals and its underlying assumptions. The six 'fundamental principles' were either never implemented or hastily withdrawn and, by the late 1950s, the very principle of insurance had been reduced to a fiction. Similarly, the underlying assumption that security could be made compatible with 'freedom and enterprise and responsibility' was compromised by the increasing impersonality and inflexibility of the state system.

The fate of the supposedly 'subsidiary' agencies of voluntary insurance and National Assistance was equally conclusive. Encouraged by tax exemption, voluntary insurance did increase, but not in the way that Beveridge had hoped. Its form became essentially selfish and, when the political need arose in the late 1950s, it proved incapable of providing benefit for all above the subsistence level. Even more significant was the increased reliance placed by government on means-tested benefit to meet needs which universal benefits were adjudged too expensive to relieve. So great, indeed, did this reliance become that Beveridge's own biographer has recently concluded:

Paradoxically, though Britain was believed to be the homeland of a 'Beveridge'-based universal insurance system, almost the opposite was really the case. It was the European countries ... which most whole-heartedly adopted a comprehensive, contributory social insurance system ... whereas Britain ... retained in addition to social insurance a substantial means-tested tax-financed welfare system, directly inherited from the Poor Law.... In other words, contrary to what most academic commentators and popular folk-lore have believed, it was not contributory insurance, but 'free' services financed out of direct taxation that was the most marked characteristic of Britain's welfare state system in the thirty years after the Second World War. (Harris 1990: 182–4)

THE REASONS FOR REJECTION

Why was there such a gulf between the fate of the Report as the expression of an ideal and as a practical guide to policy? Was it because 'timid, short-sighted or sinister persons' eventually triumphed? Was it because the Report itself was internally inconsistent and its recommendations therefore impractical? Or was it because the broad philosophical assumptions on which it was based were confused and, in the relative affluence of postwar Britain, popularly unacceptable?

Had vested interests been the principal cause of rejection, it would have been surprising, since the Report was in essence a conservative document, and, after lengthy negotiations with the Treasury, Beveridge had agreed to make substantial concessions. The Report was conservative in that it sought to minimize the role of the state, maximize individual responsibility and safeguard the work ethic. For instance, it restricted the role of government to the guarantee of a mere subsistence income, put the onus on individuals to insure themselves privately should they want higher benefits, and placed strict conditions on the acceptance of relief. Indeed, so restrictive was the Report that some modern commentators have concluded that its central concern was 'not the provision of adequate subsistence benefits but the maximising of personal responsibility and the maintenance of the conditions of social independence'; and, at the time, the realization that this might be true transformed with some alacrity instinctive opponents of the Report within the Conservative Party into supporters (Cutler *et al.* 1986: 16; Jefferys 1987: 132). Beveridge's concessions to the Treasury, such as the withdrawal of family allowances from the first child, were also substantial. They reduced the final costs of his recommendations to one-fifth of his ideal figure, and prompted Keynes to remark that, given that some measure of reform was inevitable, 'the Chancellor of the Exchequer should thank his stars that he has got off so cheap'.[3]

Nevertheless it is true that Beveridge did try to capitalize upon a favourable opportunity when many vested interests, traditionally opposed to reform, were preoccupied with war work (1942: para. 7). After the War they re-grouped to defeat, for example, the nationalization of industrial assurance. Moreover, despite Beveridge's concessions, the Treasury was never able wholly to suppress its initial instincts that any expenditure on social security was throwing 'money down the sink' (Jefferys 1984: 426). Its initial reservations were both practical and economic. Given the precedent of failed reconstruction planning after the First World War, could Britain afford so ambitious a programme? Might not USA loans be withdrawn if they were seen to be supporting such extravagance? More particularly, would poorer workers be able, and the better-off (given their lower risks) be willing, to pay their universal, flat-rate contributions? Economically, would not the necessarily high rate of taxation discourage incentive and risk-taking? Would not the 'high' rate of benefit undermine the will to work? Moreover, were the money to be raised, would it not be better spent on defence, industrial investment, or even on such social services as education and housing which had a more direct economic return?[4]

Beveridge, having been alerted to such objections during his negotiations, refuted them vigorously (1942: paras. 444–54). In particular, he argued that there was no danger of non-compliance: the employed would receive for their contributions far more than they presently received from a combination of compulsory and voluntary insurance, and employers would benefit directly from a healthier, better motivated, and hence more productive workforce. Treasury officials, however, remained unconvinced. They continued to fear that high social expenditure would offend, if not the USA, then the foreign bankers upon whom the value of sterling depended. They also strongly favoured a reduction of taxation (which, by stimulating economic growth, would increase individual welfare via the market) over the expansion, or even the maintenance, of existing levels of public expenditure.

In the short-term they had to accept the political necessity of universalism; but by the mid-1950s, when the first sustained reappraisal of postwar welfare policy was attempted, they started actively to seek a withdrawal from wartime commitments. Thus in 1957, when Thorneycroft as Chancellor wished to invoke the Report in support of increased funding for the NHS from insurance contributions, he was urged not to do so, as the Report

[3] PRO T 273/57: minute, 9 Dec. 1942; see also Harris (1990: 187).
[4] PRO T 273/57: W. Eady, 'The Beveridge Report', 22 Oct. 1942; PRO CAB 87/3, RP(43)5: 'The Financial Aspects of the Social Security Plan', the Chancellor of the Exchequer (1943).

was 'something from which we want to move away'.[5] This hidden agenda became open in the later 1950s when, for example, Treasury contributions to the Insurance Fund were cut (thereby destroying its actuarial basis), and in the 1960s when the principle of universalism was eroded by the use of means-tested benefit to target need. For the successful implementation and adaptation to changing circumstances of any major reform, a positive administrative lead is required; and it is quite apparent that throughout this period there remained, at the heart of Whitehall, interests fundamentally opposed to the spirit of the Report.

A second reason for the Report's rejection (which provides an additional justification for administrative resistance) was the internal inconsistency and thus impracticality of many of its key recommendations. These included the principles of adequacy, flat-rate contributions and benefits, universalism, and insurance. As has already been seen, the principles of adequacy and flat-rate benefit were incompatible. Until 1959, successive governments opted for the latter, and so many claimants had to top up 'inadequate' insurance benefits with means-tested National Assistance. Thus the popular expectation that social security would give 'in return for contributions benefits up to subsistence level, as of right and without means tests' (1942: para. 10) was disappointed, as was Beveridge's intention that the role of National Assistance should steadily decline. If the real purpose of the Report was to eliminate want, moreover, the choice of a 'universalist' solution was illogical, because, as Treasury officials were quick to point out, it would lead to 'a vast and essentially purposeless duplication' as contributions were collected and benefits (such as family allowances) paid back to people who were in no conceivable way threatened by want.[6] It would have been far more logical and efficient to identify those who were in genuine need and provide them with genuinely adequate help. Herein lay the justification for the erosion of universalism by targeted benefits in the 1960s.

Beveridge's practical defence of universalism was that, in Britain at least, means-testing was itself inefficient because, as a legacy of the Poor Law, it was highly stigmatized. Consequently many would not claim and help would not get through to all those in need. This was undoubtedly true, as the 1960s confirmed; but nevertheless the Treasury's practical objections to universalism did expose the financial limitations of Beveridge's proposals. These limitations were both specific and general. Specifically, to construct a potentially expensive system of social security (universalism) on very restricted financial foundations (flat-rate contributions based on what the lowest paid worker could afford) was necessarily to starve it of resources,

---

[5] Lowe (1989); PRO T 227/485/SS 226/01D: minute by Maude to Brittain, 13 Feb. 1957.
[6] PRO T 273/57: 'The Principles of the Beveridge Plan', H. D. Henderson, 4 Aug. 1942.

and thereby deny it the flexibility needed to respond to changing circumstances and expectations. This was implicitly recognized in the Report itself. There was, Beveridge admitted, no scientific definition of adequacy, and estimates would 'change upwards' in time (1942: para. 27); and yet flat-rate insurance contributions were 'either a poll-tax or a tax on employment, justifiable up to certain limits, but not capable of indefinite expansion' (1942: para. 415). How then were 'adequate' benefits to be financed at a 'minimum participatory' level, let alone when—as in the late 1950s—public expectations came to be based on a relative concept of poverty? More generally, a social security system financed by insurance contributions at work assumed not only that most risks were insurable, but also that almost everyone had access to the labour market, either directly or through a partner. As later developments, such as the growth in the number of one-parent families demonstrated, neither assumption was realistic. For all its appearance of being closely reasoned and costed, therefore, the Report contained contradictions and financial weaknesses which jeopardized both its immediate implementation and its later development.

Surprisingly, one of the areas of greatest inconsistency within the Report, as the recent work of Jose Harris has shown, was its underlying philosophy; and in the end it is this which provides a common explanation for both its internal contradictions and its ultimate rejection. There were two broad philosophical concepts on which Beveridge might have based his vision of the future relationship between the State and the individual. The tradition of the 'free-born Englishman' was based on a concept of 'natural liberty'. All citizens had certain rights (such as freedom from poverty) which it was the state's duty to ensure. Alternatively, as was more common on the Continent, the state might be viewed as a living organism—the actual embodiment of shared values and identity—from which citizens derived certain rights, but to which they also owed certain duties. The two concepts were fundamentally opposed. One assumed rights without obligations, the other did not. Nevertheless, Beveridge borrowed from both, basing, for example, the justification for contributory insurance on the concept of natural liberty (a private contract to ensure a natural right) and that for universalism on the organicist model (the entitlement to welfare for all as members of a community). As a result his recommendations were not only contradictory but also represented 'a portmanteau set of ideas offering all things to all men'—and presumably women (Harris 1986: 249).

This ambiguity denied the Report, after its euphoric public reception, the wholehearted support of any one group in society. Beveridge was exceptional amongst social administrators for his apparent determination to identify and to base his recommendations on popular opinion. However, the opinion poll which he commissioned, the Nuffield College Social Reconstruction Survey, was notoriously flawed (Harris 1983) and his perception of public

opinion was both partial and self-deluding. This was evident in his commitment to both contributory and voluntary insurance. He dismissed any
alternative to contributory insurance, for example, on the grounds that
ordinary people virtuously preferred to pay their own way rather than
receive charity. This conveniently overlooked the fact that much of its
popularity rested on the more cynical calculation that it established rights
upon which government would be unable to renege. Similarly, his advocacy
of voluntary insurance was based on a desire to maintain the nineteenth-
century tradition of self-help—whereas friendly societies were essentially
the creation of a poverty culture and had been in decline since the start of
the century (Cutler *et al.* 1986: chap. 2). Their revival was highly unlikely
in a period of full employment when, as one later poll of affluent workers
was to discover, the 'solidaristic collectivism' of the past had been exchanged
for 'more privatized forms of existence' and advance (Goldthorpe *et al.*
1968: 75–6). In short, the postwar workforce overwhelmingly preferred
private rights to communal responsibilities. This was consistently demonstrated by its rejection of calls for wage restraint and, indeed, by its
attitude towards social security where 'getting what you paid for became a
touchstone of virtue in the popular postwar welfare state ideology' (Harris
1986: 295).

This rejection of the solidaristic assumptions of universalism was not
confined to manual workers but affected also the middle class. Its initial
acceptance of social security reform was based not so much on altruism,
but on calculated self-interest. Amongst the formerly self-reliant, there were
now those who felt themselves to be at risk for both economic and
demographic reasons (the relative decline of certain professions and the
increasing cost of old age, in terms of pensions and health care). There
were also those who calculated they would benefit from any redistribution
of resources. They therefore welcomed universalism and, in so doing,
succeeded in shaping it to their advantage (Baldwin 1990: 10–21, 133).
Thus, in defiance of Beveridge, full pensions were paid immediately (to the
relative advantage of the affluent) whilst sufficient resources could not be
found to lift more claimants out of means-tested benefit (to the disadvantage
of the poor). Other areas of the welfare state which had escaped Beveridge's
attention, such as tax allowances, were similarly turned to their advantage.

Ironically, the philosophical inconsistencies within the Report even led
to its effective rejection by those who sought to save it from increasing
attack in the 1960s by mounting a 'back to Beveridge' campaign. The
essential concern of this campaign was to protect Beveridge's broader
vision—the maintenance of full employment, the provision of family allowances, and the construction of a system of non-means-tested social security.
Some of the Report's original recommendations had inevitably to be
modified—in order to provide, for example, benefit as of right to certain

'uninsurable' groups of claimants, such as one-parent families. Nevertheless, as the Fowler review correctly divined, certain other recommendations central to Beveridge's 'blueprint for national life' were blatantly overlooked (DHSS 1985: paras. 2.14–15). These included the deliberate restriction of the State's role to the provision of subsistence benefit so that voluntary insurance and thus 'individual incentive, opportunity and responsibility' could be maximized. Above all, however, they included the rejection of any major redistribution of income.

In the broadest sense, the Report was not inegalitarian. Freedom from the fear of poverty, for example, gave to all an equal status and a peace of mind which had previously been the privilege of the rich. However, in relation to the equality of income, Beveridge was quite explicit that any redistribution should be mainly within, and not between, families and classes. As he insisted:

Abolition of want cannot be brought about merely by increasing production, without seeing to correct distribution of the product; but correct distribution does not mean what it has often been taken to mean in the past—distribution between the different agents in production, between land, capital, management and labour. Better distribution of purchasing power is required among wage earners themselves— as between times of earning and not earning, and between times of heavy family responsibilities and of light or no family responsibilities. (1942: para. 449).

In sharp contrast, poverty by the 1960s had been redefined as 'relative deprivation', and no significant reduction could be achieved without a major redistribution of resources between classes.

Contradictions within the underlying philosophy of the Report, therefore, not only led to inconsistent recommendations, but also denied it effective popular support. For the majority the communal assumptions behind the principle of universalism were an unwanted intrusion into the enjoyment of private rights. For a minority, the emphasis on private rights provided an equally unwelcome impediment to the realization of its broader vision.

CONCLUSION

Despite conventional historical accounts, therefore, there is a remarkable disparity between the success of the Beveridge Report as an expression of an ideal and as a practical blueprint for the postwar welfare state. Its success as an expression of an ideal, which has so bewitched later commentators, rested upon the holistic vision inspired by its three assumptions— full employment, a national health service and family allowances—and the right to subsistence-level benefits without recourse to a means test. It contained, however, few practical details about how the three assumptions could be realized. To the extent that they were, the achievement was dependent upon the work of others. Moreover, of the six fundamental principles which were to underpin the social security system, two were never implemented and the others were soon either abandoned or heavily qualified.

The practical rejection of the Beveridge Report was not, in the main, the result of the obduracy of any vested interest group. Rather it was a consequence of the inconsistency of its own recommendations and underlying philosophy, which impeded its immediate implementation and denied it both the flexibility and the popular support its later adaptation required. This disparity between its visionary and practical success, however, was far from unique. It affected many other services within the postwar welfare state, not least the one which rapidly overhauled social security in popularity: the National Health Service. As an ideal—guaranteeing the best possible medical care, free to all, in time of need—it was unassailable. Impenetrable bureaucracy, lengthening waiting lists and a misallocation of resources between preventive and curative medicine, however, raised serious questions about its effectiveness as a practical deliverer of health care.

REFERENCES

Baldwin, P. (1990), *The Politics of Social Solidarity*. Cambridge: Cambridge University Press.

Beveridge, J. (1954), *Beveridge and his Plan*. London: Hodder and Stoughton.

Beveridge, W. H. (1942), *Social Insurance and Allied Services*, Cmd. 6404. London: HMSO.

—— (1944), *Full Employment in a Free Society*. London: Allen and Unwin.

—— (1948), *Voluntary Action*. London: Allen and Unwin.

Cronin, J. E. (1991), *The Politics of State Expansion: War, State and Society in Twentieth-Century Britain*. London: Routledge.

Cutler, T., Williams, K. and Williams, J. (1986), *Keynes, Beveridge and Beyond*. London: Routledge and Kegan Paul.

Deacon, A., and Bradshaw, J. (1983), *Reserved for the Poor*. Oxford: Blackwell.

DHSS [Department of Health and Social Security] (1985), *Reform of Social Security*, Cmnd. 9517. London: HMSO.

Donnison, D. (1982), *The Politics of Poverty*. Oxford: Martin Robertson.

Goldthorpe, J. H. *et al.* (1968), *The Affluent Worker*, ii. Cambridge: Cambridge University Press.

Harris, J. (1983), 'Did British Workers Want the Welfare State?' in J. Winter (ed.), *The Working Class in Modern British History*. Cambridge: Cambridge University Press.

—— (1986), 'Political Ideas and the Debate on State Welfare', in H. L. Smith (ed.), *War and Social Change*. Manchester: Manchester University Press.

——(1990), 'Enterprise and Welfare States: A Comparative Perspective', *Transactions of the Royal Historical Society*, 40.

Harper, S., and Thane, P. (1989), 'The Consolidation of "Old Age" as a Phase of Life, 1945–1965', in M. Jefferys (ed.), *Growing Old in the Twentieth Century*. London: Routledge.

Hill, M. (1990), *Social Security Policy in Britain*. Aldershot: Edward Elgar.

Jefferys, K. (1984), 'R. A. Butler, the Board of Education and the 1944 Act', *History*, 69.

——(1987), 'British Politics and Social Policy During the Second World War', *Historical Journal*, 30.

Lowe, R. (1989), 'Resignation at the Treasury: The Social Service Committee and the Failure to Reform the Welfare State, 1955–57', *Journal of Social Policy*, 18.

——(1993), *The Welfare State in Britain Since 1945*. London: Macmillan.

Minister of Reconstruction (1944), *Social Insurance, Part I*, Cmd. 6550. London: HMSO.

Phillips Committee (1954), *Report of the Committee on the Economic and Financial Problems of the Provision of Old Age*, Cmd. 9333. London: HMSO.

Pimlott, B. (1985), *Hugh Dalton*. London: Macmillan.

Political and Economic Planning [PEP] (1961), *Family Needs and the Social Services*. London: Allen and Unwin.

9

Beveridge meets Bismarck:
Echo, Effects, and Evaluation of the
Beveridge Report in Germany

FRITZ GRÜNDGER

1. PRELUDE

On his first visit to Germany in 1890, William Beveridge was too young to meet Prince Bismarck personally (Beveridge 1954: 30). On his second visit, in 1907, he was too late (ibid.: 55 f.). He was not too late, however, to meet the spirit of this conservative revolutionist and to pay tribute to the heritage he had left in the form of the German social insurance.

Meanwhile, Beveridge himself had become an expert and committed social security theorist. His study trip led him to intensive talks with the Reich Insurance Authority, the Reich Statistical Office and the Reich Ministry of the Interior. Besides Berlin he visited Nuremberg, Cologne, Munich and Frankfurt-on-Main (Harris 1977: 135).

Confronted with the institutions Bismarck had created two decades before, Beveridge found his own ideas of social insurance as a weapon against mass poverty in a modern industrial society fully confirmed. The German example showed him not only that the principles of a contributory compulsory insurance for wide sections of the population could become reality, but also that its positive effects, from the workers' point of view, had led to internal peace without weakening the productive resources of the economy.

As is generally known, his knowledge of the Bismarckian system of social insurance, now deepened by examination, was manifested in a series of articles for the *Morning Post* in September 1907. They were followed by several statements on contributory old age pensions in the debate on the introduction of tax-financed means-tested pensions in May 1908. They already contained in a nutshell the ideas to materialize in the Beveridge Plan, thirty-four years later (Beveridge 1954: 55 f.).

It should be mentioned here that the social insurance in Germany was (and still is) by no means a uniform and consistent system. Since they were set up, its institutions have partly followed quite different lines. This can be explained not only by social history in general, but also by the precarious political majorities in the German Reichstag with which Bismarck had to comply (Hentschel 1983: 13–21).

However, from their beginnings all branches of German social insurance have had common characteristics:

> Claims not based on individual indigence and means-testing, but on level and duration of contribution (insurance principle);
> Income-related contributions for equal services and benefits in kind, but contribution-related cash benefits (achievement principle);
> The connection between compulsory contributions and self-government;
> Organizational diversity and fragmentation (Hentschel 1983: 12 f.).

In 1907, the year of Beveridge's second visit,[1] German social insurance was strictly sectionalized and rested on only three pillars: statutory insurance against sickness, industrial accidents, and disability (including old age). Unemployment, a very special concern of Beveridge's, was at that time widely regarded as a non-insurable risk (Fischer 1982: 84; Ritter 1989: 110). Allowing some simplifications and generalizations, the contemporary picture which might have impressed the British visitor in that time was as follows.[2]

Since 1883 *health insurance* had covered all workers and most salaried employees (up to a certain salary limit) in the branches covered by the law, i.e. 13 million insured persons. The benefits comprised free medical care and provision with related services and benefits in kind, as well as cash payments in case of sickness, death, and maternity. Medical treatment was given by licensed independent doctors, paid by the insurance fund for any treatment item given to the patient according to a detailed fee schedule. About 23,000 local, industrial, guild, or certificated 'free' insurance funds and special community institutions were charged with the administration, their budgets being financed by employees and employers at the rate of 2 : 1 (today 50 : 50).

Accident insurance (from 1884) was a compulsory insurance for all undertakings to replace the former private liability insurance of employers. In the case of industrial accidents (and occupational diseases as well from 1925) the cost of medical treatment was covered. In case of disability a pension was paid which in case of death went to the surviving dependants. The responsible agencies were 114 co-operative associations of private employers and 535 civil service offices. The contributions were fully paid by the employers (including the state authorities). In 1907 19.7 out of 22.0 million dependent employees enjoyed accident insurance coverage.

---

[1] On his third visit in 1909 he was mainly interested in the administration of labour exchanges (Harris 1977: 155).

[2] See Zöllner (1982: 28–30) and Frerich (1987: 80–92). Figs. for 1907 taken from (and partly calculated on the basis of) Kaiserliches Statistisches Amt (1909), mainly ch. 16: 330–46.

Pensions insurance covered all workers and salaried staff (the latter up to
the same income level as for sickness insurance), i.e. 15 million members,
administered by 31 regional institutions and 10 for railway employees and
miners. Pensions were paid in case of disability and at the age of 70 (today
generally 65 years). Pensions were financed by equal contributions from
employees and their employers, complemented by a flat-rate state subsidy
to each pension.

By 1942 the German system had undergone many changes, not, however,
of substance, but through expanding the categories of persons to be insured
and, except for the grave reductions in the early thirties, through the raising
and enlargement of benefits. Among the most important innovations of the
period in between were, firstly, the introduction of unemployment insurance
as the fourth autonomous pillar of social insurance in 1927, thereby bringing
Germany belatedly into line with international developments (Fischer 1982:
84; Ritter 1989: 110); and secondly, in 1930 medical help for non-working
family members without additional contributions became an obligatory
benefit of the statutory health insurance (Bethusy-Huc 1987: 84).

Taken all in all, Bismarck's socio-political legacy, both as to the principles
and the institutions of social insurance, had survived the political and
economic tides of the Empire and the Weimar Republic remarkably well.
It now had to stand the twofold challenge of Hitler's ideology and the
constraints of a wartime economy.

2. WITH THE EYES OF THE ENEMY

The reception given to the liberal reformer, Beveridge (in the form of his
Report), by Bismarck's heirs was more than unkind. In truth, the circumstances could not have been more unfavourable. By November 1942
the official war propaganda and indoctrination had reached a level where
an unbiased public judgement on British conditions and politics could no
longer be expected. Radio and the press had been streamlined or directly
put in charge of the Reich Minister of Propaganda, Dr Joseph Goebbels.
His ministry dictated to editors, partly going into detail, the form and
content of their reporting. The eagerness of convinced or opportunistic
journalists took care of the rest.

The publication of the Beveridge Report could not be totally concealed,
for the German government had to take into account that information
about it would be spread by Radio London (BBC) and Swiss sources.
Herald and trailblazer of the propagandistic attack deemed necessary was
the official Party newspaper *Völkischer Beobachter* (*VB*). In a short notice
of 29 November its Stockholm office had already described the Report, just

announced, as being 'so primitive that it can be easily identified as what it really means: political agitation looking for a sucker'.[3]

The publication of the Report itself was met by the *VB* on 4 December with the loud headline 'Plutocratic fraud on the English people confirmed: England half a century behind socially. British capitalists expect continuing unemployment of millions'.[4] A day later it reported: 'Dr Ley gives capital's servant Beveridge hell. In Germany one word of the Führer—in England six hundred thousand words in Parliament'.[5] The trilogy was finished off with the sneering title 'Beveridge already almost unrigged. The British financial world says: "Not feasible"'.[6]

The second article mentioned above refers to a contribution by Dr Robert Ley, the chief of the German Labour Front (DAF), an early disciple of Hitler and devout believer in him, until his own miserable end in an American prison (Smelser 1988, 1989 *passim*). The text was written for the newspaper of his organization, *Der Angriff* (The Attack). There he talks of 'the Utopia of Mr Beveridge' and says: 'And then ..., the first basic ideas of the future provision for the aged in Germany having been discussed, they charged one of their nimblest and shrewdest economists ... to prepare something like this, too'. He calls him the 'bad and smudgy copyist of national-socialist principles'.[7]

Dr Ley quotes here the Führer's order—given to him allegedly on 15 February 1940—to plan the building up of a comprehensive social organization for the postwar period, comprising, among other things, tax-financed old age pensions following those for public servants. In mid-September 1940 he announced his social programme to the foreign press with the remark: 'The German people shall be rewarded for the sacrifices of the war by a carefree old age. In ten years' time Germany will be changed beyond recognition. Then a people of proletarians will have turned into a *herrenvolk*. In ten years the German worker will be better off than an English lord today' (quoted in Recker 1985: 98).

The launching of three large party-official articles on the Beveridge Report in a row, all on the front page, and two of them as feature reports, shows how seriously the news from London was taken. As for the daily press, they all repeated the *VB*'s opinion, whether on direct instruction or in anticipating obedience.

The echoes of most of the rest of the press differed from the texts mentioned above in their tone and style, but generally took a negative line as well. The distinguished weekly paper *Das Reich* reported in two larger

[3] *Völkischer Beobachter*, 29 Nov. 1942: 4.
[4] Ibid., 4 Dec. 1942: 1.
[5] Ibid., 5 Dec. 1942: 1.
[6] Ibid., 6 Dec. 1942: 1.
[7] *Der Angriff*, 5 Dec. 1942: 1 f.

articles full of pity and haughtiness on a 'late discovery'. Compared to German conditions, the Beveridge Plan was a 'poor allotment garden lacking fertilizer' (Brech 1942). At the same time, another, concerned with British press commentaries, asks whether 'England can afford social policy' (Vermehren 1942). Other serious periodicals, too, discussed in detail the controversy on the Beveridge Plan in the British public, and questioned its political feasibility,[8] feeling themselves later proved right by the mid-February 1943 debate in the Commons.[9] There were only a few relatively sober descriptions of the Plan in some periodicals,[10] but no echo at all in the academic journals.

A remarkable amount of space is given to the person and biography of Beveridge, and not without paying some tribute to him. It is not always in the ironic sense of the *VB*'s 'famous Sir William Beveridge',[11] when they talk of the 'leading expert on social insurance issues'.[12] But there is no unanimity as to whether he is 'England's best-known social politician' (Gehnich 1943: 8), 'one of the best-known economic politicians',[13] or no politician at all (Rasch 1942). To some authors the liberal Beveridge is not only 'known as a conservative',[14] but even an 'enrolled member of the Conservative Party' (Brech 1942). Only once he is described as a politically unsuccessful publicist, as a tragic figure (Rauecker 1943: 162).

There is a most revealing find which is typical of the tactics the Nazi government applied, in order to absorb information about the Beveridge Plan, to defuse it by manipulation and turn it into counter-propaganda. In an article for the *Observer* (8 July 1951)[15] Beveridge told of two documents marked as 'secret', found in Hitler's bunker in August 1945 and passed into his hands. Both papers, presumably from the personal archives of the Minister for Propaganda, Dr Joseph Goebbels, are annexes to an unknown third document. As they date from no earlier than the second half of December 1942 (Beveridge 1954: 194), they do prove that the Nazi government regarded the Beveridge Plan as more than a short-term threat to their policy.

The first paper is an order to avoid dealing with the Plan, that is to say, avoid publicity, unless the international debate demands it. If a discussion

---

[8] See *Der deutsche Volkswirt*, 17/10 (4 Dec. 1942: 292 f.); 17/11 (11 Dec. 1942: 321 f.); *Wirtschaftsdienst*, 27/50 (11 Dec. 1942: 41).

[9] *Reichsarbeitsblatt*, 23/V6 (25 Feb. 1943: V89–V91).

[10] A short one in *Soziale Praxis*, 52 (1943: 20–2); a more detailed and in some points even positive report in *Wirtschafts- und Sozialberichte* of the DAF's central office, 10–12 (1942: 216–27). See also Stephan (1943).

[11] See n.3.

[12] *Wirtschafts- und Sozialberichte* (see n.10: 223).

[13] *Wirtschaftsring*, 15 (1942: 1053).

[14] Ibid.

[15] See German transl. ('Goebbels über den Beveridge-Plan') in *Englische Rundschau*, 1 (1951) 11: 128.

was necessary, the Plan should be depreciated as a diversion of the public, mere shop window advertising, and dreams of the future. On the other hand, propaganda should avoid a detailed comparison with the German system, and confine itself to the counter-arguments of Left and Right in England, more than a dozen being quoted subsequently (Beveridge 1954: 195 f.). Finally, referring to paragraph 24 of the Report (on financing social insurance), 'the Beveridge Plan should be mentioned as an especially obvious proof that our enemies are taking over national-socialistic ideas' (Beveridge 1954: 197).

In opposition to that, the other document, explicitly meant for the members of the Foreign Office, is a decidedly positive assessment of the Beveridge Plan. In this view the Beveridge Plan is 'no "botch-up" and no "patchwork", but a consistent system ... of remarkable simplicity.... superior to the current German social insurance in almost all points' (Beveridge 1954: 198).

3. A GERMAN BEVERIDGE PLAN?

The starting point for the repeated speculations on the influence Dr Ley's reformist ideas might have had on the British plan is the fact that the Beveridge committee was set up in June 1941, the very month when Ley published his 'Principles of the Provision of the Aged', both showing similar innovations, such as a flexible retirement age.[16] Answering to the charge of plagiarism, Beveridge remarked in his address to the Manchester Luncheon Club on 11 December 1942:

In spite of Dr Ley the Report owes nothing to German influence. In former times it was worthwhile studying German methods of social reform, without imitating them, but not today. There is nothing and has never been anything in Germany which is even faintly similar to this project.[17]

For a better understanding of Ley's personal journalistic intervention and his irritated attack, something has to be said of the history of the Sozialwerk des Deutschen Volkes (Welfare Organization of the German People) envisaged by him, which earned him the posthumous name of a 'German Beveridge' (Hockerts 1983*b*: 309; see also Smelser 1988: 307). He obviously felt himself personally badly hurt. For him not only the superiority of his conception was at stake, but also that it had been first chronologically.

When the Nazis came to power on 30 January 1933, they took over a system of social security whose structures and functions were deeply rooted

[16] Cf. *Wirtschafts- und Sozialberichte* (see n.10: 226); referring to the 'plagiarism' as to point 15 of the party programme of the NSDAP, cf. Rauecker (1943: 164).
[17] Re-translation from quotation in Pfeffer (1943: 165).

in the basic principles of Bismarck's reform measures in the 1880s. The institutions of social insurance had been badly weakened by the accumulated consequences of inflation, unemployment and the general financial crisis of the public sector and the economy as a whole. The growing intricacy and continuous economy measures and cut-backs had heavily shaken people's confidence in the functioning and reliability of social insurance. Previous endeavours to consolidate the existing system were continued in 1933, mainly sustained by the Reich Labour Ministry (RAM) and the management of the social insurance authorities. These 'traditionalists' were soon confronted with ambitious efforts towards a comprehensive reform of social law, coming from the DAF.

The DAF as an organization of the Party had replaced the trade unions and employers' association 'in order to form a real national and productive community of all Germans' ('wirkliche Volks- und Leistungsgemeinschaft aller Deutschen'; quoted in Brusatti *et al.* 1962: 273). It was a powerful instrument of the Party, and became more and more the radical antagonist of the departmental bureaucracy, mainly interested in the financial stabilization of social insurance. Within the Party, however, ideas of transforming social insurance into a corporatist institution structured by vocational categories (Teppe 1977: 207 f.), or into a uniform insurance (ibid. 216–19), were to be found.

The Act of 5 July 1934 abolished the self-government of the social insurance authorities, but the traditional sub-division into the separate organizations of health, accident and pensions insurance was preserved. The DAF had not succeeded in its objectives against the Labour Ministry, the vested interests, the insurance establishment, or finally, the Nazi party leadership. This political defeat of the DAF led to continual antagonism with the Ministry, whose attempts to achieve, within the traditional framework, a simultaneous consolidation and improvement of benefits, were crowned by the Pensions Insurance Consolidation Act of 21 December 1937 (ibid. 233).

In opposition to that, in 1935 Dr Ley had already stressed the necessity to convert social insurance into a 'Social Commitment', a collectivist national provision for all employees, financed by contributions connected to income tax (ibid. 238–40). For him in the national community to be formed no room was left for institutions relying on the principle of self-help.

Dr Ley insisted on his intentions and finally felt the wind behind him when Hermann Goering, the Commissioner for the Four-Year Plan, charged him on 3 March 1939 with the chairmanship of an inter-ministerial committee to deal with problems of medical welfare and old age provision. As early as 16 March he submitted a printed paper, 'Der Deutsche Volksschutz' ('German National Protection', ibid. 241). To the main features of the document belonged not only a strict regulation of the labour and health laws, but also the replacement of social insurance by an old age pension system providing flat-rate pensions at subsistence level, financed by an income-related social tax. Nevertheless, Ley's suggestions were unanimously rejected by the ministries involved (ibid. 242 f.).

At last, the persistent activities of Dr Ley induced Hitler, on 15 February 1940, to charge his devoted companion officially with working out propositions for the development of comprehensive provision for the aged. Leaning on his Führer's order (Führerbefehl), Ley started, among the Party and the public, an unprecedented propaganda campaign for his project, and early in November submitted a Bill on the Versorgungswerk des Deutschen Volkes (Provision System of the German People). Thereupon Hitler himself, in several speeches, linked up the call for increased efforts to win the war with the announcement that the German welfare state would be turned into the most excellent in the world (Recker 1985: 83).

The equating of social insurance and Bismarck was deeply-rooted, not only with the traditionalists of the RAM and the social administration, but also among the people. The academic staff of the DAF, therefore, tried to give an additional historical legitimation for their master's reform project. They wanted to show that his conception came much closer to Bismarck's original intention than did social insurance (Teppe 1977: 244). And indeed, Bismarck had something different in mind when starting to pacify the German workers. It was only parliamentary resistance in the Reichstag to which we owe: the insurance principle; the decentralized self-government of the institutions; and the legal claim to benefits founded on contributions of the claimant. If it had depended totally on the conservative Prince, the German social security system would be characterized by: the principle of state welfare and provision; a centralized state-ruled office; and financing by taxes and employers' contributions.[18] Such a 'neat Bismarck' model would actually come somewhat closer to the Beveridge Plan; Dr Ley was about to create it.

The Ley model was to replace the diversity of existing social insurance and provision institutions, and was only subdivided into the three fields of old age, disability, and family. Benefits did not depend on contributions, but on previously earned income (for the disabled, an imputed one). The old age pension could be granted after at least 25 years' professional activity, at the age of 65. It should amount to 60 per cent of earned income, the minimum being 50 Reichsmark, the maximum 250. A special bonus was to be paid for those working beyond retirement age, and families should get additional household and children's allowances. For financing, a 'social tax' integrated in the income tax system was planned.

---

[18] Hentschel (1980: 47); for more detail see Hentschel (1983: 13 ff.).

Compared with the original conception the new plan had retained an essential institutional simplification of the security system, but had given up the principle of flat-rate pensions. All in all, this was the most advanced version of Ley's endeavours to put the policy of social security into the service of the National-Socialist state.

The right to a pension was not a legal entitlement, but offered as reward for loyal performance of one's duties to the national community. Beyond professional achievement, it depended on social good behaviour, and could be withdrawn for 'hostility to the nation'. Thereby the total economic dependence of all citizens on State and Party was guaranteed, an essential condition of totalitarian rule. In the end it was the political objective and not structural deviations which made the crucial difference from the ideas of Beveridge.

But this bill also met with the categorical opposition of the ministries, headed by the RAM. When during 1941 Dr Ley tried to get through his own health programme, he worried not only the Party and government agencies, but the medical profession and public health officials too. This was an untimely problem in a critical war situation. On 11 January 1942 the Chancellery of the Reich informed him that Hitler was not prepared to comment further on old age provision before the end of the War, and did not want any further legal preparation. Obviously, Ley refused to accept this, and continued his persuasive efforts; so in two letters (2 June and 21 November) these points had to be confirmed to him by Hitler's secretary, Martin Bormann (Teppe 1977: 248). Ley's last attempt to realize some ideas of his plan, at least for the miners, was also defeated (Recker 1985: 214).

The news of the publication of the Beveridge Plan, then, hit Ley at the very moment when he himself had his hands definitely tied, instead of realizing a comparable programme which he regarded as his life's work and dream. To personal frustration was now added envy of a man on the enemy side, who, not only in his own country but all over the world, knew appreciation and criticism, and was receiving attention and publicity. In any case, until his suicide in late October 1945, Ley regarded the social programme of the DAF as his failed life's work, and remained fixated both on the Plan and the person of his pretended antagonist. As his biographer quotes from the records of his interrogators, 'his emotions ... manifested themselves in tears ... when he referred to social security plans of his drafting which may never come to fruition and by the side of which "Beveridge" is very small beer' (Smelser 1988: 293).

In the last year of the War, considerations of structural changes in social insurance flickered up once more in Germany (ibid.: 275 ff.). In order to conform with the heavy pressure of the government for manpower cuts, on 25 August 1944 the RAM submitted a draft of a decree on the adaptation of social insurance for warfare purposes, which comprised some measures of unification and simplification, but also carried certain improvements in benefits. For psychological reasons, it was said, the minimum provision aimed at should 'if possible exceed comparable benefits abroad, particularly in the western democracies' (ibid. 283). The draft was not only rejected by the Reich Chancellery, and the ministries of economics and of finance, but Dr Goebbels, now the 'Generalbevollmächtigter für den totalen Kriegseinsatz' (Plenipotentiary for the Total Mobilization of Labour) stated in his letter of 7 October 1944, 'the reference to the *English* publication' (italics by the author) failed to see that these were postwar plans, whose realization was rather doubtful (ibid. 283). That statement may be taken as the late echo of the fact that immediately after its publication a German word-for-word translation of the Beveridge Report had been made 'for official use only' with the RAM, and had obviously been taken very seriously (Teppe 1977: 249; Beveridge 1954: 195). Now it was evident that the Beveridge Report had had lasting effects with other authorities, too, and that it was still regarded as the most prominent example of progressive social schemes abroad.

4. A REPRIMAND FROM SWITZERLAND

In contrast to the scorn and derision Beveridge and his Report earned from the public opinion of Nazi Germany, and the silence of German academic circles, in Switzerland arose a vivid, but both objective and controversial discussion. In the spring of the year 1943 the Europa Verlag in Zurich published the first authorized German translation of the Report (Beveridge 1943). Shortly afterwards a voluminous summary and documentation with commentary was given by the noted Geneva economist, Edgar Michaud.[19] Beside the sometimes enthusiastic approval in left party and union circles,[20] there were other opinions, such as the analysis for the Swiss government; it paid tribute to the Report, but concluded that Beveridge's propositions neither matched Swiss circumstances nor the needs of the Swiss people, and recommended instead 'to keep to the historical development of social insurance in our own country and gradually expand its activities'.[21]

A strikingly harsh rejection came from a colleague of Michaud's, the exiled German professor Wilhelm Röpke, also teaching in Geneva. Röpke repeatedly and on quite different occasions uttered his bitter criticism of the Beveridge Report and its author. To him Beveridge was one of those 'collectivist intellectuals', whose books, 'in their mixture of well-meaning

[19] For a broad discussion of the British and German social plans see *Die Weltwoche*, 26 Feb. 1943: 16.
[20] Early voices from the Swiss press quoted in Michaud (1943: 232–8).
[21] *Neue Zürcher Zeitung*, 10 May 1943.

idealism and a sociological and politico-economic lack of understanding make such a desolate impression' (Röpke 1942: 384).

In Röpke's opinion the Beveridge plan must be judged 'as another questionable step towards collectivization and socialization of society and the paralysis of the market economy' (1943: 560 fn. 5). And Röpke finally puts his scathing judgement on the English nuisance in the words: 'As a matter of fact, the worst and most decisive things for which the Beveridge plan, and the social philosophy it stands for, are to be condemned, are its rooting in completely proletarian concepts and its suitability for vigorous extension of proletarianization, for it is nothing other than a radical cure for the symptoms of proletarianization' (1944: 31).

Röpke's reaction is especially remarkable in so far as this prominent neo-liberal economist and social philosopher, together with von Hayek, Eucken, Böhm and Miksch, formed the Freiburg School circle, uniting the intellectual pioneers of the Social Market Economy conception of Ludwig Erhard. After the war he accompanied the economic and social policy of the Federal Republic as a stern critic and admonisher until his death in 1966. So still in 1956 he warned the advocates of a 'dynamic people's pension' against the dangers of an 'inflationary and collective welfare state' (Röpke 1956).

5. POSTWAR PLANS À LA BEVERIDGE

When Hitler's Reich had broken down, the bell for a new round in the 'noble contest' (Beveridge 1946: 8) between the two systems of social insurance was sounded. At the end of the War, the defeated Germany faced a political and economic shambles, and was forced to create a new system of social security as well as needing to secure the bare survival of the population in a widely destroyed country, and to remove the immediate war-induced damage.

On his visit to Germany in August 1946, Beveridge lectured in Hamburg on the basic ideas of his plan, but did not forget explicitly to honour Bismarck as a pioneer of national social insurance. He expressed his conviction that for now England was in the lead (ibid.: 7 f.). To this the subsequent Chancellor of the Federal Republic, Dr Konrad Adenauer, answered in a mass rally of the Christian Democratic Union (CDU): 'Social insurance must be preserved for us. We are proud of it. And as to the proposition Beveridge recently made in Hamburg, I can only say that we've had similar things in Germany already for thirty years' (quoted in Hockerts 1980: 329). But only in time, with extensive and objective information, could a wider public take notice of the Beveridge Plan and the measures of the Labour government to realize it.[22]

---

[22] *Inter alia* Möller (1946), Alvermann (1947), and Schieckel (1947).

For the time being the political responsibility for the reconstruction of the social security system was with the military governments of the four occupying powers, the USA, Britain, France, and the Soviet Union. In the Potsdam Treaty they had agreed to treat Germany as one economic unit during the period of occupation. Accordingly, in December 1946 the Manpower Directorate of the Allied Control Council submitted a bill for a 'Compulsory Social Insurance Law for Germany' which was not very similar to German social insurance. Especially in extending the liability to insure to all citizens, and in integrating all insurance branches (with their multitude of institutions) into a uniform insurance system, the bill came very close to the Beveridge Plan (Hockerts 1980: 26 ff.).

The supposition that here the influence of British experts might have been embodied is not justified for two reasons. Firstly, it was a proposal made by the Soviet delegate in October 1945. Together with German experts, each of the four military governments had prepared a bill, all of them being very similar in their basic ideas. As by rotation the Soviet delegate was in the chair, their bill was chosen (ibid. 25). The Soviets had already pushed forward in their own zone. Only a few days after the end of the War they had put existing institutions out of action and set about creating a uniform insurance organization for sickness, accident, old age, and disability. It came into force on 1 July 1945, oddly enough on the very day when the three western allies officially took over the administration of their sectors, and were now confronted with a *fait accompli* (Baker 1977: 24).

Secondly, the British delegates had by no means come to Germany as missionaries, but with the explicit instruction to preserve, as far as possible, the traditional German systems of social insurance. They therefore used the literal English translation of a bill prepared by a former senior official of the Reich Ministry of Labour (Hockerts 1980: 24 f.; 1982: 326 ff.). This bill, in contrast to the British scheme, implied financing solely by contributions. What was envisaged was a social security system which could function, with very modest benefits and with administrative costs as low as possible, and completely without any government grants. This austerity policy was not least meant to prevent the British taxpayer being called on to aid the financial problems of the occupied territories (Hockerts 1982: 326 ff.).

Co-operation between the Allies and their respective German experts and politicians differed. The British military government initially refused the demand to give a share in the decision-making to the advisory board of their zone, consisting of German party politicians, trade unionists, and civil servants. At last the unionists managed to persuade Beveridge to intercede personally in London, which was successful (Hockerts 1980: 34 f.; Eckert 1948: 21). Though more and more German experts and politicians succeeded in being heard with their opinions, there was little room left for influence.

It took some time before more than a bare contribution to the organizational conversion of the new principles was granted to Germans (Hockerts 1980: 35 f.).

The strongest advocates for the realization of the reform bill were the Soviets. Early in 1947 they were the only ones to enact it in their own zone of occupation, somewhat modified, and with reservation as to a later common solution. The negotiations on the bill for such an Allied Control Council Act were conducted, more and more half-heartedly, by the western Allies who were facing growing opposition from the bodies representing interests in West Germany (Hockerts 1980: 67 ff.; 1982: 331).

Meanwhile in the three western zones opposition was heard not only from the middle-class, but also from the Social Democrats (SPD) and parts of the unions. The private insurance companies and the employers, the associations of the medical profession, the self-employed, and the salaried occupations strongly protested against the generalization and unification of social insurance. Major parts of the unions and of the SPD objected above all to the cutback of benefits and the planned abolition of government grants (Hockerts 1982: 328 ff.; for more detail 1980: 36 ff.). On 7 October 1947 the SPD stated in the Parliamentary Council, the predecessor of the Bundestag, that 'the social insurance, seventy years ago developed from German action, now again should be renewed by German authorities' (Hockerts 1982: 329).

Besides, the Bismarckian social legislation was one of the few national achievements which had been a model for a long time, even abroad, and was still appreciated, as Beveridge proved time and again. For the German public it was an unincriminated slice of history of which they need not be ashamed (ibid.). In the end both large parties, the Christian Democrats and the Social Democrats, agreed with the unions that an all-embracing reform should be based on the classical principles of Bismarck's social insurance, the basic decisions being left to a German parliament still to be formed. Partly from conviction, partly from tactical considerations, it was held that, with the ideology and politics of the Nazis as a whole, Dr Ley's ideas of a uniform insurance were completely discredited with the German people.

Towards the end of 1947 the three western Allies braced themselves for concluding negotiations with the Soviets, and early in 1948 the bill was even submitted to the Control Council, the highest common body of the four Allies. But it did not pass, for already in the month of March the Soviet representatives finally withdrew their co-operation in the Control Council. Thereupon in July the Americans and the British finally declared the reform of social insurance an internal German affair and retired from the bill for good (Hockerts 1980: 331 f.).

In view of the now open conflict between East and West, it had long ago become more important for the three western Allies to come to good terms with political circles in western Germany than laboriously to bring about an agreement with the Soviet Union. But a fundamental reform of the social legislation did not take place until the foundation of the Federal Republic of Germany in 1949.

6. FROM BEVERIDGE TO THE DYNAMIC PENSION

The parliamentary debates and the legislative activity of the first German Bundestag were determined by numerous problems concerning the reconstruction of destroyed towns and cities, the installation of an administration both democratic and efficient, a working economy, the integration of millions of refugees and expellees from the eastern territories, and the fight against unemployment.

Only in the course of a series of separate socio-political acts to overcome the continuing consequences of the Nazi period, war, and expulsion, did a comprehensive reform of social insurance come up for a discussion which was to end only with the pensions reform in 1957. The whole process started with a motion of the opposition SPD in January 1952 to set up an independent study group for social security. Following the model of the Beveridge Committee, its activity was to lead up to a plan for social security in Germany (Hockerts 1980: 216 f.).

This initiative went back to the 1948 Social Programme of the SPD, comprising the explicit demand for a 'general national security system' modelled on the Beveridge Plan. In the sitting of 21 February 1952 this motion was rejected by the coalition parties led by Dr Adenauer's Christian Democrats. The government could not deny the necessity of a social reform, but was not prepared at any price to let the initiative for reshaping social security slip out of its hand. Instead, a motion was carried to appoint an advisory council of experts under the chairmanship of the Minister for Labour (ibid. 219).

A few weeks later, in a lecture given in Bonn on 21 April 1952, Beveridge encouraged the Germans to follow his example and critically scrutinize their system of social insurance. Excerpts and summaries of this appeal were published in several socio-political periodicals (Beveridge 1952: 107). And, in fact, in 1952/1953 'with a certain lag of time ... attempts of a comprehensive reform planning started, the model of the Beveridge plan having considerable influence—positive or negative' (Hockerts 1982: 334). It all began with an intensified study of the Beveridge Plan and its political realization, which can hardly be explained by Beveridge's Bonn address or the tenth anniversary of the Beveridge Report (Liefmann-Keil 1952).

Perhaps the strongest motivation was due to the common unease with the 'hopeless muddle' (Mackenroth 1957: 43) which the socio-political

tinkering of the years before had left. It was felt that the time for a long-
term solution had come, and a reference point was needed. Maybe the
fascination of the Beveridge approach was not so much in its substance,
but in the fact that in difficult political circumstances a comprehensive
scheme had been developed, and that under difficult economic circumstances
essential parts of the reform had been tackled, and had obviously stood the
first test.

Already in autumn 1952, a paper on the principles of a comprehensive
social plan had been worked out for the executive committee of the SPD.
It can be regarded as the preliminary stage of the detailed Social Plan for
Germany which the Social Democrats submitted in 1957. As to its contents,
the 1952 plan was an attempt to adjust the principles of the Beveridge Plan
to German circumstances. Thus a full employment policy was accepted as
a precondition, there was a tax-financed national health service, and the
payment of children's allowances from public funds was provided for. The
core of the social security scheme was to be a uniform basic pension for
every citizen analogous to the Beveridgian 'flat national minimum'. In
contrast to the Beveridge Plan, it was to be tax-financed. Additionally, with
wage-related complementary pensions, financed by wage-related contributions, the German tradition of an achievement-oriented old age provision was to be taken into account (Hockerts 1982: 337 ff.).

This programmatic work had been substantially influenced by Walter
Auerbach, a senior administrative expert, known to be well-informed on
the English system. During his exile in London he was on the side of the
unions indirectly involved in the preparation of the Beveridge Plan. Evidence
shows that at the turn of the years 1952/1953 he exchanged letters with
Beveridge (Hockerts 1980: 221 f.; Harris 1977: 465 fn.48).

In January 1953 a study trip to London was undertaken by nineteen
prominent German economists, politicians, and administrative experts.[23]
This socio-political pilgrimage was in itself quite extraordinary, not to
mention its consequences for the political discussion. At London University
they had within the scope of a conference two weeks of intensive talks with
British social security experts, with Professor Richard Titmuss in the chair.
The result was a series of detailed reports to be published in the course of
the year 1953, involving all major socio-political periodicals.[24]

One of the first highlights of the following discussion was the dialogue
between two participants, Ludwig Preller and Heinrich Lünendonk, the
chairmen of the party committees for social policy of the Social Democrats
and the Christian Democrats respectively. They discussed the advantages,
disadvantages, and problems of the English system as compared to the

[23] For a complete list of participants see Lünendonk (1953: 59).
[24] See e.g. Auerbach (1953), Glock (1953), Lünendonk (1953), and Oeter (1953).

German one. Here it was made clear that in the CDU there was a genuine willingness to examine the ideas of Beveridge as well as those of the political adversary. But the chairmen were not inclined to deviate from the principles of self-help and provision by contributions (Preller and Lünendonk 1953).

Chancellor Adenauer tried hard to get a design for a comprehensive scheme of social benefits. As to the contents, neither Beveridge nor British social policy seemed to have impressed him. What he had in mind was a further development of the German security system, aiming at a combination of liberalism and Catholic social doctrine (Hockerts 1982: 341). He thought of a reform 'which does not put on the Bismarckian acts the thousandth or the thousand and first act but from the bottom up adapts the whole social legislation to the present time' (Hockerts 1980: 282).

Adenauer was much more impressed by the form and method of working of the Beveridge Committee. As the government had appointed the advisory council in 1953, but its work dragged on without getting to satisfying results, in February 1955 Adenauer secretly charged four distinguished social scientists (including one participant from the London excursion)[25] to prepare an 'overall conception for reorganizing the system of social security' (Hockerts 1980: 279 ff.). When, early in June 1955, Adenauer presented this document, the 'Rothenfels Memoir', to his cabinet, he called it the outcome of an independent commission 'following the English model' (ibid. 297).

In mid-July 1955 Adenauer himself took the chair of a new inter-ministerial committee for social reform (ibid. 300). In September 1955 the Social Democrats put pressure on the government by submitting a motion on old age pensions. After that the government gave up the search for an overall conception and concentrated on practical steps towards pensions reform (ibid. 307).

The decisive turn in the discussion was made when in July 1955 the Cologne economist Wilfried Schreiber presented a plan for the pensions reform, comprising two revolutionary innovations: a break with the financing of pensions by saving for a stock of capital, instead financing by current membership contributions (apportionment method); coupling and continuous adaptation of pensions to the income development of gainfully employed people (dynamic pension scheme) (ibid. 309). For the government the Schreiber Plan was the key to the pensions reform to come. Meanwhile the Social Democrats had given up their endeavours for an overall social plan, too, and envisaged—together with the trade unions—pensions adapted to the general development of wages and salaries (ibid. 331).

The bills the SPD and CDU submitted to parliament in April and May 1956 respectively did not rest on common ground, but had much in common.

[25] Professor Hans Achinger, Frankfurt-am-Main University; see Hockerts (1980: 280) and Lünendonk (1953: 59).

Compared with the Beveridge pattern, neither succeeded in preparing an overall scheme of social security; nevertheless both of them provided a reorganization of the whole of old age, disability, and survivors' insurance. In contrast to its Social Plan of 1953, the SPD bill no longer offered a tax-financed basic pension for all citizens, but now regarded a pension as a wage substitute instead of an allowance. On the other hand, the CDU had accepted the principle of 'rehabilitation before disability pension'. For both, the traditional organizational structure with a separately organized insurance for salaried employees remained unchanged. A clearly non-Beveridge element in both bills was the confinement of compulsory insurance to gainfully employed people (ibid. 352 ff.).

Whether the common novelty, the adaptation of the pensions to the current wage level, follows a non-Beveridge or even anti-Beveridge line, is not easy to decide. With the principle of dynamizing the pensions the step was made from securing a minimum income to cover subsistence level, towards securing the relative social status acquired during the active part of life. The point is not compensation for increased cost of living, which Beveridge refused, but the proportional participation of all recipients of a pension in the prosperity of the active population. That was compatible with paragraph 27 of the Beveridge Report, which does not exclude a simultaneous increase of benefits and contributions. Beveridge spoke against an income-related old age pension, but had individual incomes in mind, and not the national one (Harris 1977: 463 f.).

After five days and a final debate of fifteen hours (the 'pensions battle'), the Bundestag passed the Pensions Reform Act late at night on 22 January 1957 with the overwhelming joined majority of Christian and Social Democrats. Now Germany obviously had the lead again in the 'noble contest' for the better scheme of social security. And when, shortly after, the British Labour Party presented its plan of a national superannuation, it was reported that this time it was the Crossman Commission who had been studying the German pensions reform thoroughly (Reichenbach 1957: 171).

The first slight correction, of course, towards Beveridge was the introduction of a children's allowance in 1964. A larger step in this direction was the Pensions Reform Act in 1972. Like 1957, it was again the common child of the now governing Social Democrats, the opposition Christian Democrats, and the smaller group of Liberals. It introduced a flexible retirement age, an income-independent minimum pension of 75 per cent of the average wage, and the extension of statutory pensions insurance to housewives and the self-employed. And the general trend with the large parties and the unions was still towards a 'people's insurance' (Brück and Eichner 1974: 23 f.). Despite worsening economic conditions during the Seventies, yet another small step in this direction was taken by opening social insurance up to artists in 1981.

7. FINAL NOTES

But beyond the Fifties the development of German social insurance had already regained its own weight and profile and left behind the Beveridge Plan and the English system of social security as a reference system. When the press, on the occasion of his death, paid tribute to Lord Beveridge, his name was only a faint memory. Today his name is no longer mentioned in German textbooks of social policy. And yet overall reform of the German social security system is not only unaccomplished as yet, but it has become more urgent than ever. The decline of the birth rate is jeopardizing the generational treaty of social insurance. The costs of the health system are exploding, the finance of unemployment insurance is in a critical situation, the growing number of welfare recipients empties the municipal treasuries, and politicians are looking for a solution to the problems of nursing. In addition, there are the problems of a total reorganization of the social security network in the eastern Länder of the Federal Republic. Germany seems to be waiting for the next encounter of Bismarck and Beveridge.[26]

REFERENCES

Alvermann, F. (1947), 'Nutzanwendung aus dem Beveridgeplan', *Versicherungswirtschaft*, 2/1.

Auerbach, W. (1953), 'Beveridge-Plan: 10 Jahre danach', *Soziale Sicherheit*, 2/5, 2/6.

Baker, H. W. (1977), 'Beginn der deutschen Sozial- und Arbeitspolitik unter der Militärregierung', in Bartholomäi *et al.* (1977).

Bartholomäi, P., Bodenbender, W., Henkel, H., and Hüttel, R. (1977) (eds.), *Sozialpolitik nach 1945. Geschichte und Analysen*. Bonn/Bad Godesberg: Neue Gesellschaft.

Bethusy-Huc, V. von (1987), *Familienpolitik*. Tübingen: J. C. B. Mohr.

Beveridge, J. (1954), *Beveridge and his Plan*. London: Hodder and Stoughton.

Beveridge, W. H. (1943), *Der Beveridgeplan. Sozialversicherung und verwandte Leistungen*. Zurich: Europa.

——(1946), *Soziale Sicherheit und Vollbeschäftigung*. Hamburg: Hoffmann and Campe.

——(1952), 'Jede Generation hat ihre eigenen Probleme', *Sozialer Fortschritt*, 1.

Boettcher, E. (1957) (ed.), *Sozialpolitik und Sozialreform*. Tübingen: J. C. B. Mohr.

Brech, J. (1942), 'Späte Entdeckung. Beveridge und der englische Sozialismus', *Das Reich*, 13 Dec.

---

[26] For a discussion of recent trends and developments in Germany from a comparative Bismarck–Beveridge point of view, see Reinhard (1992).

Brück, G. W., and Eichner, H. (1974), *Perspektiven der Sozialpolitik*. Göttingen: Otto Schwartz.

Brusatti, A., Haas, W., and Pollak, W. (1962) (eds.), *Geschichte der Sozialpolitik mit Dokumenten*. Vienna: Lentia.

Conze, W., and Lepsius, M. R. (1983) (eds.), *Sozialgeschichte der Bundesrepublik Deutschland*. Stuttgart: Klett-Cotta.

Eckert, J. (1948), *Öffentliche Meinung zur Reform der Sozialversicherung*. Schliersee: Dr Gruber.

Fischer, W. (1982), *Armut in der Geschichte*. Göttingen: Vandenhoeck und Ruprecht.

Frerich, J. (1987), *Sozialpolitik*. Munich: Oldenbourg.

Gehnich, K. (1943), ' "Safety First Society": Zum Beveridge-Plan', *Monatshefte für NS.-Sozialpolitik*, 10.

Glock, G. (1953), 'Die soziale Sicherheit in England', *Die Ortskrankenkasse*, 35.

Harris, J. (1977), *William Beveridge: A Biography*. Oxford: Clarendon Press.

Hentschel, V. (1980), *Deutsche Wirtschafts- und Sozialpolitik, 1815 bis 1945*. Königstein/Ts.: Athenäum.

——(1983), *Geschichte der deutschen Sozialpolitik 1880–1980*. Frankfurt am Main: Suhrkamp.

Hockerts, H. G. (1980), *Sozialpolitische Entscheidungen im Nachkriegsdeutschland: alliierte und deutsche Sozialversicherungspolitik 1945–1957*. Stuttgart: Klett-Cotta.

——(1982), 'Deutsche Nachkriegssozialpolitik vor dem Hintergrund des Beveridge-Plans. Einige Beobachtungen zur Vorbereitung einer vergleichenden Analyse', in Mommsen (1982).

——(1983*a*), 'Die Entwicklung vom Zweiten Weltkrieg bis zur Gegenwart', in Köhler and Zacher (1983).

——(1983*b*), 'Sicherung im Alter. Kontinuität und Wandel der gesetzlichen Rentenversicherung 1889–1979', in Conze and Lepsius (1983).

Kaiserliches Statistisches Amt (1909) (ed.), *Statistisches Jahrbuch für das Deutsche Reich*. Berlin.

Köhler, P. A., and Zacher, H. F. (1982) (eds.), *The Evolution of Social Insurance 1881–1981*. London: Pinter.

——(1983) (eds.), *Beiträge zu Geschichte und aktueller Situation der Sozialversicherung*. Berlin: Duncker and Humblot.

Liefmann-Keil, E. (1951), 'Beveridgeplan: Grenzen der Einkommens-Umverteilung–zehn Jahre nach Beveridge', *Deutsche Versicherungszeitschrift*, 6.

——(1952), 'Fürsorge—Versicherung—Versorgung: Zehn Jahre Beveridge-Plan', *Deutsche Zeitung und Wirtschaftszeitung*, 7:87.

Lünendonk, H. (1953), 'Soziale Sicherung in England: Eine Deutsch-Englische Konferenz in London', *Sozialer Fortschritt*, 2.

Mackenroth, G. (1957), 'Die Reform der Sozialpolitik durch einen deutschen Sozialplan', rep. in Boettcher (1957).

Michaud, E. (1943), 'Der Beveridge-Plan', *Annalen der Gemeinwirtschaft*, 18/2.

Möller, H. (1946), 'Der Beveridge-Plan', *Versicherungswirtschaft*, 1/6, 1/7.

Mommsen, W. G. (1982) (ed.), *Die Entstehung des Wohlfahrtsstaates in Großbritannien und Deutschland 1850–1950*. Stuttgart: Klett-Cotta.

Oeter, F. (1953), 'Gesundheitsdienst und Wohlfahrtseinrichtungen in England', *Ausländische Sozialprobleme*, 3.

Osterkamp, K. (1953), 'Soziale Sicherung in England', *Gewerkschaftliche Monatshefte*, 4.

Pfeffer, K. H. (1943), 'Hintergründe des Beveridge-Planes', *Das XX. Jahrhundert*, 5.

Preller, L., and Lünendonk, H. (1953), 'Das englische Sicherungssystem und Deutschland', *Sozialer Fortschritt*, 2.

Rasch, H. (1942), 'England entdeckt sein soziales Herz: Der unehrliche und rückständige Plan des Herrn Beveridge', *Der Angriff*, 6 Dec.

Rauecker, B. (1943), 'Das spezifische Gewicht des Beveridge-Planes', *Volk und Reich*, 19.

Recker, M.-L. (1985), *Nationalsozialistische Sozialpolitik im Zweiten Weltkrieg*. Munich: Oldenbourg.

Reichenbach, B. (1957), 'Labours Plan für die Alterssicherung', *Soziale Sicherheit*, 6.

Reinhard, H. J. (1992), 'The Beveridge Report and the German Pension Scheme', paper delivered to the International Conference, 'Social Security Fifty Years After Beveridge', Univ. of York, Sept.

Ritter, G. A. (1983), *Sozialversicherung in Deutschland und England*. Munich: C. H. Beck.

——(1989), *Der Sozialstaat*. Munich: Oldenbourg.

Röpke, W. (1942), 'Die internationale Wirtschaftsordnung der Zukunft. Pläne und Probleme', *Schweizer Monatshefte*, 22/7.

——(1943), 'Weltwirtschaft und internationale Geldordnung nach dem Kriege', *Schweizer Monatshefte*, 22/10.

——(1944), 'Die ärztliche Versorgung nach dem Beveridgeplan', *Schweizerische Ärztezeitung*, 25.

——(1956), 'Probleme der kollektiven Alterssicherung', *Frankfurter Allgemeine Zeitung*, 25 Feb.

Schieckel, H. (1947), 'Der Beveridgeplan', *Deutsche Rechts-Zeitschrift*, 2.

Smelser, R. (1988), *Robert Ley: Hitler's Labor Front Leader*. Oxford: Berg.

——(1989), 'Robert Ley: Der braune Kollektivist', in Smelser and Zitelmann (1989).

——and Zitelmann, R. (1989) (eds.), *Die braune Elite*. Darmstadt: Wissenschaftliche Buchgesellschaft.

Stephan, W. (1943), 'Atlantik-Charta und Beveridgeplan', *Auswärtige Politik*, 10.

Teppe, K. (1977), 'Zur Sozialpolitik des Dritten Reiches am Beispiel der Sozialversicherung', *Archiv für Sozialgeschichte*, 17.

Vermehren, P. (1942), 'Gefahr für geheiligte Interessen. Kann sich England Sozialpolitik leisten?', *Das Reich*, 13 Dec.

Zöllner, D. (1982), 'Germany', in Köhler and Zacher (1982).

10

Pensions Policy in Poland after 1945: Between 'Bismarck' and 'Beveridge' Traditions

MACIEJ ŻUKOWSKI

INTRODUCTION

As a product of specific, national circumstances, postwar development of pensions policy in Poland was affected by various direct and indirect foreign influences; it is considered here against a background of two broad European traditions ('models') of pensions systems, as well as of social security generally—see Schmähl (1981: 652) or Alber (1982: 40 ff.).

The first is called the 'Bismarck' tradition here, because it derives from the social insurance system under Bismarck, although the German pension insurance actually created in 1889 differed in some important respects from the plans of the Chancellor (Ritter 1983: 40 ff.). It is characterized by such main elements as:

the function of benefits being to protect living standards (earnings replacement; earnings-relation of contributions and pensions);

coverage limited to categorically separated groups of employees and (later) self-employed; and

the limited role of the state in administration and financing of the system.

The second, called 'Beveridge', derives its name from the Beveridge Report (1942) and is based on:

stressing the function of preventing poverty in old age (flat-rate pensions, financed from taxes or similar contributions, and leaving space for additional sources of provision);

universality of coverage; and

a major role of the state in administration and financing of the system.

In Poland, the 'Bismarck' traditions clearly prevailed in the interwar period which is discussed briefly in section 1. Section 2 describes postwar developments which can be seen as a substantial departure from 'Bismarck' towards 'Beveridge'. Section 3 tries to assess the character of this system and briefly considers possible future developments.

Throughout the paper the subjects of interest are limited to retirement pensions (usually regulated together with invalidity pensions and pensions for dependants), and mainly those of employees: clearly the largest group, on whose regulations those of other groups are also based.

1. DEVELOPMENTS 1918–1945

At the time when the first state pension schemes in many European countries were being created, there was no Polish state. Since the end of the eighteenth century, Poland had been divided between its three powerful neighbours: Prussia (Germany), Russia, and Austria. The Polish state as recreated in 1918 (its borders were actually fixed by 1922) consequently consisted of three parts with large differences between them, among others, in the field of (public) pensions (Piątkowski 1983; 1991).

In the former German territories, pension insurance covered (in separate schemes) wage-earners and salaried employees; and in the previous Austrian territories the coverage was limited to salaried employees (under the law of 1906). Additionally, in both parts miners were covered in separate schemes. In the former Russian territories there was virtually no pension scheme. Under these circumstances, the main objective of the Polish state in this field was to unify the pension schemes and to replace regulations dating from the time of annexation with Polish law. The task was difficult, given the objective that previous rights should not be weakened, and it was not achieved by 1939. Two main pieces of legislation in the area of pensions came from 1927 and 1933.

In 1927 a unified Polish pension insurance for salaried employees was established. It was more generous than the former German and Austrian provisions, and so could replace them. The system followed broadly the traditions of German or Austrian pension insurance:

it was financed by the contributions of employees and employers;
it covered old age, invalidity, and death with surviving dependants;
the entitlement to an old age pension depended on satisfying two conditions: old age (normally 65 years for men and 60 years for women) and a minimum period of insurance (five years);
the level of an individual's old age pension was related to the individual's earnings during the whole period of insurance: with 40 years of insurance, the old age pension reached 100 per cent of the average life salary.

The earnings on which pensions were based were not revalued, so in fact the replacement rate was not as high as that, but the level of pensions was still quite generous (Święcicki 1960: 279).

The pensions insurance for wage-earners created after many years of debate in 1933, based on broadly similar social insurance ideas, was much less successful, for two main reasons. First, its coverage was narrower than that of the salaried employees' scheme, mainly because a big group of farm-workers—about one third of all employees (Piątkowski 1991: 148)—was not covered. Second, the benefits offered by the scheme were less generous. There was no separate old age pension, and normally reaching 65 years for both men and women was regarded as equivalent to invalidity, and gave entitlement, when satisfying contribution conditions (at least four years' contributions), to an invalidity pension. A pension consisted of two parts, one being flat-rate for all pensioners, the other related to average earnings during the whole period of insurance, whereby the whole pension could not be higher than 80 per cent of those earnings. Because of the limited coverage and level of pensions, the system did not replace all provisions in the former German part of the country. The first pensions for wage-earners were paid in 1938, so the history of this part of the pension system in prewar Poland was very short.

There was also additional pension insurance for miners, and many groups of employees of the state, local authorities and other public employers, such as railways, were covered by separate non-contributory schemes.

The influence of German ('Bismarck') concepts of social insurance on Polish pension policy and other parts of social insurance in the interwar period is thus clear:

The German Reich Insurance Code of 1911 which, to some extent, remained valid (with Polish amendments) till the end of the interwar period in the western parts, and especially in Upper Silesia, influenced clearly the concepts accepted in Polish legislation [of social insurance]. It found its expression inter alia in construction of pension insurance, covering risks of invalidity, old age and death, in the separation of the insurance of salaried employees, and in many detailed regulations. (Szubert 1991: 467)

In parallel, new ideas, based on domestic concepts, were embodied in Polish social insurance legislation at that time. In particular, the organization of the whole of social insurance, including pensions, was gradually unified by 1935, which contrasted with segmented, decentralized administration in Germany, and expressed the unity of social insurance, an idea championed by some specialists in this area (Krzeczkowski 1936: 105–6, 116–17, 134 ff.).

During the Second World War, under the German occupation, social insurance for Poles was dramatically limited (Szubert 1987: 33–4). After the War, it had to be rebuilt, and in many areas it had to be built again from scratch.

2. DEVELOPMENTS AFTER 1945

This section describes the main developments in pension policy in Poland between 1945 and 1991 (see especially Pławucka 1991), leaving the issue of 'Bismarck' versus 'Beveridge' influences to the next section.

2.1. 1945–1953

The situation just after the War was in many respects quite different from that in 1939. First, Poland was destroyed, having lost during the War about 6 million citizens (almost one sixth) and about 40 per cent of its prewar economic wealth. Second, the state had new borders, having lost one-third of its prewar territory to the Soviet Union, and gained nearly one-third of its new territory from Germany. Third, communists strongly dependent on Moscow ruled the country. All these factors were important for the development of social insurance: the need for protection was very great and economic possibilities were very limited; the system had to be introduced and unified over the whole territory; and the ruling powers wanted to introduce structural changes into it, alongside the concepts of the new political system.

During the first years after the War the main objectives of pensions policy were to rebuild social insurance administration, to introduce a unified legislation over the whole territory and to start paying benefits. The prewar legislation was introduced by 1946 over the whole country, and the rest of the old social insurance law from the time of annexation was removed. During this period, some important structural changes were also introduced into the old system.

Thus, social insurance contributions for employees became payable only by employers (companies); employees' contributions were abolished. The differences between wage-earners and salaried employees were gradually removed and coverage was extended to some new groups, not covered by pension insurance before the War (farm-workers, 1953), or covered by non-contributory schemes (between 1950 and 1954 civil servants and public employees, but not soldiers or policemen, were integrated into social insurance). In parallel, the administration of the whole of social insurance was integrated and centralized in the Social Insurance Institution (ZUS), and only employees of the State Railways retained a separate pension administration. In 1949, hitherto-existing separate autonomous insurance funds in individual social insurance branches were wholly integrated into the state budget. Social insurance became a part of the state planned economy. Accordingly, in 1951 social insurance contributions were fully integrated and covered from then on all insurance risks. On the benefit side, from 1951 entitlement to pensions became dependent not on specific contribution records but only on employment records (whether or not contributions had actually been paid during those periods).

The first pensions, paid from 1947, were flat-rate, equal for all. From 1949 some limited earnings-relation was reintroduced. Pensions were generally very low during the first years after the War due, first, to very limited resources and, second, to the political choice to concentrate those limited resources on the economically active population, rebuilding the economy, and on the youngest; in social insurance, on benefits connected with health, maternity, and family (Winiewski 1968: 1).

To summarize, many very important, systematic changes were introduced in pension insurance during the first years after the War. As a result, a unified social insurance system for nearly all employees was established, covering different social risks (old age being one of them), financed only by companies' contributions, integrated into the state budget, administered centrally with a high degree of state power, and paying pensions not dependent on contribution record, which were low and (at the beginning) flat-rate. These were serious departures from 'Bismarck' traditions (see Section 3).

2.2.   1954–1989

The three main regulations of the pension system for employees in the time of communist Poland were passed in 1954, 1968, and 1982. All the legislation followed the model of joint provision for pensions for old age, invalidity, and death with surviving dependants; in what follows, only old age pensions are discussed.

The decree of 1954 on general pension provision for employees and their families, as amended in 1956 and 1958, introduced a unified pension system for all employees, based on concepts unknown before the War, and most of these concepts remained valid until the late 1980s; some of them have remained valid until now.

The decree actually unified the pension rights of almost all categories of employees, *inter alia* by removing the remaining differentiation between wage-earners and salaried employees, and abolishing the additional insurance system for miners. On the other hand, some groups (e.g. miners) were to get or retain separate regulations, although generally on a similar basis; and *within* the general system of employees some differentiation between groups of employees was introduced. The latter was done by dividing employees into two 'categories of employment', on which both qualification conditions and level of old age pension were dependent. This differentiation was justified not only in terms of the need for protection by social insurance, but also by politico-economic considerations: it was to encourage people to take up work which was regarded as especially important for the development of the socialist economy.

To qualify for an old age pension one had to satisfy two general conditions:

a period of employment (not insurance) of at least 25 years for men and 20 years for women, with some periods regarded as equivalent to employment; and
old age; for employees of the first category of employment—60 years for men and 55 for women, for those of the second category—65 and 60, respectively.

Old age was thus accepted as a risk separate from invalidity (as opposed to the prewar regulations for wage-earners).

Some earnings relation of pensions was reintroduced, which was partly influenced by prewar traditions, and partly by incentive considerations. The level of pension was related to the average monthly earnings of a given person in the previous twelve months of employment, or (after amendments in 1956) in two consecutive years within the last ten (later, twelve) years—this was the 'assessment basis' of pensions. Its level was originally limited. In fact, after amendments in 1956 and 1958 those limits were removed and the formula used for assessment of a pension was degressive (see Table 10.1). In 1956 a minimum pension was introduced. In 1958 its level was equal to the minimum wage; afterwards it was lower. Several categories of additions were introduced, *inter alia* for dependants, for the period of work as a miner, for scientific workers, for holders of certain state honours, and for honours degrees.

In 1958 the principle of suspending pension payments in case of employment or receipt of other income by pensioners (under a stated limit) was introduced. The situation in the labour market of permanent shortages of workers gave rise to gradual and extensive relaxation of these limitations.

The average level of pensions rose substantially, as a result of the new, more generous assessment formula for new pensions and reassessment of 'old' pensions on new lines in 1958. Between 1955 and 1965 the average old age pension nearly doubled as a percentage of average earnings (Table 10.2).

The principles of the pension system of employees established between 1954 and 1958 proved to be very stable. The coverage of the system was much wider than before the War, and the system departed substantially from previous social insurance concepts (see Section 3). The degressive assessment formula implied redistribution from richer to poorer and was strongly equalizing, and with the 'degression threshold' expressed in absolute terms and with only discretionary changes, it led to a gradual falling of relative pension levels. Thus, the new pensions of people retiring under a

Table 10.1.　Formula of Retirement Pension Assessment (as % of Assessment Basis),[a] 1958–1990

Year	Lower limit as % of average earnings	Lower limit (zł.)	% applicable	Range (zł.)	% applicable	Upper limit (zł.)	% applicable
1958	89.0	1,200	75	1,200–2,000	15	2,000	15
1968	71.2	1,500	80	1,500–2,000	55	2,000	25
1977	45.2	2,000	90			2,000	40
1978	42.7	2,000	90			2,000	45
1979	39.2	2,000	90			2,000	50
1980	33.1	2,000	90			2,000	55
1983	20.7	3,000	100			3,000	55
1990	0.3	3,000	100			3,000	55

[a] Average monthly earnings of the person from the last 12 months or from two consecutive years within the last 10 (12) years of employment.

Sources: Pławucka (1991); GUS (1981: table I, 1991: table I); own estimates.

Table 10.2.　Average Retirement Pension[a] as % of Average Earnings in Socialized[b] Economy, 1955–1991

Year	%
1955	27.5
1960	48.5
1965	52.8
1970	64.9
1975	48.4
1980	54.4
1985	56.1
1990	64.1
1991	76.2

[a] Excluding pensions of individual farmers.
[b] 1991 in the whole economy.

Sources: ZUS (1987: tables 35, 80); ZUS (1992: 13); GUS (1992: tables 293, 304); own estimates.

given assessment formula became relatively lower with time, as the proportion of earnings exceeding the 'degression threshold' rose (Table 10.1). Once in payment, however, pensions were not systematically indexed, and their level stayed systematically behind those who retired later. The latter problem of 'old pension portfolios' was a recurring theme throughout postwar pension history in Poland (Table 10.3).

Table 10.3. Average Current Retirement Pension[a] as % of Average New Retirement Pension,[b] 1965–1988

Year	%
1965	95.4
1970	89.4
1975	84.0
1980	74.4
1985	63.4
1986	69.6
1987	80.6
1988	87.6

[a] All pensions payable in the given year; excluding pensions of individual farmers.
[b] Pensions which started to be paid out in the given year; excluding pensions of individual farmers.

Sources: ZUS (1987: tables 41; 70); GUS (1989: tables 251; 254).

The main objective of the new pension law of 1968 was to increase the level of pensions. This was done by: relaxing the degression in pension assessment (Table 10.1); introducing increments for period of employment in postwar Poland above the minimum qualifying for a pension: for each year 1 per cent of the assessment basis, up to 10 per cent of it (for the first time the level of pension was related to the employment record); introducing increments of pensions (by 5–15 per cent) for some employees in the first category of employment; and increasing the minimum pension. Old pensions were also to be reassessed alongside with new rates (gradually, between 1968 and 1970). As a result, the level of pensions rose substantially over that time (Table 10.2).

The act also changed terminology from 'old age pension' to 'retirement pension' and from 'old age' to 'retirement age', which fulfilled old claims (for instance, Modliński, 1959: 237) and was intended to stress the character of the benefit related to long work and reaching an advanced age.

In 1968 another important change on the finance side of the pension system took place: the Pension Fund was created, separated from the state budget, from which all pensions for employees, and later also for the self-employed, were paid out. However, this was without any separation of pension contributions from general social insurance contributions, which remained unified and paid only by companies.

The act of 1968 was amended ten times by 1981. The objective of most of these changes was to adjust pensions to increases in earnings (pensions fell substantially behind earnings, especially in the early 1970s: Table 10.2). The pension formula was modified, *inter alia* by reducing the number of 'degression thresholds' from two to one (Table 10.1). Pensions in payment were increased in 1975–80, which stopped the fall in the relative level of pensions (Table 10.2). However, the changes introduced which were not structural were not able to stabilize those ratios or, in particular, to narrow the gap between 'older' and 'newer' pensions (Table 10.3).

The main novelty of the act of 1982 was the introduction of a *mechanism* for pensions uprating, which was seen as the actual solution to the 'old pension portfolios' problem. All pensions in payment were to be uprated annually in line with the rise in average earnings. Because of financial problems, however, the mechanism was to start only in 1986 which, given the fall in real level of pensions between 1983 and 1986, led to emergence of 'new old pension portfolios' (Table 10.3). The latter could not be prevented by reassessment of old pensions along new lines, as in 1983–5. The act of 1983 introduced also some changes into the assessment formula, but within the old structure (Table 10.1), and into pension increments (*inter alia*, increments for the period of employment were no longer limited by the ten per cent ceiling, and a system of increments for employment in 'special circumstances' replaced the old categories of employment).

The indexation mechanism which started in 1986 and additional discretionary increases were partly successful in improving the relationship between older and newer pensions (Table 10.3), and between pensions and earnings (Table 10.2). However, the problem became dramatic when the inflation rate was about 61 per cent per year in 1988, 244 per cent in 1989 and 586 per cent in 1990. The response to this were changes in the pension system in 1990 and 1991 (see next section).

Between 1962 and 1977 also several pieces of legislation were passed which expanded coverage by pension insurance to different groups of the self-employed. This is considered only very briefly, as the main focus of interest in this paper is the general system for employees, which covers about 93 per cent of all insured persons registered in the Social Insurance Institution, apart from individual farmers (Table 10.4).

The latter group, which included in 1985 about 4.9 million persons (ZUS, 1987: 9), was the last category of working people covered by pension insurance in Poland, actually under the act of 1977 (with several steps before, having started in 1962). The other categories covered, for which separate acts were passed, but whose pensions are based on a broadly similar basis to those of employees and administered by ZUS, were members of agricultural cooperatives (from 1962), craftsmen and other self-employed people outside agriculture (from 1965), artistic workers (from 1973), and people working as agents for companies within the 'socialized economy' (from 1975).

Table 10.4. Insured Persons, Registered with Social Insurance Institution,[a] 1985 and 1991

	1985 000	%	1991 000	%
TOTALS	14,042	100.0	13,629	100.0
Employed	13,232	94.2	12,604	92.5
Self-employed	810	5.8	1,025	7.5

[a] Excluding individual farmers; average in the year.
Sources: GUS (1990: table 335; 1992: table 302); own estimates.

In summary, then, the period between 1954 and 1989, i.e. that from the first regulation of employees' pension schemes to the end of communist Poland, was characterized by the expansion of coverage of pension insurance (both within the system for employees and to the self-employed), and the durability of general solutions accepted in the 1950s. Among the latter were: integration of the whole of social insurance (its financing and administration); no employees' contributions; relating the entitlement to pension to employment (not contribution) record; relating the level of pensions to earnings over a very short period; a strongly degressive assessment formula for pensions; and only discretionary up-rating of benefits. The last two points caused the problem which seemed to be the most important throughout the period and was a motive for many acts of legislation: the instability of the levels of pensions from different years ('old pension portfolios', Table 10.3), and of the relations between pensions and earnings (Table 10.2).

2.3. 1990–1991

In 1989 Poland was the first country in Central and Eastern Europe which broke with communism and started the transition to democracy and a market economy. The transition began in a very difficult economic situation, especially with hyper-inflation, which pushed towards changes *inter alia* in pensions. Social insurance, and especially pensions, proved to be a relatively protected area of public spending, not least because of their political importance. Thus the financial problems of social insurance have been growing as a result both of increasing expenditures, especially following rapidly increasing unemployment (*inter alia* in the form of pensions for the early retired) and of decreasing revenues (also caused to a high degree by unemployment, resulting in a drop in the number of insured persons— Table 10.4). This situation has given rise to plans for structural changes to the pension scheme. The possible future developments go outside the scope of the paper and will only briefly be mentioned at the end of Section 3.

Between 1990 and 1991 three pension acts were passed concerning all pension systems for employees and the self-employed (apart from individual farmers) which introduced important changes on the benefit side, deeper than those between 1954–8 and 1989.

The act of 1990 (Nowogórska Kuźnik 1990: 3–10) was mainly a response to the dramatically high inflation at that time which enhanced the problems known from the whole postwar pension history. First, the assessment basis became equal to the proportion of current average earnings in the economy which the earnings, or income, of the insured person had reached in his/her best 3 following years within the last 12 years. Second, indexation was made more frequent, to be done each quarter, and pension increases were related to the current (i.e. from the last quarter) increase of average earnings. Another change whose aim was to secure the relative level of pensions was to relate the minimum pension level to average earnings in the economy: no retirement pension was now to be lower than 35 per cent of average earnings in the country (in a given quarter). Some other minor changes, *inter alia* concerning certain periods equivalent to periods of employment, were also introduced.

The second act of 1990 concerned the reassessment of benefits of pensioners aged over 80, from all pension systems, using a quite new assessment formula which was then, in a slightly amended form, introduced as the new assessment formula in 1991 (Kobierska 1991: 9–12).

The changes of 1990 were generally successful in securing the real level of pensions, which was not only stabilized, but rose substantially between 1990 and 1991 (Table 10.2).

Finally, the Act of 1991 (Januszek 1992: 3–9) introduced structural changes into pension law in all branches (apart from that of individual farmers), concerning both qualifying conditions and assessment of benefits, and was certainly one of the most important pieces of legislation in this field after the War.

Apart from the unchanged retirement age, the entitlement to retirement pension depends now on contribution, not employment, periods and non-contribution periods; the first are periods in which social insurance contributions are paid (with some equivalent periods, e.g. military service); the latter include many categories of activities, such as periods of receiving social insurance benefits, periods of care of children, of higher education, etc. The total length of non-contribution periods can only make up one-third of the total length of contribution periods; minimum requirements have not been changed: 25 years for men and 20 years for women.

Pensions are assessed on the basis established in 1990 with the extension of the period from which earnings are taken into consideration by one year each year (from 3 years within the last 12 years in 1992, to 10 years within the last 20 years in 1999). The personal assessment basis cannot, however, exceed 250 per cent of current average earnings.

The assessment formula is based on quite new lines. Each pension consists of two parts; the first is equal for all (24 per cent of current average earnings), the second related to the length of insurance coverage: 1.3 per cent of the assessment basis for each year of contribution periods and 0.7 per cent of the assessment basis for each year of non-contribution periods. The number of pension additions has been drastically reduced to only three: family allowance, invalidity allowance, and orphan's allowance. All the other additions, especially many categories of increments for people employed in certain types of companies or in certain activities, have been abolished. The possibility of drawing a pension and continuing to work has also been strictly limited.

All previous pensions were reassessed on the new basis: this was intended as a unification of the relative level of all pensions, using the same criteria for all, and so resolving the problem of 'old pension portfolios'.

In summary, in the last two years structural changes on the benefit side (financing and administration structures were not changed) of pension systems in Poland have been introduced. These changes generally stress the dependence of entitlement to a pension, and the level of pension paid, on the length of the insurance period and on relative earnings. It leads us to the question of assessing the character of these changes against the background of the postwar pension policy.

3. BETWEEN 'BISMARCK' AND 'BEVERIDGE'

As we saw in section 1, the traditions of social insurance as it had developed in Germany (i.e. the 'Bismarck' model) prevailed in Polish pension policy before the Second World War. After describing in Section 2 developments after the War, several questions emerge. First, were departures from those traditions so substantial that one could talk about breaking with the 'Bismarck' model? Second, to what extent, and in which way, if any, did the 'Beveridge' model influence Polish postwar pension policy? Third, what

were the main reasons of the postwar changes? And fourth, in which
direction will (or should) the system develop in future?

Table 10.5. 'Bismarck' and 'Beveridge' Elements in the Polish Pension System

'Bismarck'	'Beveridge'
Separate regulations for employees and several groups of the self-employed	Comprehensive coverage
	Unity of administration (ZUS)
Joint regulation of pensions for retirement, invalidity and death	Substantial role of the state in administration of the system
Earnings-related contribution	One contribution for the whole of social
Earnings-related benefits	insurance; one Social Insurance Fund
Retirement pensions main source of income in old age	Stress on function of securing a common minimum (preventing poverty)

There is no clear answer to the first question. Just after the War the
prewar legislation was the basis for the rebuilding and development of the
pension system, but at that time important structural changes were already
introduced (section 2.1) which created the basis for the postwar character
of the system. What remained from the 'Bismarck' model (Table 10.5)?
First, the comprehensiveness of new regulations notwithstanding, these were
separate for different categories of insured persons, with separate regulations
even within the system for employees (miners, railway workers), and with
differentiation within the general employees' system, e.g. two 'categories of
employment'; and, adding to this, different categories of the self-employed
were gradually covered by separate pension provisions (section 2.2). This
was thus following the 'Bismarck' way of gradual, categorical extension of
coverage. Second, the model of joint regulation within the pension system
of pensions for retirement, invalidity, and death with remaining dependants
was maintained. Third, benefits were financed by contributions which were
earnings-related, and not flat-rate. Fourth, benefits were also generally
earnings-related rather than flat-rate (with the exception of the first years
after the war), although the actual form of this relation changed over time
(section 2). Generally the influence of length of insurance coverage on the
level of pensions was at the beginning non-existent, then limited, and only
after the recent changes (section 2.3) substantial. Similarly, individual
earnings from only a very short period (12 months) were the basis for
pension assessment, again with recent developments towards longer periods.
Retirement pensions, fifth, were seen as the main source of income for the
elderly, with practically no place for private and voluntary provisions.

To sum up, some important elements of the old traditions remained and
grew in importance in recent years, which allows one to conclude at least
that the 'Bismarck' model is still, to some extent, evident in the Polish
pension policy. In a recent work Szubert concludes:

These facts clearly confirm the importance of the output from the interwar period, on which the development of social insurance in People's Poland was based; continuity of this process has been unquestionable. (1991: 466)

There are certainly also departures from 'Bismarck' traditions which can be called 'Beveridge' elements (Table 10.5). Less important in this context, although characteristic, has been the different terminology used in the postwar legislation: the acts concerned pension 'provision' (not 'insurance'). More important were the real changes in pension policy. First, coverage has been comprehensive: almost all of the population was covered by the combined pension provisions, with great similarity in solutions for all groups covered, especially in recent years when the regulations were almost unified (section 2.3). Second, the administration of the whole social insurance system has been united in the Social Insurance Institution (ZUS). It has had, third, the character of a governmental department with almost no autonomy. Fourth, there has been only one contribution for the whole social insurance scheme, and one fund into which the receipts from the contribution went (for a long time it was fully integrated into the state budget). Finally, and on the benefits side probably most importantly, securing a common minimum, the prevention of poverty, was stressed as the function of pensions, at least in parallel to protecting accustomed living standards. This has broken the relation between contributions and pension entitlement, by means of a strongly equalizing assessment formula and a relatively high minimum pension. Recent changes continue to combine both functions (section 2.3).

To what extent were these changes influenced by the Beveridge Report? It was known in Poland and its importance was widely recognized. But so were the limitations of the possibilities for directly 'importing' its concept to a country with different circumstances. In an earlier work Szubert concluded:

A common and universal social security system can be realized, as mentioned before, only on the base of the general wealth of the society and the previous development of insurance institutions. Therefore, the Beveridge plan has a specifically English character and cannot be regarded as a model worth full imitation under all circumstances. Each country faces within the area of social security different problems, and has to look for solutions which suit its socio-economic structure, specific conditions and needs, the psychology of its citizens, etc. Mechanical imitation of foreign patterns cannot bring good results in this area. It is always possible and appropriate, however, to use foreign experience and solutions with respect to a country's own needs. The Beveridge Plan offers in this sense a lot of valuable material, bringing many original concepts concerning the structure of insurance risks, construction of benefits, methods of financing etc. These concepts deserve closer attention, regardless of attitudes towards the general construction of the Plan. They can also have importance for the reform of Polish insurance which has been so far too one-sidedly based on German patterns, full of defects and structural shortcomings. (1946: 21–2)

The Beveridge Report had an indirect rather than direct influence on the direction of postwar changes in Polish pension policy, as well as—probably even more—in the whole social security system. The importance attached in Poland after the War to conditions—a high employment level, a comprehensive health service, children's allowances—which Beveridge regarded as necessary for the functioning of social insurance is characteristic.

This policy agenda, however, as well as changes within the pension system itself, were rather more strongly influenced by Communist ideology and solutions implemented previously in the Soviet Union. This influence was especially strong on the organization and finance structures of the whole of social insurance (Szubert 1991: 468).

The ideology of the socialist state generally had a very strong influence on the development of pension policy in People's Poland. The state's declared aim was meeting needs; the method used to achieve that aim, provision by the state. Social insurance of the 'Bismarck' type, with its fragmentation, the limited role of the state, and the self-organization of insured groups, did not suit the aims of the socialist state. Substantial departures from that model took place, therefore, towards a more comprehensive system, with a high level of state involvement, stressing the function of securing a general minimum. The latter was certainly also influenced by generally low living standards, under which the guarantee of a certain minimum was regarded as the first aim of pensions (Piotrowski 1966: 321). On the other hand, pensions were nearly the only source of income in old age (apart from earnings from continued employment, which was possible only to some degree) because market sources, like private insurance, were totally rejected for ideological reasons. This contrasted sharply with Beveridge's strategy.

Thus, solutions similar to those advocated by Beveridge were used in Polish social security only where they suited the aims of state policy, and the methods were chosen under the strong influence of ideology. To some extent similar solutions were thus implemented under different ideologies, and the influence of the Beveridge Report on Polish pension policy was indirect; this influence was also not admitted, as it came from a capitalist country, especially in the 1950s when the structural changes took place.

Although not so decisively, recent changes (section 2.3) can be regarded rather as strengthening 'Bismarck' elements in the Polish pension system. The advocates of this direction for the future argue especially that it is more likely to achieve social and political support (*inter alia* because of traditions), which is necessary, given the political importance of the system; that changing to a structurally-different system, especially one limited only to a flat-rate minimum, with additional, funded schemes, would cause serious troubles for the 'transition' generation: they would have to provide for the older generation (under PAYG) as well as starting to build new resources for their own future pensions (in funded schemes); that such a change would be enormously costly; and that the 'Bismarck' type of pensions which relates benefits to the contribution record supports work effort, and can be very helpful in the process of developing a market economy.

There are also advocates of structural change to the system, by reducing its role only to guarantee a common minimum, and creating additional, funded schemes whose role would be to protect living standards. Such a solution is regarded as both guaranteeing better and safer (funded) pensions, and supporting the process of economic transformation: the creation of pension funds could be connected with privatization.

Further discussion of this problem—choosing between 'Bismarck' and 'Beveridge' for the future of Polish pensions policy—goes, however, outside the scope of this paper.

CONCLUSIONS

Polish pensions policy after the Second World War both continued some important elements of the prewar 'Bismarck' traditions of pension insurance, and departed from them in many important respects towards a system with many 'Beveridge' elements. It is not possible to weigh exactly the shares of both models. It can only be argued that the 'Beveridge' features tend to concern the administration and financing of the system, and the 'Bismarck' elements its legislation and benefits. There have also been some changes over time, with a further strengthening of the 'Bismarck' side, as far as benefits are concerned, in recent years.

There are some important differences in the ways in which both traditions influenced Polish pensions policy after 1945. The 'Bismarck' model of social insurance directly influenced Polish legislation in this area in the interwar period and proved able to survive to some extent after the War. The Beveridge concepts had rather indirect influence: in this case it is probably better to speak about similarities than influence.

The ideology of the communist state was an important factor in developments in the pension system after the War. The 'Beveridge' model, although born under quite different ideological circumstances, better suited the objectives and methods of the state than 'Bismarck'. However, postwar pensions history in Poland shows also that ideology is only one of many factors in the development of social security, and that traditions in this area are another important factor: certain solutions, like 'Bismarck' in Poland, can survive under different ideologies.

REFERENCES

Alber, J. (1982), *Vom Armenhaus zum Wohlfahrtsstaat. Analysen zur Entwicklung der Sozialversicherung in Westeuropa*. Frankfurt: Campus.

Beveridge, W. H. (1942), *Social Insurance and Allied Services: Report by Sir William Beveridge*, Cmd. 6404. London: HMSO.

GUS (various years), *Rocznik Statystyczny*. Warsaw: Główny Urząd Statystyczny.

Januszek, Z. (1992), 'Emerytury i renty na nowo', *Służba Pracownicza*, 19/1.

Kobierska, K. (1991), 'Rewaloryzacja emerytur i rent dla osiemdziesięciolatków', *Służba Pracownicza*, 18/3.

Krzeczkowski, K. (1936), *Idee przewodnie ubezpieczeń społecznych*. Warsaw: Instytut Spraw Społecznych.

Modliński, E. (1959), 'Kilka uwag o systemie zaopatrzeń emerytalnych w świetle ostatnich zmian', *Państwo i Prawo*, 14/2.

Nowogórska-Kuźnik, H. (1990), 'Zmiany w systemie emerytalnym', *Służba Pracownicza*, 17/7–8.

Piątkowski, M. (1983), 'Świadczenia emerytalno-rentowe ubezpieczeń społecznych w okresie międzywojennym', *Studia i Materiały z Historii Ubezpieczeń Społecznych*, 1.

——(1991), 'Ubezpieczenie emerytalne', in *Rozwój ubezpieczeń społcznych w Polsce*. Warsaw: Ossolineum.

Piotrowski, J. (1966), *Zabezpieczenie społeczne. Problematyka i metody*. Warsaw: Ksiąka i Wiedza.

Pławucka, H. (1991), 'Świadczenia emerytalne i rentowe', in *Rozwój ubezpieczeń społecznych w Polsce*. Warsaw: Ossolineum.

Ritter, G. (1983), *Sozialversicherung in Deutschland und England. Entstehung und Grundzüge im Vergleich*. Munich: C. H. Beck.

Schmähl, W. (1981), 'Soziale Sicherung im Alter', *Handwörterbuch der Wirtschaftswissenschaften*, 6. Stuttgart: G. Fischer.

Szubert, W. (1946), *Plan Beveridge'a*. Warsaw: Polski Instytut Służby Społecznej.

——(1987), *Ubezpieczenie społeczne. Zarys systemu*. Warsaw: Państwowe Wydawnictwo Naukowe.

——(1991), 'Uwagi końcowe. Refleksje nad rozwojem ubezpieczeń społecznych', *Rozwój ubezpieczeń społecznych w Polsce*. Warsaw: Ossolineum.

Święcicki, M. (1960), *Instytucje polskiego prawa pracy w latach 1918–1939*. Warsaw: Państwowe Wydawnictwo Naukowe.

Winiewski, M. (1968), 'Rozwój zaopatrzenia emerytalnego w Polsce', *Praca i Zabezpieczenie Społeczne*, 10/4.

ZUS [Zakład Ubezpieczeń Społecznych] (1987), *Rocznik Statystyczny Ubezpieczeń Społecznych 1946–1985*. Warsaw: ZUS.

——(1992), *Ważniejsze informacje z zakresu ubezpieczeń społecznych*. Warsaw: ZUS.

11

Beveridge Fifty Years On: Second Youth or Early Retirement?

SASKIA KLOSSE, TEUN JASPERS, AND MIES WESTERVELD

Netherlands
H55
N44

INTRODUCTION

In this paper the fiftieth anniversary of the Beveridge Report has been seized upon as an occasion to rethink the foundation upon which our social security system has been built. In a nutshell, the system in the Netherlands rests on two pillars. The first pillar reflects ideas taken from Beveridge, the other from Bismarck. Although cast in different moulds, no choice has been made in favour of the one or the other. Because of this duality, one may best characterize the Dutch system as a mixed system, or as a Bismarck building with a Beveridge façade.

Due to three striking developments, this originally solid looking structure now appears to be unsteady on its foundations. First, the steady growth in the number of people entitled to benefits (in particular the increasing numbers of pensioners and disability beneficiaries) has led to a serious shrinking of the active labour force and, in consequence, of the load-bearing proportion of the population upon which the social security system rests. The necessity for drastic reform brought about by that development is intensified by the movement towards European integration. In turn, this movement impels a reining in of the cost of our social security system, at least if one does not wish, in economic terms, to price oneself out of the internal market. In addition to all this, international legislation in the field of equal treatment of men and women has obliged the legislature to move to the emancipation of claims to social security. As these three developments, each in its own way, gnaw at the existing structure of the social security system, the call for revision of the Dutch system is ever louder (WRR 1990; Wolfson 1992; FNV 1992).

Against this background, this paper aims first to indicate to what extent the principles embodied in the Beveridge Report were incorporated into the Dutch social security system. Then the significance of those principles in 1992 will be reflected on. Are they out of date or can we still learn some valuable lessons from the ideals Beveridge presented fifty years ago? Given that the present system is shaking on its foundations, this is a topical question in the Netherlands; the above developments are compelling the legislature to examine critically the existing structure of the social security system. The issue is whether a structure founded completely on Beveridge pillars is possibly the more suitable basis for the social security system, or whether alternatives should be sought.

1. INFLUENCES OF BEVERIDGE IN THE DUTCH SOCIAL SECURITY SYSTEM

1.1 PRINCIPLES

1.1.1. Social Security: Responsibility of Government and Individual

Although Beveridge's ideas were not completely integrated into the Dutch social security system, nevertheless clear traces can be identified. The basis thereof lies in the perception of government's role in the field of social security. Since 1945 the role of government has been perceived to be that of guaranteeing social security and protection against hardship for all citizens, on condition that they themselves act reasonably to provide that social security and to protect themselves against hardship (Van Rhijn 1945). In comparison with the situation prevailing before the Second World War this constituted an expansion of the system. It was no longer sufficient to protect only workers in employment against loss of income as a result of certain 'Bismarckian' social risks, such as industrial injury and occupational disease (covered by the Workmen's Compensation Act, 1901), illness (covered by the Health Act, 1913), and invalidity, old age, and death (covered by the Invalidity Pension Act, 1919).

The view of Beveridge that the government, in organising social security, should not stifle the responsibility of the individual to provide for his own needs, is echoed in the Dutch perception of the role of government that has been current since 1945. As to married women, the Netherlands legislature (like Beveridge) allowed for an exception. In principle the individual's personal responsibility to provide for his own needs does not apply to her; responsibility for her needs rests with her spouse. This principle, known as the family principle, has been incorporated into most of the regulations that have been added to the Dutch system since 1945. This will be expanded in sections 1.2.4.1 and 2.3.1.

1.1.2. Guaranteeing Income Security

The responsibility of the government to provide its citizens with social security extends primarily, according to current views in the Netherlands, to offering a certain income guarantee. Thus, social security is ascribed only a narrow role.

The Beveridge Plan also proceeded on the basis of social security in a narrow sense. It was emphasized there that sufficiency of income is not sufficient in itself. A satisfactory system of social security assumes, in addition, that the government also ensures maintenance of employment (that is to say avoidance of mass unemployment), establishment of comprehensive health and rehabilitation services accessible to all, and allowances for dependent children.

Beveridge referred to these three matters as necessary conditions for success in social insurance. An effective policy designed to fulfil these conditions will ensure that assurance of a certain income remains restricted to those cases where persons nevertheless find themselves unable to meet their own needs.

In the Netherlands the first two matters are also deemed to be complementary to the provision of a certain income guarantee. However, its effective implementation leaves much to be desired: the government's employment policy, (industrial) health policy, and the social insurance system operate in isolated circuits. It is only recently, by means of agreements on co-operation, that an attempt has been made to effect a change in this. Children's allowances are seen as a form of income security. Such payments, therefore, fall within the Dutch system of social insurance. As for some time now these child benefits have been financed from general taxation, they have in fact been taken outside the social insurance system.

1.1.3.   *Freedom, Equality, and Solidarity*

The question of to what level the government ought to provide its citizens with income security has not been answered entirely in conformity with the ideas presented by Beveridge. A structural choice for flat-rate benefits at the subsistence level has not been made. Such benefits do actually exist, but are made in addition to benefits that are related to the most recently enjoyed income. Given the high levels of the latter benefits (which on the basis of agreements between employers' organizations and trades unions can be supplemented up to 100 per cent of previous income) the room or need for personal initiative within the Dutch social security system is more restricted than in the Beveridge model. Personal 'freedom' to decide on the level of supplementary income security by means of private insurance is accordingly less obviously present in the Dutch system.

Though Beveridge's ideal of freedom can be traced to some extent in the Dutch system, that is certainly not the case in respect of his ideal of 'equality'. The principle that every insured person should pay the same sum for the same level of security has not been adopted into the Dutch system. In the first place, it follows from the distinction drawn between flat-rate and income-related benefits that there is no question of the same level of security. Secondly, the Netherlands legislature has given the concept of solidarity between rich and poor a content that better squares with a sense of justice. By choosing expressly for the principle that the broadest shoulders must bear the heaviest burden, rich and poor in the Netherlands are not treated alike. The rich in the Netherlands pay more than the poor because the contribution is always a percentage of the income. As no contribution is levied on income above a certain amount, the principle of the broadest shoulders is not taken to its limits. By virtue of this restriction there is certainly no question of solidarity of the rich with the even richer.

An important consequence of the choice for income related contributions is that the contribution is not dependent on the extent of the individual risk. Instead, a system of pooling of risks is employed, a system of which Beveridge also was a proponent. A different form of solidarity is expressed in such a system: the solidarity between the strong (the 'good' risks) and the weak (the 'bad' risks). The latter are admitted to the system without hindrance and pay no higher contribution because they constitute a 'bad' risk. This emphasizes the social character or, to put it even more strongly, the essence of the social security system.

1.2. ELABORATION OF THE PRINCIPLES

1.2.1. *Income Security Through Insurance and Assistance*
In accordance with Beveridge's ideas, income security in the Netherlands is primarily guaranteed by the institution of compulsory social insurance, with social assistance and voluntary insurance as subsidiary methods. At first sight this appears to square with Beveridge's views. However, substantive differences exist in the concrete actualization. These result to a large extent from the manner by which the principal instrument, compulsory social insurance, has been given substance.

1.2.2. *Employment Insurance and National Insurance*
The fact that Beveridge's ideas have only partially been implemented in the Dutch system may mainly be ascribed to the circumstance that the Netherlands legislature did not choose to introduce one compulsory social insurance covering all citizens against general social risks. Instead, it opted to maintain the existing system of social insurance for employees, derived from the German system. This meant a preference to hold fast to a system that offers cover against risks directly related to full or partial inability to perform contracted labour, such as illness, industrial injury, invalidity, and old age. Yet after 1945 a number of typical Bismarck features were discarded. This especially applied to those features which were thought to be out of date or had proved to be inadequate: the *risque professionnel*, the notion that old age was to be equated with a form of invalidity, and the principle that

benefits (like pensions) accumulate in proportion to the contributions that had been paid.

As these features lay at the bottom of the existing disability system, a thorough revision of this system was deemed to be necessary. A progressive and totally different disability scheme resulted from this. First of all, the legislature expressly excluded the *risque professionnel*. The juridical ground for a separate regulation for loss of income caused by industrial injury thereby came to an end. The decisive factor here was the notion that it does not really matter *how* one becomes disabled; what really matters is *that* disability has occurred and that something has to be done about that. On the basis of this line of argument the risk of loss of income caused by industrial injury or occupational disease was subsumed under the general disability scheme. As a result, the Dutch system no longer possesses a separate Industrial Injury Act. Secondly, the risk of old age was no longer considered to be equated with a form of invalidity. Consequently, the old age risk was unlinked from the disability system; it was argued that this risk, being a general risk, would be more properly dealt with by national insurance. Additionally, the principle that benefits (like pensions) accumulate in proportion to the contributions that have been paid was dropped. Instead, the principle of earnings-related benefits was introduced. Henceforth to fully-disabled employees a benefit of 70 per cent of the most recently-enjoyed income would be awarded without regard to the payment of contributions. Partially-disabled employees would receive benefits at a lower level according to the degree of their incapacity for work. Thus a generous and relatively easy, accessible disability scheme came into being in 1967.

Moreover, as a consequence of the government's role described above at section 1.1.1, the Dutch system was enriched by the addition of two new employment insurances (concerning unemployment and medical expenses) and a number of national insurances covering all citizens against certain general risks, such as old age, death, exceptional medical expenses, and the costs resulting from having children.

The choice in favour of a combined system of national insurance and employment insurance implies that the concept of social insurance in the Netherlands is bipartite. This choice also leads to the Dutch system being composed of separate regulations built around each insured risk, a system that Beveridge, with his separation of legislation and administration, considered so undesirable.

1.2.3. *The Comprehensiveness of Social Insurance*

Despite the existence of separate regulations built around separate risks, the Dutch social security system does comprise at least those risks which Beveridge considered had to be brought within such a system. The national insurance systems cover the risk of income loss as a result of:

old age (AOW: Algemene Ouderdomswet (National Pensions Act) 1957);
death (AWW: Algemene Weduwen en Wezenwet (National Dependent
Surviving Relatives Act) 1959);
the costs resulting from having children (AKW: Algemene Kinder-
bijslagwet (National Child Benefits Act) 1963);
the risk of exceptional medical expenses (AWBZ: Algemene Wet Bijzon-
dere Ziektekosten (National Act on Exceptional Medical Expenses) 1968);
and
(long-term) disability (AAW: Algemene Arbeidsongeschiktheidswet
(National Disability Act) 1976).

The employment insurances offer in addition cover against the risk of
income loss as a consequence of:

illness including pregnancy and birth (ZW: Ziektewet (Health Act) 1913);
unemployment (WW: Werkloosheidswet (Unemployment Act) 1949);
the risk of (unexceptional) medical expenses (ZFW: Ziekenfondswet
(National Medical Expenses Act) 1966) and
(long-term) employment disability (WAO: Wet op de arbeidsonge-
schiktheidsverzekering (Employment Disability Insurance Act) 1967).

1.2.4. The Adequacy of Social Security

1.2.4.1. Adequacy of Benefits in Amount. Apart from the regulations
governing medical expenses, which provide help in kind, benefits are supplied
without a means test. In contrast to the Beveridge system, the level of
payment depends on the question of whether the contingency is covered by
employment insurance or by national insurance. In the former case the
payment will amount to a maximum of 70 per cent of most recent income;
in the latter case a flat-rate benefit is provided which corresponds to the
(statutory) minimum income needed for subsistence. The level of this
payment varies in accordance with the family circumstances. In this latter
case one can recognize Beveridge type ideas.

The regulations governing the position of married women, whether
working or not, is, to an extent, in line with Beveridge's ideas. No separate
'housewife insurance' was ever created for her in the Netherlands, nor was
she allowed the choice to enter the social security system. The Netherlands
legislature has given form to the family principle in other ways, namely,
either by keeping the married woman outside the insurance (AWW) or by
denying her any right to payment of benefits in certain circumstances
(AAW) or by allowing the insurance covering the married man to extend
to his wife (AOW). A consequence of this latter approach is that the
married woman has no independent right to an old age pension. As a higher
level of benefits is made to married persons than to unmarried individuals,

this is not generally regarded as a problem: the payment that is made to her spouse is sufficient for both of them.

Seen in this light the widower comes off badly in the Dutch system. Proceeding from the point of view that only wives and children can be left behind and unprovided for, he can derive no rights from the AWW.

Whether the manner in which the Netherlands legislature has anchored the family principle in the Dutch system is still tenable in 1992 will be discussed in section 2.3.

1.2.4.2.   Adequacy of Benefits in Time.   In Beveridge's view benefits should not only be adequate in amount but also in time. This latter view implies that in principle benefits will continue indefinitely, without means test, so long as the need continues. This should be offset by the obligation on the person entitled to receive payment to do everything reasonably possible to return to employment, and to co-operate fully with those measures aimed at bringing to an end as soon as possible the situation that has led to benefits being paid.

This view is only partially traceable in the Dutch system. In the first place, most regulations impose a time limit for receipt of benefits. In the case of illness, for example, benefits end after 52 weeks, and benefits for disability and widow's pension end upon attaining the age of 65. Unemployment benefit deviates most strikingly from Beveridge's views. Payment of this benefit, conditional upon the past employment history of the recipient, may not exceed a period of six years. Thereafter a claim for social assistance will have to be made, and that leads to a means test.

Furthermore, under the Dutch system no direct duty is imposed on beneficiaries to co-operate in returning to the labour market as soon as possible. This is seen most strongly in the case of the widow. If at the time when her husband dies or the children leave home she is approximately 40 years old she is assumed to be unable to provide for herself. As a consequence she is relieved of the duty to seek work from that moment until she reaches the age of 65. If she nevertheless enters the labour market, the income she thereupon enjoys is not deducted from her widow's pension.

This is somewhat different in the case of the unemployed. They are expected to make appropriate attempts to find suitable work and if they fail to do so that failure is generally sanctioned with a (temporary) reduction in the benefits received. By this indirect means the Netherlands legislature attempts to encourage unemployed people to accept work. The speed with which this approach leads to an ending of unemployment is primarily a question of the policy on sanctions maintained by the body paying the benefits, and the extent to which the unemployed person is sensitive to the implementation of that policy.

The same applies, to a certain extent, to persons claiming disability benefits. They also are under no direct duty to return to work as soon as possible. Their position is significantly different from that of unemployed persons in that the type of work they are capable of performing already determines the level of benefits they receive. Whether the particular individual is actually in a position to perform that work is irrelevant. This expressly stated statutory determination appears to make the disabled initially responsible for returning to the labour market. Yet the legislature has provided a number of instruments designed to promote the return to work of those (partially) incapacitated for work. Given that this aim is to be achieved primarily by means of financial incentives, it follows that in the area of employment disability also Beveridge's views have not been fully implemented by the Netherlands legislature. Honesty requires one to remark that recently a shift in the direction of Beveridge's views has been noticeable. The increasing growth in the numbers of persons claiming employment disability benefits more or less compels that shift. This will be elaborated further below.

2.   THE POSITION IN 1992

2.1. ASSAULTS ON THE STRUCTURE OF THE DUTCH SOCIAL SECURITY SYSTEM

When one looks at the Dutch social security structure in 1992 it has to be said that a number of the principles anchored in it since the Second World War have been or are now the subject of discussion. As pointed out in the Introduction, this can, to a great extent, be ascribed to a three-fold development: a narrowing of the load-bearing population base upon which the social security system rests, the movement towards greater European integration, and the need to emancipate claims to social security arising from international legislation in the area of equal treatment of men and women.

These three developments have placed the Dutch social security system increasingly under pressure. Proceeding from Beveridge's ideas, two opposing tendencies may be distinguished. On the one side there is the issue of scrapping the notions held by Beveridge. On the other, there is a tendency to identify a strengthening of his ideas; a tendency that becomes more clearly visible against the background of European integration and the pressing necessity to broaden the load-bearing base. These tendencies are examined more closely below, in order to determine whether there will be any effect on the characterization of the Dutch system as a Bismarck building with a Beveridge façade. This examination will take place against the backdrop of certain assaults made on the Dutch social security system in response to the above-mentioned developments. No separate section will be devoted to matters where European integration is involved, because this has not yet led to actual reforms.

2.2. CHANGES RESULTING FROM A NARROWING OF THE LOAD BEARING BASE OF THE SOCIAL SECURITY SYSTEM

2.2.1. Causes of the Reduction in the Load-Bearing Base

Together with the choice in favour of financing social security expenditure from income-related contributions through a 'pay-as-you-go' system, the size of the population actively engaged in income-producing work is determinative of the load-bearing base of the Dutch system. The principal cause for a shrinking load-bearing base is connected with this. The fact is that the Netherlands is confronted with a steadily increasing number of recipients of social security benefits, an increase that is coupled with a contemporaneous decline in the numbers of persons actively engaged in income producing work.

2.2.1.1. The Ageing Process. The narrowing of the load-bearing population base of the Dutch social security system may be attributed in the first place to the increasing claim on the system that is being made by persons of pensionable age. As this development is not compensated for by a contemporaneous increase in the number of young persons, the so-called 'generational solidarity' (whereby those currently at work pay for the old age pension for 'their parents' in order that 'their children' will in turn do the same for them) is thus put under severe strain. Additionally, this development places an increasing financial burden on the (simultaneously shrinking) active working population. The combination of these factors subjects the expandability of the load-bearing base to such a severe test that it is disputable whether the Dutch social security system can be maintained in its present form. In the absence of measures that lead to a broadening of the load-bearing base, a scaling-down of the system in the (near) future would seem to be unavoidable. The movement for greater integration in the European Community would also seem to prescribe such scaling-down. The high costs involved in the extensive claim on the Dutch system threaten to influence unfavourably the Dutch economic competitive position *vis-à-vis* other European countries.

2.2.1.2. The increase in the number of employment-disability beneficiaries. The fact that the number of persons at work is slowly decreasing to a worrying level is related to the decline in economic growth following the oil crisis of the 1970s. In reaction to that, employers have tended to pursue a selective personnel policy, which is demonstrated, *inter alia*, by the imposition of increasingly high standards on employees. It is true that such a tendency has led to an extremely high level of productivity among employees, but there has also been a correspondingly high price to be paid: a substantial increase in the number of persons receiving social security benefits, in particular in the number of persons with an employment disability.

Meanwhile, it may be stated quite bluntly that the steady growth in the number of employment-disability beneficiaries has been caused to a great extent by the disability system itself. The relatively easy accessibility to this system has provided ample opportunity to use these regulations as an outflow channel for employees who are less productive. Both employers and employees have profited from this. Employers could thus avoid complicated dismissal procedures and employees were able to stay out of the less favourable unemployment circuit.

However, this 'solution' also has a negative side. As a result of an inadequate policy to get disabled employees back to work, those who once find themselves in the system generally do not quickly get themselves out again. Consequently, in the course of time a large group of people with long-term employment disability benefits has come into existence. Given the small chance of their ever resuming work they are condemned to a life without paid work. In order to reverse this load-bearing reducing development, a drastic reform of our progressive but expensive disability benefits scheme seemed to be the most natural option. This reform was accomplished in 1987.

2.2.2.   Reform of the System in 1987

The guiding principle for reform in 1987 was the notion that the increasing demand made on the disability insurance system was mainly ascribable to a benefits regime which is much more favourable in the case of employment-disability than in the case of unemployment. As was demonstrated in section 1.2.4.2, people with an employment-disability can in principle continue to claim benefits linked to their most recently enjoyed salary until they are 65 years of age, whereas unemployed persons are thrown back after a period of time upon social assistance. Furthermore, the majority of employment-disabled received at that moment benefits based on full disability, while in reality that need not be the case. This was the result of the policy to grant maximum benefits to the partially disabled if the work which the claimant was considered to be capable of doing could not be obtained.

Beveridge, in his Report, had already foreseen that such a system would have a 'suction' effect. It was first necessary to experience that in the Netherlands before the difference in dealing with the unemployed and the disabled became a subject for discussion. To that end an appeal was made to the labour market, which had become enlarged under the influence of the general economic decline. The social position of the disabled, so it was argued, thereby no longer differed in any essential respect from that of the unemployed; both groups would in this situation experience difficulties in finding work. Consequently, the justification for different benefits systems became invalid.

This was translated into a statutory prohibition to award full benefits where suitable work could not be found. Such an unemployment situation ought to be dealt with by supplementary unemployment benefits. At the same time, measures were taken to strengthen the position of the partially disabled in the labour market. It was thus clearly recognised that their position in the labour market was more vulnerable than that of the unemployed, but that fact was not seen any more as sufficient reason to maintain the difference in benefits.

By now, time has told that the problem of the 'suction' effect could not be helped by this halfway solution, which did not constitute a full equivalence between the benefits systems. As the measures designed to strengthen the position of the disabled in the labour market did not lead to any significant increase in the outflow from the employment-disability system, the 1987 reform of the system, certainly from the point of view of broadening the load bearing base, has failed. In the meantime the magical figure of one million persons receiving employment-disability benefits draws ever closer. The continuing narrowing of the load bearing base that goes hand in hand with that has necessitated the preparation of new measures of reform. In September 1992 a bill to that effect was introduced in Parliament.

2.2.3. New Reforms

The new measures continue to elaborate on the trend initiated in 1987. On the one hand, by means of financial stimuli, they aim to prevent employment-disability or at least to restrict its length as much as possible. On the other hand, greater shape is given to attempts to effect equal benefits systems in the case of unemployment and that of employment-disability.

2.2.3.1. Greater Emphasis on Prevention and Reintegration. The greater emphasis on prevention and reintegration most closely approaches the system proposed by Beveridge. More strongly than ever, attempts are being made to impress on employees and employers their responsibility to co-operate as much as possible in bringing employment disability to an end. At the same time, greater attention is being paid to preventing absence from work through illness. Besides secondary prevention, primary prevention is thus also acquiring a recognized role within the Dutch social insurance system.

In Beveridge's vision only secondary prevention was recognised as falling within the scope of the social insurance system. In the Netherlands there is a slowly growing conviction of the necessity to broaden this scope of activity (Berghman 1986: 19; 1991*a*: 44–7; 1991*b*: 8–9; Van den Heuvel *et al.* 1991: 15; Viaene and Steenberge 1990: 11; Van Voorden 1991: 514–15). Besides measures aimed at restricting already-existing employment disability cases, measures should first and foremost be taken to prevent this situation from arising. If that trend is perpetuated Beveridge's restricted approach is threatened in the Netherlands in time with being dismissed as obsolete.

2.2.3.2. Renewed Efforts to Treat Unemployed and Employment Disabled Equally. Building on the path that had been laid out in 1987, the new measures also aim at dismantling even further the more favourable benefits system in cases of employment-disability. As a result the unemployed and those with an employment-disability would in the future certainly be more equally treated, although not in a manner that would have appealed to Beveridge. This time the government has chosen to effect equality of treatment by bringing the benefits system in employment-disability cases more into line with that operated in the case of unemployment. Consequently, disability benefits will henceforth, like unemployment benefits, be limited in time.

It is not only the restriction in the length of time that benefits are to be paid that runs counter to Beveridge's ideas, but also their actual implementation. In the first place, the age of the beneficiary determines the length of time that the income-related benefits are to be paid. In this way an attempt is made to do justice to the equivalence principle, a principle that is appropriate to the Bismarck model but not to the Beveridge model. Secondly, persons with an employment-disability benefit continue to be better treated. In contrast to the unemployed there is, in general, still no need for them to fall back on social assistance with its means test.

Even though the reforms described above do finally lead to a lowering of the benefit level and as a result also to a highlighting of individual responsibility with more room for personal initiative, the manner in which shape was given to these typical Beveridge features leads, on balance, to a reduction rather than to a strengthening of Beveridge's views within the Dutch system of social security.

2.2.3.3. A Glance Into the Future. To what extent the reforms outlined above will lead to the essential broadening of the load-bearing base of the Dutch system remains to be seen. Although at present the greater emphasis on prevention and reintegration seems to result in a reduction of absence through illness, it remains uncertain whether this tendency will continue to be pursued and whether, as a result, there will be a reduction in the number of employment-disability beneficiaries. If that is not the case, or only to an inadequate extent, then new assaults on the current Dutch system would appear to be unavoidable. Against the backdrop of the movement towards European integration the expectation would also seem to be justified that when these new assaults are being devised, financial considerations will encourage a move towards a 'mini system' (a system that only provides for flat-rate benefits at the subsistence level). It therefore does not appear to be excluded that, more for pragmatic reasons than from any question of principles, the Dutch system will, in time, become a Beveridge structure, albeit renovated.

2.3. CHANGES RESULTING FROM THE (INTERNATIONAL) OBLIGATION TO TREAT MEN AND WOMEN EQUALLY

2.3.1. Injunction to treat men and women equally

It has already been touched on a number of times that when the Dutch social security system was laid down the married woman was accorded a special status. The fundamental idea underlying this was that marriage ought, for her, to be the best means of providing for her needs; the responsibility for her livelihood rested in principle with her spouse. If, nevertheless, she herself earned an income, it was seen as a little something extra that did not necessarily have to be protected by compulsory social insurance. This notion, which is also to be found in the Beveridge Report, can be traced back to the usual division at that time of paid work and family responsibilities between husband and wife.

Because the roles ascribed to men and women in society have changed in the course of time, this view of family life has come under pressure. With the Third EC Directive, the legislature even became obliged to remove the unequal treatment of men and women resulting from the view of family life stated above. Given that this also meant the removal of one of Beveridge's principles from the Dutch system, the manner in which the legislature has attempted to implement this task will be examined more closely below. As the family principle in particular has been given shape in the national insurances against old age, long-term disability, and death of the bread-winner, the examination will be concentrated on changes in this area. The account turns on the removal of direct discrimination between men and women. Indirect forms of discrimination are not considered.

2.3.2. Removal of the family principle from the National Pensions Act (AOW)

The legislature has been able to discharge the obligation to effect the principle of equal treatment of men and women without too much difficulty in respect of the National Pensions Act. The direct discrimination existing in this regulation, expressed by the fact that married women had no independent right to a pension, was removed by dividing the pension formerly made to a married couple (i.e. 100 per cent of the statutory minimum income needed for subsistence) into two equal parts, instead of awarding to all men and women the pension which was usually made to unmarried people (i.e. 70 per cent of the statutory minimum income needed for subsistence). Each of the spouses can claim his or her part (i.e. 50 per cent of the statutory minimum income needed for subsistence) upon attaining the age of 65. An autonomous right to benefits was thereby created for the married woman. As to a pensioner married to a younger woman who has no income of her own, the legislature allowed for an exception to this rule. It was considered to be unfair that in such cases a lower pension would be awarded than normally would be made to a married couple. Therefore, in these situations, only a supplement is paid out in order to reach the usual married couple pension level (100 per cent of the statutory minimum income needed for subsistence). This supplement is terminated as soon as the woman reaches the age of 65.

2.3.3. Removal of the family principle from the National Disability Act (AAW)

In contrast to the National Pensions Act, the legislature had incorporated the family principle in the National Disability Act by excluding married women from those persons with a right to claim benefits. This exclusion was already removed in 1980. However, in order to restrict the financial implications of this as far as possible, a new condition was simultaneously attached to the right to claim benefits: to qualify for benefits the claimant must henceforth show that income from or in connection with employment was enjoyed in the year prior to the disability arising (the entrance requirement). Married women who were already disabled before 1980 could only claim benefits if they could meet this new entrance requirement. This was a condition that was not imposed on other, predominantly male, 'old cases'. They were entitled to keep their benefits irrespective of whether they met the entrance requirement or not.

In a number of judgements, characterized by commentators as a 'bomb explosion' in the field of social security, courts in the Netherlands held that such unequal treatment of men and women was in conflict with the Third EC Directive (CRvB 5-1-1988; RSV 1988: 104 and 198–201). In answer, the legislature finally produced regulations whereby from 1991 all 'old' claimants must meet the entrance requirement. Those among them who enjoyed insufficient income from or in connection with employment in the year prior to the disability arising in consequence still lose their benefits on the ground of not meeting the entrance requirement. Amongst these there are people who for 15 years have derived rights from the National Disability Act (which came into force in 1976). It is obvious that the equal treatment achieved by these new regulations have dramatic consequences for these persons.

2.3.4. Removal of the family principle from the National Dependent Surviving Relatives Act (AWW)

The legislation governing dependent surviving relatives, which accords a right to claim benefits only to married women, was originally excluded from the scope of the Third EC Directive due to its complexity. Yet it has not been generally realised in the Netherlands that there is another treaty that could play a role in this context: the International Convention on the Protection of Civil and Political Rights (ICPCPR). This treaty also contains a general prohibition on discrimination.

It was first confirmed by the Netherlands court in 1987 (the year of the above-mentioned 'bomb explosion'), that the ICPCPR prohibition on discrimination gives a direct right to the citizen to bring a claim. One year later the court held that the fact that only widows could derive rights under the National Dependent Surviving Relatives Act was contrary to that prohibition. As a result of that judgement all widowers have since then been able to claim benefits under the National Dependent Surviving Relatives Act. This means that men and women are entitled to a pension until they attain 65 years of age if on the day of the decease of their spouse they are older than 40 years or have dependent children, or suffer from disability.

It is not surprising that there is great concern in the Netherlands concerning this form of 'overkill' whereby, for example, a 50-year-old man enjoying a good income without children is accorded benefits upon the death of his wife. A structural legislative reform, therefore, was bound to come. The renovated Dependent Surviving Relatives Act will, on the one hand, give a statutory basis to the widower's right to a pension and, on the other, provide that all pensions paid to dependent surviving relatives will be partially income dependent. This solution actually lays the cost of equal treatment at the door of the widow. Given this result, the question arises whether a strictly implemented equality, without taking account of the social realities of the time, would not be as disadvantageous for women as was the Beveridge system in which the married woman was seen exclusively as the appendage of her husband.

3. CONCLUSIONS

The tendencies outlined above raise the question whether the fiftieth anniversary of Beveridge in the Netherlands is an occasion for Beveridge to undergo a second youth or to enjoy an early retirement. The above account has already made it clear that the question cannot be unequivocally answered. That is due in the first place to the fact that the Dutch social security system could only to a certain extent be termed 'Beveridged'. The Netherlands has never had a benefits system at the level of a subsistence standard of living under which every citizen can claim irrespective of the cause of the decline in income. The most recent proposals of the government do not proceed in that direction either.

Nevertheless, the adaptations made in 1987 and recent proposals for reform of the system in the Netherlands indicate that a movement in the direction of the Beveridge model has taken place. These measures are all aimed at removing the differences between the benefits regimes in cases of employment disability and long-term unemployment. However, the actual implementation of this does not square with Beveridge's ideas at all.

Despite the proposal to lower the level of benefits, persons with an employment disability remain better-treated than the long-term unemployed. In contrast to the former group, the latter are caught after a period of time in the safety net of social assistance with its means test. These developments point rather to an early retirement for Beveridge than to a second youth.

Secondly, the emphasis within the social security system in the Netherlands would appear to be gradually shifting to the prevention of claims on social security. Necessary instruments to effect that change, such as good and accessible industrial health care and an adequate employment creation policy, are consequently gradually becoming part of the social insurance system. Departing from the Beveridge model, in which the emphasis lay principally on guaranteeing a certain income, this means a step forward. After all, Beveridge only assumed an effective health care and employment creation policy to be necessary conditions for success in social insurance; he did not consider an effective policy in these two areas to be part of the social insurance system, which in his view was based primarily on compensation. In the Netherlands there is a slowly growing conviction of the necessity to broaden this scope. The social insurance system should become a system that primarily aims at preventing loss of income; compensation should be of secondary importance. Proceeding from Beveridge's ideals, this development can partly be described as an early retirement, and partly as a second youth for Beveridge. Nevertheless, this one swallow does not promise a second summer for Beveridge in the Dutch social security system.

Yet there could be a second youth for Beveridge on the horizon. If it should transpire that all the implemented and announced measures do not produce the desired effect, the continued crumbling-away of the load bearing basis of the system in combination with the pressure from 'Europe' to lower the levels of social security benefits, could finally lead to the implementation of a system that only provides for flat-rate benefits at the subsistence level, the so called 'mini-system'. This would imply the introduction of a system that would mesh to a significant extent with that proposed by Beveridge. Such a reform would make the Dutch system not only simple and affordable, but would also stimulate personal responsibility. By holding the level low for all benefits, people will naturally be encouraged to seek (paid) employment, or, alternatively, to take steps themselves to ensure supplementary means. As a result, benefits could, in principle, be paid indefinitely. Furthermore, such a system would no longer have any need for a safety net in the shape of national assistance, given that all benefits would be set at the minimum subsistence level.

However much the 'mini-system' corresponds with the basic ideas of Beveridge, there is one step that is not likely to be taken: the structural implementation of the principle that all insured, rich or poor, will pay the same contribution for the same security. The solidarity between poor and rich is a principle that is too deeply rooted in the Dutch system to permit that to be done. The legislature has made a very careful attempt to breach this principle by introducing a flat-rate contribution into the national insurance for medical expenses. As that insurance provides for help in kind, there would appear to be no reason to hold fast to the principle of 'the broadest shoulders'. This argument, which only applies to national insurance for medical expenses, is met in practice with such strong opposition that there is little likelihood at present that in this matter Beveridge's ideas will be implemented. The general feeling that income-related contributions must be seen as a fundamental feature of the Dutch social security system is opposed to that development.

Developments in the area of equal treatment between men and women, which have been 'steered' in the Netherlands from the European Communities, also make it impossible at this time to do full justice to Beveridge's views on social security. The need that has flowed from this development to remove the family principle does not of itself, in our view, prevent a second youth for Beveridge. That development does, however, compel a certain modernization of the Beveridge concept, which is also required by the more prominent place presently accorded to primary prevention within the Dutch system. This, supported by the Dutch leaning towards income related contributions, brings one to the conclusion that a choice by the Netherlands legislature for a social security system constructed on Beveridge pillars would certainly demand that the classical Beveridge model be renovated. Thus, if Beveridge wishes to pursue a second youth in the Netherlands he must be prepared as a minimum to undergo a facelift.

Against the backdrop of the move to European integration (a movement closely connected with the necessity to lower the cost of social security benefits), a revival of Beveridge's concept for social security (in a renovated form) seems to be an attractive option indeed. However, such a revival is not easy to effect. We are facing a European fortress which for the most part consists of Bismarckian buildings, all having their own characteristics. If the Beveridge concept were to be taken as a specification, all those buildings will have to be thoroughly reshaped. The question is to what extent this can or should be done. From this point of view it seems to be justified to conclude that the time has come to work out a new blueprint for social security, a blueprint that also reckons with the implications of the movement towards greater European integration.

REFERENCES

Berghman, J. (1986), *De onzichtbare sociale zekerheid*. Deventer: Kluwer.
——(1991*a*), 'De volksverzekeringen in de sociale zekerheid', in J. L. M. Schell, (ed.), *De toekomst van de volksverzekeringen in Europa*. Tilburg: KUB, Reeks Sociale Zekerheidswetenschap.
——(1991*b*), *Sociaal Zekerheidsbeleid anno 1992: Brabants of Europees*. Tilburg: KUB, Reeks Sociale Zekerheidswetenschap.
FNV [Federation of Netherlands Trades Unions] (1992), *Met zekerheid aan het werk*. Amsterdam: FNV.
Heuvel, F. G. Van den, Vrooman, J. C., and Wijngaarden, P. J. Van (1991), *Preventie van arbeidsongeschiktheid en werkloosheid*. The Hague: Vuga.
Klosse, S. (1989), *Menselijke Schade: Vergoeden of herstellen?* Antwerp/Apeldoorn: Maklu.
——(1992), 'Wetgeving en secundaire preventie', in Ch. J. de Wolff and S. Klosse, (eds.), *Stress en arbeidsongeschiktheid: schade vergoeden of gezondheid bevorderen?* Antwerp/Apeldoorn: Maklu.
Rhijn, A. A. Van (1945), *Sociale Zekerheid, ii: Algemene richtlijnen voor de toekomstige ontwikkeling voor de sociale zekerheid in Nederland*. The Hague: SDU.
SER (Social Economic Council) (1989), *Recommendation no. 89/8*. The Hague: SER.
——(1991), *Recommendation no. 91/15*. The Hague: SER.
Viaene, J., and Steenberge, J. Van (1990), *Hervorming van de sociale zekerheid vanuit een nieuw begrippenkader*. Bruges: Die Keure.
Voorden, W. Van (1991), *Preventie in de sociale zekerheid, mooi perspectief of ongepaste pretentie, in Sociaal Maandblad Arbeid*. Alpen a/d Rijn: Samson.
Wolfson, D. J. (1992), *Wolfson Report: Niemand aan de kant*. Amsterdam: PvdA (Labour Party).
WRR (Wetenschappelijke Raad voor het Regeringsbeleid [Scientific Council for Government Policy]) (1990), *Een werkend perspectief*. The Hague: SDU.

12

The Effectiveness of the Beveridge Model at Different Stages of Socio-economic Development: The Israeli Experience

ABRAHAM DORON

Israel
HSS
N44

INTRODUCTION

The emergence of the Beveridge social security model in the early 1940s, and its later implementation in Britain during the immediate postwar period, played an important role in the shaping of the evolution of the Israeli social security system. The overall strategic aim of the Beveridge plan was the creation of a minimum standard of living below which no person should fall, or, in Beveridge's own words, 'the abolition of want'. The implementation of this plan was to be based on insurance, i.e. on a contributory system of finance. The means by which poverty was to be relieved was by cash payments and not by benefits in kind (Beveridge 1942; Davies 1986: 10–11). These were well-known and familiar ideas. However, the most innovative idea in the plan, which moved social policy from the margins to the centre, was its commitment to the principle of universality (Silburn 1991: 84). It is universality which symbolized the model and eventually gave it acclaim. All of these features made the model appealing to the Israeli leadership of the time, one which was dominated by a Labour Zionist ideology that stressed the values of collective responsibility, mutual aid, and egalitarianism. Although the Beveridge model was not adopted in its entirety into the evolving Israeli system, it inspired the establishment of the Israeli national insurance programme and served as a blueprint for the Israeli welfare state.

A shortened version of the Beveridge report was published in Tel Aviv in Hebrew in June of 1943 (Kanevsky 1943). The publication served not only to disseminate the main principles of the Report within the Jewish community in Palestine, but it served also as a reminder of the almost total lack of any social insurance legislation in the country. The Report further served as a means to express the wishes and aspirations of the labour movement within the Jewish community that the Beveridge principles become part of the postwar social reconstruction programme in Britain, and that the colonial power accept the responsibility to adopt and implement these principles as part of its Mandate obligations in Palestine.

The Beveridge Report influenced not only the Jewish community and the labour movement, but also the Palestine government. By the end of the War the country proliferated with all types of plans for social insurance programmes. In December 1945, the Histadrut—the General Federation of Labour—submitted a memorandum to the Palestine government in which it pointed to the need for a comprehensive system of social insurance which would include protection against sickness, disability, and unemployment as well as providing for maternity, old age, widowhood, and orphanhood.[1]

The Palestine government did not reject, as it had previously, the proposal for a social insurance scheme. The Labour Department even publicly stated that the introduction of social insurance legislation might be contemplated by the government (Department of Labour, Palestine 1946: 20). By the end of the Mandate in 1948, however, no practical steps had been taken to introduce such a programme.

A short time after gaining independence in 1948, influential segments within the Jewish labour movement produced a Beveridge-style social insurance plan which included most of the demands for social legislation which the Jewish community had previously put forward to the Palestine government. The plan was published in June 1948, and recommended the gradual establishment of a comprehensive system of social security in Israel (Kanevsky 1948). It contained the essential aspirations of the Jewish community to establish in the new state the foundations of a future welfare society. However, since the country was in the midst of the War of Independence, and actually struggling for its very survival, the provisional government and public opinion were too occupied with the more urgent problems of the War for the plan to make any real impact on social policy at that time.

The government of the newly established Jewish state, however, was soon confronted with the harsh problems of unemployment, health, and social welfare, and had to decide how to deal with difficult social problems. In response to these pressures, the Government appointed an inter-ministerial committee in January 1949 to develop a social insurance programme in Israel. Mr. I. Kanev (formerly Kanevsky), a well known figure within the Israeli labour movement, was appointed chairman of the committee. Kanev was the person who was actively involved in publishing and disseminating the Beveridge plan in 1943, and was responsible for the preparation of the social insurance plan published in June 1948.

The Kanev committee submitted its report in January 1950. The report

---

[1] Submitted to the Director of the Department of Labour, 1945 (files of the Jewish Agency Political Department, General Zionist Archives, Jerusalem).

recommended the gradual establishment of a comprehensive system of social security in Israel (Kanev Report 1950). In its social philosophy, comprehensiveness, institutional features, and organizational pattern, the Kanev report was clearly inspired by Beveridge and the experience of the reforms introduced at the time by the Labour government in Britain. Kanev considered himself the father of the Israeli Beveridge plan (Kanev 1962: 164–6). In the main, the government adopted most of the Kanev recommendations, and the first national insurance law concerning old age and survivors, maternity, and work injury insurance was passed by the Knesset— the Israeli parliament—in 1953 (National Insurance Law 1955). The first phase of an Israeli Beveridge plan thus came into being. Children's allowances, unemployment and general disability insurance were added at a later stage, thus completing the adoption of the Beveridge Plan (National Insurance Law 1986).

What effect did the adoption of the Beveridge model of social security have on Israeli society? Forty years of experience shows that the effectiveness of the model was very closely related to different stages in the evolution of Israeli society. Three such stages can be discerned, especially with respect to the system of provision for the elderly population as reflected in the old age and survivors' national insurance scheme.

During the first stage, from the mid-1950s until the early 1960s, the model had a highly beneficial effect. This was a period of economic hardship and austerity. The flat-rate national insurance pensions provided the elderly population with an income far above the then existing social assistance rates. Given the circumstances of the time, this was sufficient for a minimum level of living.

The second stage, from the mid 1960s until the end of the 1970s, was a period of rapid social and economic change and increasing national prosperity. During this period the serious shortcomings of a flat-rate and essentially static system became apparent. It thus became necessary to add a second layer of selective, income-tested allowances, to supplement the flat-rate pensions of the elderly. The introduction of the additional income-conditioned supplements marked the first serious breach of the Beveridge principle of universality.

The third stage began in the early 1980s. Over the last decade Israel has become a relatively affluent society. The growing middle classes succeeded in obtaining very generous occupational pensions and, as a result, the low-level, flat-rate, national insurance, old age pensions have become largely irrelevant for most of them. Consequently, there are increasing demands from the more affluent segments of Israeli society for 'targeting' the old age pensions on those in need and transforming the Beveridge modelled universal old age insurance scheme into a traditional public assistance programme.

The particular characteristics of these three stages will now be discussed and analysed in more detail.

THE FIRST STAGE

In the early post-independence years, the old age and survivors' insurance scheme represented the major instrument of social policy for dealing with the economic problems of the elderly population in Israel. Israel's elderly population was still relatively small compared to Britain and other advanced countries, but it was growing rapidly. Moreover, most of the elderly were recent newcomers to the country. The social and political upheavals that led to their emigration to Israel, and the relatively short period of their stay in the country, resulted in very few of them being able to make any significant provisions for themselves in old age. Their dependence on government provision for their livelihood was much greater than in countries with more stable populations.

The Beveridge style old age and survivors' insurance scheme was introduced in 1954 as part of the first national insurance law. All residents were covered by the scheme, with the exception of those who had already reached the age of 60 at the time of their arrival in Israel. Pensionable age was set at 70 for men and 65 for women. Eligibility for pensions at this age was not conditional on retirement or the income of the elderly person. Men between 65 and 70 and women between 60 and 65 were entitled to pensions on condition that they partially retire from work and that their annual income from work did not exceed a certain prescribed maximum.

The old age insurance scheme was designed to provide the elderly population with a basic income floor. The pensions were thus initially set at a flat-rate level of IL 15 per month for a single pensioner. At the time, this sum was equivalent to nearly 25 per cent of the average industrial wage. The effects of inflation on the value of a fixed flat-rate pension were foreseen from the start, and benefits were thus automatically linked to the cost of living index.

Although the scheme provided for flat-rate benefits, it escaped the Beveridge pitfall of static flat-rate contributions. From the beginning the scheme was financed by a dynamic wage- and income-related contribution system. Consequently, everyone contributed to the scheme's finances according to their income, and everyone received an equal flat-rate pension. All of these features reflected the strongly universalistic and egalitarian elements of the system.

An additional feature of the scheme was the extension of coverage to all residents, both male and female, who on the day of the adoption of the law in 1953 had not attained the age of 67 years. The qualifying period of insurance for this group to become eligible for an old age pension was reduced to three years in place of the ordinary five years. In reality, this meant that a person joining the scheme at the age of 65 was entitled to an old age pension on attaining the age of 68. Coverage by the scheme of this already elderly population group made an important contribution to the well-being of those who were already aged.

In adopting the new scheme the Israeli government, as in Britain, consciously accepted a subordinate, albeit important role in the social security system for the aged, and left the field open for a broad second-tier system of occupational pensions. The government bowed in this instance to the wishes of the Histadrut, the General Federation of Labour, which was determined at the time to maintain its own occupational pension system. As in Britain, this led to the development of a private, work-place-related pension system providing income-related, status-preserving pensions, mostly to the middle classes and the stronger employee groups. In the long term this decision to create a separate two-tier system of provision for the retired elderly population has become a crucial divisive element in Israeli society, weakening broader social solidarity and reducing support for universal national insurance old age pensions.

The two major achievements of the national insurance old age pension scheme were its rapid maturation and the level of benefits it provided the elderly population.

Old age pensions were first paid out in April 1957, only three years after the inception of the scheme. By the end of the first year, in March 1958, 31,500 pensions were being paid. The numbers grew steadily, and by March 1964, the end of the first decade of National Insurance, pensions were paid to nearly 70,000 claimants. Together with their dependants, the pensioners comprised a group of nearly 100,000 people, or about four per cent of the total population. In fact, every second person in the pensionable age group was receiving an old age benefit. Moreover, the rapid maturation of the scheme also benefited the immigrant population in Israel. In March 1965, about 53 per cent of all pensioners were new immigrants who had arrived in the country after 1948 (National Insurance Institute 1954/1964: 11).

The pensions paid were rather modest. They were originally intended only to provide a minimum standard of living to the retired elderly population. It is doubtful whether this original intention was actually achieved. From the start, the Beveridge-style flat-rate pensions failed to maintain the original relationship between pensions and earnings. Under the prevailing circumstances of the period, and in comparison to the social assistance rates in effect at the time, the old age pensions were, however, rather generous. They were more than twice as high as the average assistance payments. The retired elderly population was thus effectively removed from the stigmatizing and utterly inadequate assistance system. The scheme therefore improved their social and economic status by granting them, as of right, a quite generous old age national insurance pension.

In addition, there was practically no opposition to the scheme. On the contrary, it enjoyed almost universal consensus. During this period, Israel was a rather poor country with relatively small differentials in the distribution of income and wealth. Broad support for the scheme was ensured by its universal coverage and the extent and nature of the beneficiary population. Further, the rather modest pensions provided under the scheme did not disrupt or threaten, in real or symbolic terms, the existing hierarchy of inequalities (Oyen 1986: 273).[2] Another contributing factor to the general support for the scheme was the prevailing social and political climate which was supportive of distributive and modestly egalitarian social policies.

The Beveridge model of social security, with its major premisses of universality of coverage and flat-rate modest minimum level of benefits, was thus highly effective and beneficial at this stage in the development of Israeli society. It enhanced the social and economic circumstances of the elderly population without exacerbating or creating inter- or intra-class social conflicts. It succeeded in accommodating some of the pressures for social reform by creating a social security system which was legitimated by the existing institutions of a rapidly developing capitalist-industrial society.

THE SECOND STAGE

In the decade from the mid-1950s until the mid-1960s, Israel's social and economic situation changed significantly. During this period the country was transformed, as conditions of severe austerity and rationing were replaced by those of relative prosperity and affluence. The country experienced an unprecedented increase in its Gross National Product in real terms of about 240 per cent. This was accompanied by a parallel growth in personal incomes. The increase in the real value of wages since 1954 was about four per cent per annum, although it was substantially higher among the established groups, such as professionals, civil servants, and others. These developments invariably had a profound effect on the character of Israeli society and the nature of its social security system.

Closely linked with these developments was the renewal of public interest in the country's national insurance programme in general, and in the system of provision for the elderly in particular. This change in attitude has to be looked upon in terms of a renewal, because the major political parties of the time, and especially the ruling Labour party, adopted the view that the 'welfare state' was finally established when the Beveridge-modelled national

---

[2] Some of the other analysis in this paper is also based on the Oyen model. See Oyen (1986).

insurance programme came into existence in 1954. Towards the end of the decade, however, the social consequences of the industrial transformation started to come to the fore. Long concealed social tensions became more manifest. Problems of the underprivileged groups, such as large families, the disabled, recipients of social assistance and, in particular, the aged, began to receive more public attention.

In the early 1960s it became apparent that the Beveridge style old age national insurance pensions had been allowed to fall below the minimum standard adopted in the early 1950s. Although the old age pensions were protected against inflation, they were basically designed to provide a fixed income, while under the changed circumstances the incomes of the general population were leaping ahead. Practically nothing of the real increase in the income level of the population as a whole was reflected in the level of the old age pensions. Thus, the retired pensioner population did not share at all in the growing national prosperity.

Initially, the old age pension for a single elderly person was planned to be at a level close to 25 per cent of the average industrial wage. The actual level of the pensions when they were paid for the first time in 1955 (to survivors) was only 18.8 per cent of the average industrial wage. In the following decade the old age pension level rapidly deteriorated to 14.7 per cent in 1961 and, by the end of 1965, reached its lowest level of 9.9 per cent (Lavon 1969).

In addition, at least at this stage, another major premiss of the Beveridge model—that retired people would supplement their low national insurance old age pension by income from occupational pensions and individual savings—failed to materialize. A study carried out in the early 1960s on the living conditions of the recipients of old age pensions found that about a quarter of all pensioners depended entirely on the national insurance pensions as their sole source of income; another quarter lived off the pension with some family support; and only 50 per cent of the pensioners had any additional income (Nizan 1963). Moreover, the national insurance actuarial report for 1962–3 made it clear that the monthly old age pension rate amounted to only 60 per cent of the old age pension level intended when the original law was passed by the Knesset. To achieve the original intention of the scheme the basic pension needed to be increased by about two-thirds, from the original IL 15 to IL 25 (National Insurance Institute 1963: 41).

All these factors clearly showed the inadequacy of the flat-rate, essentially static Beveridge model, at this stage of evolution of Israeli society. Inevitably, these shortcomings produced a conflict situation which became evident in the growing public criticism of the system and, consequently, contributed to the weakening of the earlier consensus around the legitimacy of the old age pension system. The resulting pressures eventually induced the pursuit of new policies to deal with the pension system. The two new major policy courses adopted in the mid-1960s and early 1970s were a clear departure from the Beveridge principle of universality and of strict adherence to flat-rate pensions. The changes did not, however, entirely abandon the Beveridge model which still remained as the core operating principle.

The first new policy adopted in 1965 was to change from a universal to a selective system of pension payments by increasing the amount of benefits paid only to those elderly whose chief source of income was the national insurance pension. In support of this policy the classical arguments for selectivity were invoked:

> that it is necessary in terms of social justice to improve the conditions of those groups of the population most in need but who are unable to obtain adequate incomes through their own efforts;

> that a selective increase in old age pensions would benefit mainly the most underprivileged among the old age pensioners;

> that it would be a more egalitarian measure insofar as it would narrow the economic and social gap among the pensioners which a uniform pension system perpetuated or aggravated; and

> that a selective policy would involve only a moderate increase in cost and would not strain the scheme's finances.

The debate about the selective policy proposal brought to an end the existing consensus on the old age national insurance pensions scheme. It also aroused considerable opposition from the Histadrut—the General Federation of Labour, the left-wing labour parties, and other groups committed to the 'insurance principle' (Ephrat 1965). Moreover, it also brought into the open the conflict between those groups that opposed a general increase in the old age pensions level, because such an increase would have a negative impact on the national economy. In place of the consensus that had existed until that time, the debate marked the beginning of a manifest inter-class conflict with regard to the system of provision for the elderly.

In the end, the policy adopted involved the introduction of a selective increase in the old age pension by the payment of a 'social supplement' to needy old age pensioners. The compromise reached was that the supplement would be paid by the national insurance system not as part of the old age insurance scheme, but as a direct grant by the government and financed entirely from general revenues. In the short run, the social supplement improved the living conditions of needy pensioners (Lotan and Nizan 1970). This new policy, however, did not solve the long-term problem of inadequate pensions.

The continuous erosion in the value of the universal old age national insurance pensions in relation to earnings led, in the early 1970s, to the introduction of a second policy measure. After a prolonged debate, it became apparent that it was necessary to abandon the flat-rate, Beveridge type formula and to set the old age pension rates as a percentage of the national average wage. An amendment to the law passed in 1973 set the pension rates, starting from April of that year, as a percentage of the average wage. The rate for a single pensioner was set at 15 per cent of the average wage, much below the level originally intended by the Kanev committee, which was incorporated into the 1953 law.

The two new policies adopted at this stage significantly improved the economic wellbeing of the elderly populations, especially those without or with very little additional income. However, as will be shown later, these changes led, in the third stage, to a system that was more vulnerable to inter-class conflicts, contributing to a further erosion of the consensus around social security.

THE THIRD STAGE

In spite of the major changes in the national insurance old age pensions in the 1960s and 1970s, the scheme enjoyed a certain degree of consensus throughout this period. However, beginning in the 1980s, this fragile consensus gradually began to disintegrate. In this period the entire social security programme, including the old age insurance scheme, became a central focus of political controversy and conflict.

The abrupt change in Israel's approach to social security policy reflects recent economic difficulties and fiscal constraints. More importantly, however, the change reflects the abandonment by Israel's ruling élites of the progressive social-democratic agenda, with its emphasis on social reform, that had been so dominant in earlier periods. This agenda has been replaced by a conservative, consumer oriented capitalism that encourages people to pursue their private individual interests and satisfaction. The political agenda in Israel in the early 1990s can be best described as a triumph for privatist and inegalitarian policies (Doron 1991), linked to the trends in many parts of the developed world.

How have these changes in the political ideology of the ruling élites affected the national insurance old age pension scheme? The change in attitude is intimately related to the remaining universalist core of the Beveridge system. The old age pension scheme at present provides the single pensioner with a uniform basic pension of 16 per cent of the monthly average wage. In a one earner couple the pension is at the rate of 24 per cent of the average wage. In addition, there is a seniority increment of 2 per cent for each year in excess of 10 years of insurance up to a ceiling of 25 per cent of the pension. There is also a deferred retirement increment up to a ceiling of 25 per cent of the pension. Because of these increments, the actual average old age pension paid in 1989 for a single elderly person was 21 per cent of the average wage, and, for a one earner couple, 31 per cent (National Insurance Institute 1991: 45).

About two-thirds of the Israeli working population is earning less than the average wage. Since pre-retirement income is not taken into account in calculating the old age pensions, the pensions therefore provide a very favourable replacement rate for the majority of the retiree population, which has earned less than the average wage throughout its working life. This system has thus a highly redistributive and egalitarian effect. For example, persons with pre-retirement earnings of only half the average wage were actually receiving basic pensions amounting to 32 per cent of their earnings in the case of a single person, and 48 per cent in the case of a one-income couple. At the same time, persons with pre-retirement earnings of twice the national average wage were receiving basic pensions of only 8 per cent of their earnings in the case of a single person, and 12 per cent in the case of a one income couple (Doron and Kramer 1991: 94).

The current attack on national insurance in Israel is thus directed at its two main characteristics: the Beveridge principle of universality, and its progressive and egalitarian benefit formula. The principle of universality is being attacked under the guise of the conservative code word 'targeting', which means limiting the payment of social security benefits to those in need only and avoiding paying benefits to the better-off. The claim made by the advocates of 'targeting', or selectivity, is that this will make the system more efficient and effective, and its redistributive impact more progressive. In the ensuing debate, the opponents of the system conveniently disregard the fact that the system is in fact highly progressive.

Although the progressive and egalitarian benefit formula has not been attacked in the same open and direct way as the principle of universality, it is actually the main source of inter-class and political conflict, and the one factor that most threatens the future of the old age insurance scheme. In effect, it reflects the dissatisfaction of the growing Israeli middle classes that have adopted the New Right conservative mode of thinking and are thus opposed to a distributive pension system from which they draw little benefit.

The dissatisfaction of the new middle classes with the existing system of provision for the elderly is based on three main factors: the financing of the old age insurance scheme; the redistributive benefit formula; and the emergence of very generous pension plans—actually a system of private welfare states—that enable the better off population groups to withdraw from the universal national insurance system.

The old age national insurance scheme is financed by a wage- and income-related contribution system in which every insured person pays a fixed percentage of his income. Essentially, everyone contributes to the system according to their ability, and everyone receives a benefit to meet their basic needs. The effect of this arrangement is highly redistributive. It carries with it, however, an inverse relationship between contributions and benefits. While this type of policy was acceptable in the political climate of the 1950s and 1960s, at the earlier stages of evolution of Israeli society, which was sympathetic to egalitarian social policies, such social policies are no longer acceptable to the new conservative Israeli middle class élites.

The same is true for the redistributive effect of the benefit formula. The disproportionate level of benefits received by elderly people in relation to their contribution and pre-retirement income poses a threat to the existing structure of income differentials of the new middle classes.

The most dangerous threat to the old age national insurance scheme lies in the growth of workplace-connected occupational welfare systems. The occupational welfare system, basically a kind of private welfare state, not only covers the strongest and most affluent groups of the Israeli population, but it also provides them with a very extensive range and extremely generous level of retirement benefits (Root 1981; Doron 1988). These private welfare provisions not only preserve the social, economic, and employment status of the better-off population groups, but they also redefine their status on the stratification ladder and in the class structure of Israeli society. Their effect in terms of working conditions, living standards, and social status and prestige, has been one of the chief factors in the consolidation of the new class divisions emerging in Israeli society. Furthermore, the middle classes in this newly emerging class structure are not prepared to tolerate a system of provision for old age which runs contrary to this trend.

The financially and socially attractive private pensions mean that the small, universal old age pension is insignificant and mostly superfluous for the well to do middle classes. This has led them not only to withdraw their support from the universalistic and egalitarian provision system, but actively to support the new selective policies of targeting benefits only to the needy. Under the guise of a radical rhetoric for selective care of the needy among the elderly, the new rich are advocating a return to a traditional means-tested relief system.

The political and social forces in power in Israel are essentially in agreement with the middle-class groups opposed to the Beveridge-modelled social security system. In reality, the Israeli government until the summer 1992 elections made no secret of the fact that its agenda includes plans to abolish the universalistic basis of the old age national insurance scheme and essentially to transform it into an old age assistance programme (Maltz 1990). In fact, it actually passed in May 1992 a resolution to introduce income testing for the old age national insurance pensions. At the last minute, however, former Prime Minister Shamir decided to freeze its implementation, most probably because of the impending elections. The new Labour government that replaced the Likud government has not yet clarified its position, although the views of the powerful Treasury lobby have remained unchanged. There is still strong opposition to this agenda in Israel, and it remains to be seen what policy the new government will follow. However, if the Israeli middle class have their way, and it is they that are the most influential group in the Israeli Labour party, the Beveridge era of social security will come to an end in Israel.

ASSESSMENT AND SUMMARY

After four decades of rapid social change, the Beveridge model of social security has lost much of its significance for Israeli society. Although the principle of universality still has considerable support, the model is generally no longer perceived as vital. Like in Britain in the midst of the hardships and austerity of World War II, so in Israel in the midst of the hardships and austerity of the immediate post-independence years, the Beveridge revolution carried with it the promise of a better future. The promised future was, however, tainted with the bleak view of the immediate past, the wasted years of the great economic crisis of the 1930s in Britain, and the difficulties of the early stages of economic development and nation-building in Israel.

Beveridge and his social security plan with a flat-rate and minimum subsistence level of benefits, and Kanev with his Israeli equivalent, were essentially proponents of backward-looking models. Like many generals in history, the focus of their effort was to fight the last war. Beveridge fought the war of the 1930s because, like the generals, he did not and could not foresee that the postwar period would be entirely different from the interwar period he wanted to reform. Neither of them could envisage the rapid economic development and attendant affluence and prosperity of the next quarter of a century, nor could they foresee the welfare backlash and the return to 1930s style, unrestrained, free market economics. The precepts of the Beveridge model contained no adequate answers to the problems facing the more prosperous societies in the postwar years, and certainly it could not address the changed circumstances of the last decade of the century.

To the extent that the Beveridge model was beneficial in the earlier stages of evolution of Israeli society, it is no longer capable of coping with the social problems and distributive conflicts of a vastly different society. At present, the model does not seem to be sufficient to address the needs of the weaker population groups, and, at the same time, it has less and less relevance to the aspirations and desires of the now-powerful new middle classes.

It seems that the basic flaw in the Beveridge model as it was pursued in Britain and in Israel was its failure to integrate the national insurance old age pensions with the occupational pension schemes into a comprehensive system of provision capable of catering to the needs of the different population groups in a more affluent society. The disjointed nature of the system which confined government provision to a rather low level inevitably led the middle classes and the stronger groups of the working population to create for themselves private- or workplace-connected systems of provision, with an extensive range of benefits to its better-off members. The Beveridge model, in fact, lent a hand in an indirect way to the creation of these separate welfare states for the more affluent population groups. In the changed political climate, the middle classes who are enjoying the privileges of their private-pension systems no longer see the need of the government to cater to the needs, even at a low level, of the elderly population as a whole. The lesson that can be learned from this experience is that only a fully-integrated pension system that takes into account the needs of the various population groups carries with it the vitality and the promise of having political and social support in a rapidly-changing environment.

The most vivid sign of the loss of vitality of the Israeli system can be seen in the various parts of the coalition currently attacking its national insurance programme. In addition to the traditional conservative groups and supporters of the New Right, the most vocal opponents of the universal features of the existing social security system are some of the leading figures of the Israeli Labour Party who have embraced the currently-fashionable new conservative creed.[3] In the 1950s it was the leadership of the Israeli labour parties that was responsible for the adoption of the Beveridge model of National Insurance. Ironically, however, it now appears that the leaders of the Labour Party may become instrumental in dismantling the remaining core of the Beveridge edifice.

Like any revolution, the Beveridge revolution carried within it the seeds of its own destruction. In Israel this revolution has apparently come to a dead end. The challenge facing Israeli society is to produce a new model capable of preserving the universalistic features of Beveridge, while at the same time serving the needs of a changed and more affluent society where sizeable pockets of poverty continue to persist.

---

[3] Leading members of the Labour Party, such as Members of Knesset Hayim Rimon and Yossi Beilin, and even the contender for the party leadership, Ora Namir, who have now ministerial posts in the new Rabin government, repeatedly express their views against universality and advocate a return to a selective system.

202   *Doron*

REFERENCES

Beveridge, W. H. (1942), *Social Insurance and Allied Services*, Cmd. 6404. London: HMSO.

Davies, S. (1986), *Beveridge Revisited: New Foundations for Tomorrow's Welfare*. London: Centre for Policy Studies.

Department of Labour, Palestine (1946), *Annual Report for 1945*, 10.

Doron, A. (1988), 'The Histadrut, Social Policy and Equality', *Jerusalem Quarterly*, 47.

—— (1991), 'Social Security in Israel in Transition: The Effects of Changed Ideology', *Bitachon Sotziali—Social Security*, 36 (Hebrew).

——and Kramer, R. (1991), *The Welfare State in Israel: The Evolution of Social Security Policy and Practice*. San Francisco: Westview Press.

Ephrat, A. (1965), 'National Insurance on the Agenda', *Al Hamishmar*, 24 and 31 Jan. and 15 Feb. (Hebrew).

Kanev Report (1950), *A Social Insurance Plan for Israel*, Report of the Inter-ministerial Committee for Social Insurance Planning. Tel Aviv: Ministry of Labour and Social Insurance.

Kanev, I. (1962), *Society in Israel and Social Planning*. Tel Aviv: Am Oved (Hebrew).

Kanevsky, I. (1943), *The Beveridge Plan*. Tel Aviv: The General Federation of Labour (Hebrew).

—— (1948), 'A Social Insurance Plan for the State of Israel', *Khikrei Avodah—Labour Studies*, 2/1–2 (Hebrew).

Lavon, Y. (1969), *The Level of Living in Israel*. Tel Aviv: General Federation of Labour in Israel, Institute for Economic and Social Research (Hebrew).

Lotan, G., and Nizan, A. (1970), *Supplementary Benefits to Old Age and Survivors Pensioners*. Jerusalem: National Insurance Institute.

Maltz, J. (1990), 'The Treasury Prepares a Proposal to Reform the National Insurance Pension', *Ha'aretz*, 22 Oct. (Hebrew).

National Insurance Institute (1954/1964), *Annual Statistical Report*. Jerusalem: NII.

—— (1963), *Balance Sheet and Financial Report for the Year 1962–63*. Jerusalem: NII (Hebrew).

—— (1991), *Quarterly Statistics*, 20/4: Jan.–March.

National Insurance Law (1955), Legislative Series 1953, Israel 3. Geneva: International Labour Office.

—— (1986), Consolidated Version: 5728–1968. Haifa: A.G. Publications.

Nizan, A. (1963), *Living Conditions for the Aged in Israel*. Jerusalem: National Insurance Institute (Hebrew with English summary).

Oyen, E. (1986), 'The Muffling Effect of Social Policy: A Comparison of Social Security Systems and their Conflict Potential in Australia, the United States and Norway', *International Sociology*, 1/3.

Root, L. S. (1981), 'Employee Benefits and Income Security: Private Social Policy and the Public Interest', in J. E. Tropman *et al.* (eds.), *New Strategic Perspectives on Social Policy*. New York: Pergamon Press.

Silburn, R. (1991), 'Beveridge and the War Time Consensus', *Social Policy and Administration*, 25/2.

13

The Deterioration of the Swedish Pension Model

TOR ERIKSEN AND EDWARD PALMER

1. INTRODUCTION

As Swedish social insurance passed its 100th anniversary in 1991 it did so in the midst of heated debate and demands for radical change. Old age and disability, work injury and sickness, and medical care insurance are all under fire. Will the storm blow over? Or are we in the dawn of a new era for Swedish social insurance? It is our thesis that Swedish social insurance in general and the pension system in particular are in the midst of a fundamental change.

The direction of change is clear. We are approaching what might be called a third stage. Stage one was the development of minimal universal income maintenance, i.e. protection against dire poverty. In the decade following the publication of the Beveridge Report in 1942, Sweden would begin its journey on a new course. Instead of opting to improve the minimal guarantee levels of social insurance, by the mid-1950s it was clear that Sweden had chosen an alternative. The emerging second stage involved the introduction of comprehensive social insurance coverage for income loss due to sickness, work injury, unemployment, disability, and old age, but still with a pronounced element of income redistribution.

One of the explicit objectives behind the design of the pension and medical care systems emerging in the 1950s was the redistribution of income from the working generation to persons retiring from the labour force in the 1960s and 1970s. These workers, one could argue, had contributed with their life's work to the transition of Sweden from an agrarian to an industrial society. The return on their human capital had, however, been seriously and permanently impaired by a long period of political and economic turmoil. As real growth soared at a rate of 3–6 per cent in the 1950s and 1960s, there was also considerable room for a redistribution of income to the elderly.

Other social currents would also make themselves felt during the postwar years. The movement of women into work outside the home became an important socio-political issue in the Sweden of the 1950s. If women were to be able to enjoy suitable work-related pension benefits based on their own labour force participation, the coming universal work-related pension system would have to contain generous rules for the number of years required for full benefits. The era of the 1950s to the 1970s was characterized, in general, by considerable socio-political legislation aimed at strengthening the independent status of women.

The women's movement led to the emergence of public daycare centres, social insurance for maternal leave at childbirth and coverage for parental care of sick children, independent tax status for married couples, and much more. When ATP (*Allmänna Tjänstepension*), the new income-related universal old age and disability pension insurance was introduced in 1960, one of the arguments for the 15–30 year rule for full benefit qualification was that women would normally be able to work full-time only a limited number of years. Hence, women would be favoured if benefits were based on the insuree's 15 best earning years, with 30 years for qualification for full benefits.

What, then, is the third stage in the development of social insurance in Sweden? Nowhere is it more evident than in the debate on the future of the pension system, that stage three will entail a move closer to a pure insurance system. Individual benefits within the obligatory, universal system will— given a minimum guarantee level sufficient to maintain a minimum acceptable standard of living—be related directly to the individual's own earned income. The pension system will no longer be used as an instrument for redistribution *between* individuals, other than in the pure actuarial sense.

The present process of change is easiest to understand when viewed within a historical, socio-political perspective. In fact, it would be wrong to judge the events of social insurance history with today's measuring rod. They can only make sense when viewed within the framework of the times in which they were discussed and enacted. Our aim in this paper is to examine the development, and, as it turns out, the seeds of deterioration of the present Swedish pension model. We shall go back to the time of the present system's conception, which can be dated to a Social Democratic proposal to parliament shortly after the publication of the Beveridge Report in Britain in 1942.

2. THE EVOLUTION OF PRESENT OLD AGE SOCIAL SECURITY IN SWEDEN

The legislation for the first old age and disability insurance in Sweden dates back to 1913. As in many other countries, this legislation was preceded by legislation regarding work injury insurance, and, in the case of Sweden, sickness insurance (compensation for income loss). Among the Nordic countries, Sweden and Denmark were the first to have statutory pension schemes. Norway and Finland came considerably later. On the other hand, all four countries had statutory work injury legislation by the turn of the century. The dates of the first social insurance legislation in the Nordic countries are provided in Table 13.1.

Table 13.1. Dates of First Social Insurance Legislation in the Nordic Countries

	Denmark	Finland	Norway	Sweden
Pensions	1891	1937	1936	1913
Sickness	1892	1963	1909	1891
Work injury	1898	1895	1895	1901
Unemployment	1907	1917	1906	1934
Child allowances	1952	1948	1946	1947

Even if at first appearance the old age and disability scheme in Sweden seemed to resemble relief payments for the poor, it differed in principle from the usual form of relief payments, in that the recipient did not have to establish need to qualify for a benefit. Both universality and the absence of means-testing have been fundamental principles of Swedish social insurance from the very outset.

Prior to the Second World War, old age benefits were not generous. A pension in the mid-1930s amounted to 70 kronor plus 10 per cent of total contributions, which in turn varied from 6 to 20 kronor per year (Jerneman 1938: 86). This can be compared with an average annual wage of around 3,300 kronor for men and 1,700 kronor for women working in industry (Sterner 1938: 14). The basic pension could be augmented slightly with a supplement based on geographic location and, in this case, means. The pensioner had thus a right to receive a supplement if his/her income did not exceed 457 kronor in the least expensive areas of Sweden and 743 kronor in the most expensive. All workers aged 18 to 65 were required to contribute to the basic pension. The supplement was financed from general revenues.

The origin of the present social security legislation is usually traced back to a legislative proposal presented to Parliament by the Social Democratic Party in 1944 (Molin 1965: 11). Here, the Social Democratic Party established three of the basic principles they would maintain throughout the coming decade and a half of public debate, and three successive parliamentary reports on the future of the pension system. The three principles were that pensions should be universal, fixed in legislation, and mandatory.

When the Beveridge Report was published in 1942 it created quite a stir even in Sweden. The doctrine of Beveridge, combining flat-rate subsistence benefits with private supplementation to fulfil additional needs, was not to gain acceptance in the Swedish Social Democratic thinking of the times. Its rejection did not come without due trial, however. Gustav Möller, then the Minister of Health and Social Affairs, was strongly influenced by the Beveridge Report and had it translated into Swedish (Larsson 1943). In 1946 Möller presented a new model for sickness insurance and health care to Parliament that closely resembled the Beveridge principle of providing a minimum standard of public assistance supplemented by private initiative.

The Möller proposal for sickness insurance and health care support was adopted by Parliament, but its implementation was postponed and eventually abandoned. In 1951 Möller left the political arena, and with his exit the Beveridge principle lost its foothold in Swedish Social Democracy. The Social Democratic model developed instead in the direction of comprehensive income-related social insurance, replacing a large part or all of income loss due to sickness, disability, and old age.

After the War, in 1946, the amount of the basic pension was increased substantially. The fact remained, however, that the basic pension was intended to provide only a subsistence living, and the vast majority of blue collar workers had no collective insurance supplement to this basic benefit. Employer representatives, the unions, and politicians of all colours were all agreed that the current social security benefit level was not sufficient. Something had to be done.

At the same time, state and local government employees and white collar private employees all had separate benefit schemes that provided a substantial supplement to the basic social security pension. Public employees could look forward to a replacement rate of 60–70 per cent, and private white collar workers to 45–50 per cent of their final wage (Classon 1986: 28). The higher rate of 60–70 per cent would become a goal for the labour movement and the Social Democratic Party in the ensuing political debate of the 1960s.

In 1947 a parliamentary commission was formed to consider the future of the pension system. The group completed its work with the presentation of its Principles Report in 1950. The following general principles for an earnings-based, national supplementary pension scheme were presented in the commission's report (Pensions Commission of 1947, 1950: 70–3).

THE BASIC PENSION'S PURPOSE: TO PROVIDE MINIMUM SUBSISTENCE

From the very outset through to the present time, the purpose of the basic pension was to provide a minimum standard of living. The Principles Report set out that the basic pension should be universal. Furthermore, it should serve as a base for a supplementary earnings-related system. And, this is indeed how it turned out in practice.

Today, just as in the 1930s, the basic pension can be topped up with what is now a housing allowance. The size of the housing allowance is determined by where the pensioner lives and his/her other economic means. The supplement to the basic pension, for persons without other means, has been the only means-tested benefit throughout the history of Swedish social security. Today, practically all disability and old age pensioners receive, at the very least, minimum benefits through the basic pension scheme. These just meet the official poverty level.[1]

THE SUPPLEMENTARY PENSION'S PURPOSE: TO PROVIDE AN EARNINGS-RELATED PENSION WITH A REASONABLE COMPENSATION RATE

In its Principles Report of 1950 the commission argued for an earnings-related supplement to the basic pension. The general earnings-related pension should offer reasonable benefits with regard to the worker's economic situation and standard of living while active in the labour force.

The commission stressed that earned pension rights should be the same irrespective of type of employment, type of workplace, etc. Pension rights should, thus, be portable, a condition that, in principle, is normally fulfilled by a comprehensive national scheme. It was also agreed that the same contribution rate and benefit formula should apply universally. Whether the system should require the participation of the self-employed was, however, an open, and politically controversial question.

The farmers in particular, and the important Farmers Party, were opposed to compulsory social security for the self-employed. Instead, this special-interest group was more interested in increasing the size of the basic flat-rate benefit, for, they could argue, their pension capital was tied up in their agricultural estates. When the new system was eventually legislated and enacted in 1960, it would permit the self-employed to join on a voluntary basis. This concession was later deleted from the law, however, as the farming community decreased in relative number and as opting-out proved in practice to be more of a disadvantage than an advantage.

In addition, the committee stressed the need financially to 'secure' pension rights, either with funding or by some other suitable means. This meant, apparently, that although there was political consensus that the system should be universal, obligatory and, as we have just seen, provide uniform rights and obligations for all employees, there was disagreement in the general debate as to whether the earnings-related supplement to the basic pension should be fully funded or run on a pay-as-you-go basis. A fully

[1] In 1992 around 70,000 kronor for a single adult or, using an exchange rate of 6.0, just under 12,000 dollars.

funded system could, in principle, be an obligatory, but private insurance scheme. Pay-as-you-go would be 'secured' by the state.

On the other hand, the commission stressed that it was undesirable to build up funds of an order of magnitude of the social insurance fund that, not so long ago, in the 1930s, had been abolished. The commission also stressed that it was none the less important to create enough funding to cope with future demographic pressures.

In principle, a compulsory system based on the principles of universality and uniformity could be organized privately, with some sort of public re-insurance or guarantee. Differences in opinion on this issue would also be debated in the interim decade between the publication of the Principles Report in 1950 and the introduction of ATP in 1960. The Social Democratic Party favoured a public scheme, while the parties to the right were interested in creating a private solution. These differences in principle have remained to the present time, and are as important in the present debate as they were in the 1950s.

In 1952 a new commission was formed. This commission delivered its report to the government in 1955. In their report the commission agreed once again on the need for pension reform. The report did not present a proposal, however. In 1956 the government commissioned yet another group, this time to work on a proposal. This commission finished their work in 1957. In their report they recommended a further increase in the basic pension, and they were also agreed that some form of earnings-related supplement was necessary. However, they could not agree on a model; instead, their report contained three alternatives.

The first alternative was supported by the Social Democratic Party and Sweden's largest union, LO (*Landsorganisationen*), the confederation of blue collar unions. Whereas LO was a part of the Social Democratic movement, TCO (*Tjänstemännens Centralorganisation*), the confederation of white collar unions was not. Non-partisanship was regarded as essential for recruitment of white collar workers by TCO. During the preparation of the Social Democratic pension bill, changes were implemented that were aimed explicitly at gaining TCO's support. Recall that both the 60 per cent replacement rate and the 30-year rule to qualify for full benefits resembled closely benefits that many of TCO's members already had, which can be compared to the 40 per cent replacement rate for lifetime income discussed in the Principles Report.

Given the inevitable split with the Farmers Party in the ensuing election, owing primarily to different stances on the pension issue, the Social Demo-crats saw the possibility of winning a majority of the electorate by cajoling white collar support with a pension reform containing promised benefits in line with those to which this group had become accustomed. And a parliamentary majority would be essential to enact the Social Democratic proposal. This was also clear to LO, and hence catering to TCO and its membership was an obvious strategy.[2]

The emerging proposal concluded a campaign of more than two decades by LO, 'spearheaded as in many other instances by the metalworkers' union' (Martin 1984: 214). According to this proposal, the new, earnings-related, supplementary pension system should be a mandatory pay-as-you-go system financed with employer contributions. The system should also build up a buffer fund to meet future demographic pressures. Pension rights would be computed in terms of points. Points would be calculated in terms of so-called base amounts (*basbelopp*) which would be inflation-indexed. In principle, then, the base amount would retain a constant purchasing value. Full benefits would require 30 years of labour force participation, and would be based on points from income exceeding one base amount with a ceiling of 7.5 base amounts.[3] Pension benefits would be based on an average of the wage earner's best 15 years. For the first 30 years there would be a transitional rule that would give full benefits for points earned during 20 of 20 possible years, 21 of 21 possible years, etc. up to the long-run rule of 30 years.

Representatives of the Conservative Party, the Liberal Party and the Confederation of Employers felt that the proposed increase in the basic pension was sufficient for the public system. Instead of developing the coverage of the public system, they favoured a development where supplementary pensions would be based on collective labour contracts or individual initiative, much along the lines of Beveridge. The private supplementary systems would be fully funded and in their opinion would lead to an increase in saving and, hence, future welfare. In the ensuing debate this became alternative number two.

The Farmers Party's representative in the commission presented a third alternative. This involved a more liberal increase in the uniform basic pension with the possibility of privately contracting further social insurance above the basic uniform pension. The Farmers Party feared that the Social Democratic alternative would create too great a burden on small enterprise, and, in particular, farmers.

It was not possible to reach an agreement in Parliament, so the question was put to the people in a referendum in 1957. The Social Democratic proposal won 45.8 per cent of the votes cast, while the Farmers Party's proposal, the third proposal, won 35.3 per cent. The second proposal won 15 per cent. This indecisive result led to the dissolution of the coalition between the Social Democratic and Farmers Party, and, consequently, the fall of the government in 1958. In the following election the Farmers Party

[2] See Martin (1984) for a comprehensive discussion surrounding the politics of ATP.
[3] In 1992 a base amount is 33,700 kronor.

gained ground at the expense of the Liberals. True to its principle of neutrality, TCO took a neutral position in the election, undoubtedly to the dismay of the Social Democrats who had catered so specifically to TCO membership. A new minority government was formed by the Social Democratic Party, whose voting strength, with the support of the Communist Party, exactly equalled that of the parties to the right.

The Social Democratic proposal, the first alternative described above, but without compulsory participation for non-employees, won by one vote in Parliament. One of the members of the Liberal Party refused to bring down a universal supplementary pension scheme and abstained. The new system, called ATP, was introduced in 1960. From the beginning the pension age was set at 67, although an actuarial reduced pension could be taken out at age 60 and an augmented benefit could be earned by working additional years up to the age of 70. In 1976, the pension age was lowered to 65.

Aside from the reduction in the pension age, the ATP rules have remained unchanged since 1960. Nevertheless, as we shall see, the circumstances surrounding the rules have helped to create an entirely different picture of the system's viability than what was imagined prior to its introduction.

Compared with the original legislation, the minimum benefit level has been increased substantially since the enactment of ATP. For the system viewed as a whole, the redistributional element has, thus, increased in the 30 years since the introduction of ATP, as can be seen in Table 13.2.[4]

Table 13.2. Combined Replacement Rates of ATP and Basic Pension (Excluding Housing Allowance) for a Single Beneficiary[a]

	Wage prior to retirement expressed in base amounts (BA)		
	1 BA (%)	4.5 BA (%)	7.5 BA (%)
The Parliamentary Commission's proposal (1958)	90	67	64
Present law (1992)	144	68	65

[a] Benefits as % of the average wage (pre-tax) prior to retirement.

For more than 20 years, the contribution rate for ATP was set so that contributions exceeded what was required to pay current benefits. Even during the 1980s the sum of contributions and the return on the fund more than sufficed to pay current benefits. In this way a fund has been built up progressively over the system's first decades of existence, and at present its

---

[4] Social insurance benefits are also supplemented in Sweden by a third tier of benefits negotiated between employers and employees (see Eriksen and Palmer 1988).

asset value is over 500 billion kronor, or around 35 per cent of GDP. The basic pension is financed separately from ATP, today with around 75 per cent employer contributions and 25 per cent general tax revenues. These percentages have varied considerably over time.

3. THE CURRENT PENSION DEBATE

The pension system has been the subject of heated debate during the 1980s. Some of the discussion is a clear echo of the debate of the 1950s, some is new and has more to do with the deficiencies revealed by over thirty years of experience with the system. Let us outline briefly the major issues.

INCREASING MISTRUST OF POLITICIANS

As political animals, one could argue, public pension systems can, by definition, have an entirely different approach to running their operations from private insurance schemes. Among other things, politicians and actuaries operate from entirely different time perspectives and define and deal with risks in entirely different ways.

What the past decades of experience indicate is that it is extremely difficult to have an open, objective discussion of the public scheme's risks. Politicians tend to line up either to attack or defend the system, basing their rhetoric more on political conviction than anything else. This usually leads to conflicting interpretations of the 'facts' and hence utter confusion for the public. Not surprisingly, conflicting claims in the pension debate have undermined confidence in the system, and, hence, have contributed to growing mistrust of government and politicians.

With regard to the pension system, there is political confusion on a number of points (Eriksen 1992: 24):

The purpose of social insurance is no longer clear.

The transfer system is generally inflated and ineffective.

The legitimacy of the transfer systems in general and the pension system in particular can be questioned.

It is unclear within the present legislation where the responsibility of the public system stops and where the responsibility of the top tier of negotiated supplementary benefits begins.

How 'contributions' relate to benefits is unclear.

The conditions of the political contract are unclear. All the 'loose ends' provide considerable room for political manipulation.

The meaning of these points will become clearer as we consider the problems of the system in greater depth.

WHAT IS WRONG WITH THE PENSION SYSTEM?

The Cost Burden on the Working Generation Varies with Growth

The system's first problem has to do with the fact that benefits are based on past economic performance whereas they are paid out of current wages of the next generation. This is of course the whole point of a pay-as-you-go system. The problem is that, everything else being equal, a system with this sort of design costs more, relatively speaking, when real economic growth is low, and less when growth is high. This is illustrated by Table 13.3.

Table 13.3. Income Replacement Rates for ATP With Various Real Rates of Wage Growth

	Annual rate of change in real wages (%)				
	−1	0	1	2	3
Average of 15 best earning years as % of final wage	116	107	100	87	77
ATP benefits as % of final wage	64	60	56	52	49
ATP benefits as % of an active wage-earner's wage after 10 years as a pensioner	71	60	51	43	37

As the figures in Table 13.3 indicate, the cost burden of the ATP system is almost twice as great for permanent growth of − 1 per cent as it is for permanent growth of 3 per cent. There is an obvious way of coping with this problem. Instead of indexing pension credits and benefit payments solely with respect to price inflation, one can index to account for both inflation and real wage growth. Since the Swedish system does not contain the latter component, projections of its future 'health' must always hinge on what we believe about the economy's future growth prospects.

Originally the designers of the system calculated the costs of the system for different rates of growth between 1 and 4 per cent. What they believed in, however, was growth of 3 per cent or more. This must have played an important role in the commission's decision to settle for the generous compensation rate of 60 per cent with regard to the worker's 15 best earning years. It is noteworthy that a 40 per cent rate was discussed in the Principles Report of 1950, and as we have already seen was what private sector white collar employees could expect from their collective scheme prior to the introduction of ATP.

In the current debate, different forms of indexation have been discussed. Since all the conceivable alternatives for indexation must entail a reduced compensation rate, at least when growth is poor, it has so far been difficult to gain widespread support for a reform of this kind. At the same time the necessity of such a reform is widely acknowledged.

The Present Ceiling on Pension Qualifying Income Makes the Future Pension Status of the Younger Generation Unclear

A second problem with ATP is that the present ceiling on income carrying pension entitlement must be indexed to real growth if the pension system is to retain its relative importance for coming generations of workers. Initially, the ceiling was set so that only the very highest incomes were not fully covered. Today something like 10 per cent of all workers have income above the ceiling that is not insured by social security. With annual real growth of 2 per cent, an industrial worker who is 25 years old in 1990 will reach a point soon after his fortieth birthday, and long before he reaches his 15 best years, where his income will progressively exceed the ceiling. In sum, in the long run the system will no longer be earnings-related. Instead, if the ceiling is not indexed to the rate of growth, the ATP will gradually evolve into a new flat-rate pension system.

Table 13.4. Calculated Costs for ATP and the Basic Pension (incl. Housing Allowance) with Real Growth Indexation of the Ceiling (% of Contribution Base)

Year	Annual real growth in GDP (%)			
	0	1	2	3
1990	24.3	24.3	24.3	24.3
2000	29.0	25.5	22.9	20.7
2010	38.1	30.4	24.8	20.8
2020	46.6	34.3	26.5	21.3

Source: Pensions Commission (1990: 538).

Table 13.4 illustrates two points. The first is the fact that the system is impossible to finance with the present rules if long-run growth falls to 1 per cent or less. The second is that, with indexation of the ceiling, the cost of the system is relatively manageable with real growth of 2 per cent. Based on the latter observation, the National Social Insurance Board has recently proposed indexation of the ceiling as described here, as well as indexation of both earned credits and benefits. The latter would have 2 per cent growth as a norm, which means that, after indexation, all growth alternatives diverging from 2 per cent would be automatically indexed back to the outcome with 2 per cent growth—the third column in Table 13.4 (NSIB 1991).

Under the circumstances it would seem to be a simple matter to index the ceiling with real growth. The increase in costs for the public system is not especially great, and, if the present replacement rates are to be maintained in the future, the alternative is not a decrease in overall pension costs, but, rather, a transfer of the cost burden to the third-tier systems.

The fact that recommendations from the National Social Insurance Board that the government should consider indexation of the ceiling have thus far enjoyed little support undoubtedly has to do with various political interests. As it turns out, just about every political interest group has something to gain in the short run by taking a passive position.

Those who opposed the system from the outset, the parties to the right of the Social Democratic Party, still oppose it on the same grounds as in the 1950s. For them, the ceiling is a blessing in disguise. It provides a new opportunity for discussing how the relative importance of social security can be reduced, and the importance of private insurance increased, in the future.

Since contributions to the system are at present levied on the entire wage bill, the ceiling also involves an element of income redistribution from higher incomes to lower incomes. This may explain why LO (still the only confederation of blue collar unions) and the Social Democratic Party have taken the position throughout the 1980s that the pension ceiling is a problem that can be put off until some distant time in the future. At the same time, construction workers, who are affiliated with LO, have already reached the 'danger zone'. As more groups reach the ceiling and are forced to choose private alternatives, the conservative vision will come closer to fulfilment. There will be no turning back.

The Link Between Contributions and Benefits is Weak and Ambiguous

A third problem often discussed in the current debate is that the link between what individuals contribute to the pension system and the benefits they receive is weak. In economic terms, contributions to the pension system must be viewed more as taxes than as 'premium' payments. For example, most men work well beyond the 30 years required for a full benefit from ATP but they pay contributions in all these years. For men, then, the system contains a large element of taxation.

Prior to the introduction of ATP, as we have seen, 30 years were required for a full pension in the public sector. Since 1960 the 15–30 rule has been viewed primarily as an extra 'benefit' for women, as we have already discussed. The question is whether it is important to retain this redistributional element in the future.

As new cohorts of women now entering the workforce are expected to show much the same participation patterns as men, many believe that a new reform could move in the direction of a pure insurance system. In the 'simulated' insurance system all years between, say, 16 and 65 would be potential pension-qualifying years, with perhaps some norm for compensation, for example 50 or 60 per cent of lifetime income being set in terms of 40 years of earned pension credits.

The simulated insurance system would have to be modified in at least two respects. The first is that credits would have to be given for some reasonable number of childcare years. Although it is already possible to get credits in the Swedish system, the 'pure' insurance system would require imputing an income for some specified number of years. The second modification is that men and women would be treated equally in the insurance collective, in spite of their different life expectancies.

Do we Need a Purely Funded System to Enhance National Saving?

A fourth issue currently debated has to do with funding and national saving. There are really three separate issues involved here. Some stop with the claim that pensions are more secure if funded. They argue that if the income of future wage-earners stops growing for some reason—say a national health disaster—then we will at least have our funds with interest. Yet, as we all should know, negative income growth means negative real interest rates and, hence, shrinking funds and pensions. This argument *per se* does not hold water. In addition, a transition from a pay-as-you-go to a fully funded system must decrease the welfare of the transition generation.

Several studies in Sweden indicate that the saving rate of households is lower than it would be without pay-as-you-go social security (Berg 1983; Markowski and Palmer 1979; Palmer 1981). What is more, the current level of saving is considered by many to be too low at present. Would not this, they argue, be the right opportunity to make the transition to a funded insurance system? This would force an increase in saving, they claim, and thereby create productive investment and higher growth in the future. This is possible, but far from given as an outcome. Investment requires expectations of sales and profits. Saving is only a means of finance. In addition, in order to generate a savings surplus, a country must have a current account surplus *vis-à-vis* the rest of the world. This means all the sectors of the economy together must be in surplus. Creating insurance funds is not sufficient for this.

The third funding issue has to do with the demography of the social insurance problem. Demographic problems present the strongest case for partial funding of a pay-as-you-go pension system. As we have already mentioned, the Swedish system has a fairly substantial fund. Although it is presently not large enough entirely to meet the financial requirements for babyboomers around 2010, it will not require too much of a sacrifice to augment it sufficiently during the coming decade. In this way the babyboom generation can also contribute more to their own pension finances.

To sum up, we could say that the first three problems currently under debate have to do with what we could call 'faulty design' of the system.

The solutions are also clear. Other problems have resulted from an entirely different set of factors. The common denominator for these is that they are demographic in origin. We turn to these now.

4. THE PITFALLS OF DEMOGRAPHY

Even if the pension system had been designed correctly for a stable demographic trend over time, we would have still been confronted with considerable problems due to the sheer demographics of the pension problem during the past thirty years. Three trends have been important. These are increases in the life span of the population, a fundamental change in the labour force participation of women, and a substantial rise in the absolute number of disability pensioners.

Table 13.5. Persons 65 and Older as % of Total Population

Year	%
1750	6
1900	8
1950	10
1980	16
2000	17
2020	21

Source: Statistics Sweden.

As Table 13.5 indicates, it could not have been easy for the fathers of the present system to predict the relative number of future beneficiaries. In 1950 persons aged 65 and older constituted 10 per cent of the population. In 2020 they are expected to constitute 21 per cent. The latter reflects in part the aftermath of the postwar babyboom, and thus is an extreme observation, at least as far as we can judge it today.

A closer look at the demographics of the past three decades or so reveals that while the number of working age persons has been practically constant, their number relative to the number of persons over the pension age or disabled has decreased from 5.4 per pensioner to 2.7 per pensioner. (The number of people of working age has been reduced in Table 13.5 by the number of disability pensioners.) Of this decrease, the decrease in the pension age from 67 to 65 in 1976 accounted for 0.8 percentage points, demographic change for 1.4 percentage points, and the increase in disability pensioners for the remaining 0.5 percentage points.

During approximately the same period, the labour force participation of men contributing to the scheme increased slightly from around 83 per cent in 1960 to 87–90 per cent in the 1980s. The participation of women increased from 32 per cent to around 80 per cent. The picture of the development of the dependency ratio is not quite so bleak if we take the increase in the participation rates of the working age population into account, by weighting the working age population by the participation rates. This gives a dependency ratio of 3.0 in 1960 and 2.3 at the end of the 1980s.

There is less consolation in the above dependency ratio than first meets the eye, however. Whereas women in the labour force are currently contributing towards the support of contemporary pensioners with their full weight, women pensioners are on average not receiving nearly the level of benefits which younger cohorts with more workforce participation (recall the 30-year rule for full benefits) can expect to receive in the future. This is, in fact, one of the important reasons why relative costs are going to continue to increase for another decade or so, in spite of a decrease in the number of aged during the 1990s.

Table 13.6. The Demography of ATP, 1990 and 2035

	1990	2035
Total no. of beneficiaries (000)	1,589	2,546
Old age pensioners	1,160	2,016
Disability pensioners	281	334
Widows[a]	148	196
Working age population (000)		
Persons 20–64[b]	4,603	4,176
Ratio of workers to beneficiaries		
Excluding widows[c]	3.2	1.8
Including widows	2.9	1.6

[a] Full benefit equivalents.
[b] Excluding disability pensioners.
[c] Widow pension benefits are 40% of full benefits according to the rules applying through 1991. Beneficiaries have been weighted accordingly. Following lengthy transitional rules, the widows' pension will not exist in 2035. Instead, it will be replaced by an 'adjustment' benefit available to both widows and widowers for 1 year.

What, then, is in store for the future? We can gain some idea by examining the figures in Table 13.6. The ATP dependency ratio will drop from 3.2 in 1990 to around 1.8 in 2035.

Note that the dependency ratio for ATP includes *only* ATP pensioners. In 1990 about 25 per cent of old age pensioners had no ATP whatsoever. In 2035 practically all persons over 65 will have an ATP benefit. Hence, close to half of the change in the dependency rates for ATP has to do with this effect. The demographic picture clearly illustrates the vulnerability of pay-as-you-go pension systems. Given that pay-as-you-go may nevertheless be preferable to fully funded pure insurance, particularly for emerging economies designing their first comprehensive national scheme—which was approximately true of Sweden around 1950—the lesson seems to be that it is important to design systems to enable them to work in the face both of varying long-run rates of growth and of extreme demographic movements.

5.   QUO VADIS?

The Swedish pension system is presently under considerable pressure. Demographic changes, a decreasing *de facto* pension age, low growth in the labour force and weak productivity growth have brought the problems into focus. With real economic growth the ceiling will lead to the system's downfall as an earnings-related scheme. With no or poor growth the development of costs will be impossible for the working population to shoulder. All growth options will eventually lead to the system's downfall.

The system needs to be reformed for a number of reasons. Among these is not, however, the level of costs of the system, given an assumption of reasonable economic growth, i.e. something around two per cent or more. On the other hand, the state has been running a heavy budget deficit during the past decade and the need to find candidates for expenditure cuts can hardly leave social insurance untouched.

Demands for greater individual freedom of choice; the European Community's requirement of equal treatment of indigenous and foreign nationals, portability of pension rights and international allocation of costs according to the principle of *pro rata tempora*; the desire from some quarters (the Ministry of Finance) to attempt to use the pension system to increase private saving (i.e. decrease private consumption); and the need to create a more direct link between, first, payments and benefits and, second, the development of costs and the economy provide the environment for present political discussions on the system that will succeed ATP.

After six years of parliamentary investigation and political discussion, the most recent Pensions Commission presented its *Principal Report* in the late autumn of 1990 (Pensions Commission of 1984, 1990). The report, which also includes a number of expert studies, is impressively rich in information but poor in proposals. The new government formed a working committee in 1992, with representatives from all the political parties represented in Parliament and led by the Deputy Minister of Health and Social Affairs, with instructions to present a proposal for pension reform in 1993. The Committee is considering a model with benefits based on lifetime income and, perhaps, with a greater element of funding, although with more decentralized and private portfolio management.

The redistributive element of the system will thus be considerably less in the future. Instead, there will be a more direct link between payments and benefits. The losers will be persons who for various reasons have trouble in finding steady work, many migrant workers, and persons who work part-time during a considerable part of their earnings career (for reasons other than childcare, where there is a political consensus for pension rights). The winners will be the vast majority of lifetime residents who work for at least the 30 years now required for a full pension.

REFERENCES

Berg, L. (1983), *Konsumtion och Sparande: en studie av hushållens beteende*. Uppsala: Uppsala University.

Classon, S. (1986), *Vägen till ATP*. Karlskrona: Axel Abrahamsons tryckeri.

Eriksen, T. (1992), 'Vad vill vi med socialförsäkringarna?', *Rapport till ESO*, Ds 1992: 26. Stockholm: Swedish Ministry of Finance.

Eriksen, T., and Palmer, E. E. (1988), 'Economic and Social Aspects of the Financing of Pensions' in *Economic and Social Aspects of Social Security Financing*, International Social Security Association, European Series, 14. Geneva: ISSA.

Jerneman, T. (1938), 'Social Insurance in Sweden', in *Social Problems and Policies in Sweden* (Annals of the American Academy of Political and Social Science, May).

Larsson, S. (1943), *Beveridgeplanen i sammandrag*. Stockholm: Tiden Förlag.

Markowski, A., and Palmer, E. E. (1979), 'Social Insurance and Saving in Sweden', in G. M. von Furstenberg (ed.), *Social Security versus Private Saving in Post-industrial Democracies*, i. Cambridge, Mass.: Ballinger.

Martin, A. (1984), 'Trade Unions in Sweden: Strategic Responses to Change and Crisis', in P. Gourevitch *et al.* (eds.), *Unions and Economic Crisis: Britain, West Germany, and Sweden*. London: Allen and Unwin.

Molin, B. (1965), *Tjänstepensions frågan*. Gothenburg: Elanders boktryckeri.

NSIB [National Social Insurance Board] (1991), *En strategi för ATP systemets framtid*, Rfv Anser, 1991: 15. Stockholm: NSIB.

Palmer, E. E. (1981), *Determination of Personal Consumption: Theoretical Foundations and Empirical Evidence from Sweden*. Stockholm: Almqvist and Wiksell.

Pensions Commission of 1947 (1950), *Allmän Pensionsförsäkring: Undersökning och förslag av pensionsutredningen Principbetänkande* (Principles Report), SOU 1950: 33. Stockholm: P. A. Norstedt and Söner.

Pensions Commission of 1984 (1990), *The Swedish National Pension System: Principal Report of the Pensions Commission*. Stockholm: Swedish Ministry of Health and Social Affairs.

Sterner, R. (1938), 'The Standard of Living in Sweden', in *Social Problems and Policies in Sweden* (Annals of the American Academy of Political and Social Science, May).

14

Social Security and Full Employment in Australia: The Rise and Fall of the Keynesian Welfare State, and the Search for a Post-Keynesian Settlement

BETTINA CASS AND JOHN FREELAND

1. INTRODUCTION: THE KEYNESIAN HERITAGE

In 1944 William Beveridge's *Full Employment in A Free Society* was published, setting out the broad economic policy and supporting labour market policy on which his plan for a comprehensive social security system for Britain, published in 1942, was predicated. He held that 'full employment' was essential to the implementation of an adequate and comprehensive system of social protection (see Chapter 2). His definition of 'full employment', 'having always more vacant jobs than unemployed men', and in addition, 'jobs at fair wages of such a kind and so located that unemployed men can reasonably be expected to take them', reflected his view that 'society exists for the individual' and that the imposition on persons of anything more than short periods of unemployment was one of the greatest social evils. In 1945 the White Paper, *Full Employment in Australia*, was published, attributable primarily to the work of Dr H. C. Coombs, articulating the economic and labour market policies underpinning the consolidation of the social security system implemented by the wartime Curtin/Chifley Labor Governments, and continuing to provide the framework of social and economic policy during the years of the Liberal/Country Party coalition governments until the late 1960s (Macintyre 1985; Smyth 1991). The Australian White Paper also defined 'full employment' as 'a shortage of men instead of a shortage of jobs', insisting that the maintenance of full employment in the transition from a war to a peace economy could be achieved only through strong 'public capital expenditure' on a range of infrastructure and social service developments, stimulating and stabilizing private sector investment. In Sweden in the 1940s, the Rehn-Meidner model of integrating social security, labour market policies, and a solidaristic wages policy with a commitment to full employment was introduced and remained the cornerstone of Swedish welfare state policies until the late 1980s (Jangenas 1985; Marklund 1992). Similar observations have been made regarding full employment as the fundamental pillar of the Norwegian welfare state in the postwar period (Stjerno 1992). These commitments to full employment, occurring as they did in widely diverse, emerging welfare states, were predicated on the dominance of Keynesian economic theory within which postwar social policies in a number of states were framed. The heart of the matter is encapsulated in Beveridge's statement that:

The first condition of full employment is that total outlays should always be high enough to set up a demand for products of industry which cannot be satisfied without using the whole man-power of the country: . . . Who is to secure that the first condition is satisfied? The answer is that this must be made a responsibility of the State. No one else has the requisite powers; the condition will not get satisfied automatically. It must be a function of the State in future to ensure adequate total outlay and by consequence to protect its citizens against mass unemployment . . . (Beveridge 1944: 29)

In similar vein, the White Paper on *Full Employment in Australia* asserted:

The policy outlined in this paper is that governments should accept the responsibility for stimulating spending on goods and services to the extent necessary to sustain full employment. (The Parliament of the Commonwealth of Australia 1945: 3)

The necessity for governments to set full employment as a matter of social priority, and then to establish the required public investment and additional labour market policies as the core of both economic policy and welfare state provision, provided the Keynesian parameters in which the emergent Australian welfare state (and a number of others) was situated.

Despite the similarities apparent in these developments, current analyses of western welfare states, in particular the work of Esping Andersen (1990), emphasize the clustering of various welfare state types, usually categorizing Australia within the 'liberal welfare state regime' with other Anglophone countries, to denote the relative reluctance of governments to intervene in market arrangements, particularly labour market arrangements, and to provide comprehensive systems of social protection. There has been one valiant attempt to reconsider this categorization in respect of Australia by establishing the direction and quantum of redistribution through the taxation/benefit system as the central analytical question (Castles and Mitchell 1992). This analysis concludes that, in the light of the historically formative role played by the labour movement in institutionalizing both minimum wage protection through centralized wage-determination, and redistribution rather than contribution as the core of income support arrangements, by instituting a fully social assistance system of social protection with no social insurance base, Australia is more appropriately designated a 'radical redistributive' welfare regime.

What is missing in most of the literature is an appreciation of the interconnections of labour market, incomes, and social security policies, interconnections which were placed at the centre of Australian social policy debates from the turn of the century, and particularly in the periods of Labor Government between 1942 and 1949 and from 1983 to 1992. Developments in the Australian welfare state cannot be understood comprehensively if these three elements are not fully explored.

This chapter examines the changing relationships between economic and labour market policies and welfare state arrangements in Australia at various key stages since the turn of the century, paying particular attention to the postwar period. Section 2 delineates the concept of 'provisional settlement', while Sections 3 and 4 outline the continuities and differences between the major provisional settlements of the early 1900s and the 1940s, in the latter period when the commitment to full employment was introduced into economic and social policy. The expansionary welfare state developments under the Whitlam Labor Government (1972–5), and the onset of the era of contractionary policies from 1974, including the policies of the Fraser Coalition Government, are outlined in Section 5. Section 6 analyses the economic and social consequences of 'the end of full employment', focusing on the period of the Hawke/Keating Labor Governments (1983–93) and the competing economic and social policies presented by the Government and the Liberal/National Party Opposition in the early 1990s, a period of severe domestic and international recession, when the promise of achieving 'full employment', or even of seeing any credible government commitment to that goal, appears more elusive than at any other stage in the postwar period in Australia and in most other OECD countries. The concluding Section 7 attempts a re-categorization of the characteristics of Australian market/state relations, steering a path between the polarities of liberalism and 'radical redistributivism', in the light of the various political alliances forged in the contested development of Australian welfare state arrangements.

2.   CONFLICTS OF INTEREST AND PROVISIONAL SETTLEMENTS

Castles (1988) has identified conflicts of interest based on differential locations in the structures of economic advantage, focusing on class relations as the determining factor in the processes of Australian public policy formation. In contrast, Shaver (1990) notes that in privileging class relations and class conflict as the primary determinants of welfare state outcomes, most analyses of welfare state regimes ignore the multi-dimensionality of power relations. She argues that power relations in the domains of gender and sexuality, race and ethnicity, religion and culture also influence the structures, processes, and meanings of welfare state regimes. In this analysis we examine only two of these intersecting domains of power—class and gender relations—in shaping Australian welfare state outcomes.

Also, it is important to extend Castles's analysis of conflicts of interest by seeing them as based on differential locations in the structures of economic, political, and social advantage and power. The conflicts are fought out within arenas of public policy, the market and civil society which develop their own dynamics and assume degrees of autonomy. The parties to any particular contest can arrive at a set of mutually acceptable terms and conditions for the cessation of unproductive conflict and the constrained continuance of the conflict within agreed parameters. These conditions constitute what Castles (1988) has termed an 'historical compromise'. The concept of 'provisional settlement' is preferred because it does not have the pejorative connotations of 'compromise' and because it indicates the contingency and temporality of the 'agreement'. Provisional settlements establish the parameters for ongoing disputation: what the participants can disagree about; the limits on action taken by the parties in pursuit of their interests; and the mechanisms for resolving conflicts which emerge within the parameters. As such, provisional settlements do not rigidly determine either the precise agenda for future developments or the explicit courses of action for participants.

3. THE 1900S LIBERAL/SOCIAL-DEMOCRATIC SETTLEMENT

The 1890s started with major droughts, a collapse in export prices and a major trial of strength between the trade union movement and employers, who were backed by the Colonial governments. In 1901, the Colonies were federated, and the Commonwealth formed, but the States retained the bulk of legislative powers under the terms of a liberal free market Constitution. By 1910 a strategic alliance between liberal and social democrats against conservative free traders had set in place a number of related 'settlements' which constituted a composite 'provisional settlement' known as the 'new protection'. Emerging from a conflict over tariff policy, this settlement was the product of an alliance between the Protectionists, who were primarily concerned with securing industry protection, and the Australian Labor Party, part of whose agenda was concerned to secure a 'fair and reasonable' wage and old age and invalidity pensions.

The constituent elements of the 'new protection' settlement included: tariff protection for employers who provided fair wages and conditions; the 'White Australia' immigration policy; the centralized industrial relations and wage determination system; the setting of a fair and reasonable *male* 'living wage' based on a conception of family needs; and the introduction of a general, revenue-based, flat-rate, means-tested social security system, with the introduction of old age and invalidity pensions (Baldock 1988; Macarthy 1976; Macintyre 1985; Markey 1982). It should be noted that the outcome of political debates about the financing of pensions for the aged and disabled, focused as they had been around either contribution through social insurance (following European models) or general revenue financing, in entrenching the latter as the basis of the Australian social security system, established the principle of redistribution through tax/benefit arrangements (Castles and Mitchell 1992).

Castles (1988) has analysed this provisional settlement as a product of the politics of domestic defence in the face of national vulnerability, and has drawn attention to the split between liberals and conservatives on the issue of free trade, a split which facilitated the alliance between industrial labour, the Australian Labor Party, and protectionist liberal democrats. Macintyre (1985; 1989) also sees significance in this strategic alliance, arguing that the settlement was marked by an historically significant acceptance of state intervention. A comparatively high level of state intervention was implemented in the form of public pensions, the Commonwealth Court of Conciliation and Arbitration, anti-monopoly legislation, and state-run enterprises in banking, insurance, railways, telecommunications and post, shipping, munitions, woollen mills, sawmilling, brick-making, and, in Queensland, state-run butcher shops! In short, there was a widespread acceptance that the state had a responsibility to intervene in the market to ensure economic security, a view which informed the decision of Justice Higgins when determining what constituted a fair and reasonable wage in 1907.

It is beyond the scope of this chapter to detail the marked gender inequalities in wage determination established by the setting of a 'living wage' for adult men (based on assumed family responsibilities) and the setting of the female minimum at 50–54 per cent of the male rate. However, various such judgements in the first two decades of the twentieth century established policies and practices which enforced gender segregation in the labour market and wage injustice for women for more than sixty years. The principles underlying these practices persisted, but moves toward wage equality were introduced under the unique wartime labour market conditions, again in the 1950 Basic Wage case and then from the late 1960s, culminating in the 'equal pay' measures introduced by the central arbitration system in 1972–5, all propelled by the advocacy and organization of women's organizations both inside and outside the unions (Baldock 1988; Curthoys 1988). Prior to this history of contest, however, the deep entrenchment of gender inequality in wage-determination indicates that the provisional settlement of the Federation period, while incorporating a variety of interests around state intervention into market relations, also reinforced and perpetuated gender divisions in paid work, unpaid work in family and household, and women's access to market incomes.

4. THE 1940S KEYNESIAN WELFARE STATE SETTLEMENT

The Keynesian-based welfare state settlement was negotiated in the 1940s, building on and extending the 'new protection' settlement. These far-reaching developments were deeply influenced by Australian experiences of the 1930s Depression; strong involvement in World War II and the total mobilization of the economy, the labour force, and civil society around the war effort; and by Australian economists' and policy makers' interpretations of Keynesian thought (Roe 1976; Coombs 1981; Black 1984; Cornish 1981; Smyth 1991). The major reforms included: the Commonwealth government's acquisition of all income-taxation powers in 1942 in the context of pro-secuting the war effort at national level; the creation of the National Welfare Fund as the source of central revenue financing for an extended social security system; the introduction of a number of new social security pensions, benefits and allowances: child endowment (1941), widows pension (1942), increased maternity allowances (1943), funeral benefits (1943), unem-ployment, sickness, and special benefits (1944), and pharmaceutical benefits (1947); the publication and acceptance of the 1945 White Paper, *Full Employment in Australia*; and the creation of the Commonwealth Employ-ment Service to manage and sustain the transition to full employment in peace-time.

The White Paper's commitment to full employment and the associated social security and welfare reforms built on and sought to rectify the inadequacies of the 1900s liberal/social democratic settlement. The aspir-ations and promises of the early years of the century had not been fulfilled, as the mass unemployment of the Depression, unalleviated by any national system of unemployment benefit, had made abundantly clear to the labour movement (Macintyre 1985; Smyth 1991); and war had reinforced the belief in central government intervention to pursue national priorities. It was widely, but certainly not universally considered that Keynesian economic theory provided a more effective path to the 'working man's paradise' than did discredited neoclassical economic theory. As argued by Dr H. C. Coombs, Director General of the Ministry of Post War Reconstruction in Australia:

The choice before us is to go back or to go on, to attempt to rebuild the so called 'free' economy based here upon individual choice, freedom of enterprise, unemployment, and the alternation of booms and slumps; or to go on ... to an economy, still predominantly one of private ownership and enterprise, but with an increasing responsibility on the Government for the allocation of resources, the prime purpose of which will be the achievement of social objectives of a high and stable level of employment, of rising standards of living for all people, of the development of our national resources and security and opportunity for the individual. (Coombs 1944: 98–9)

Even conservative politicians such as Menzies, leader of the opposition Liberal Party, endorsed the need for full employment and government intervention:

It is elementary knowledge to all that it [full employment] involves direction and control. The days of uncontrolled capitalism are gone. I do not object to controls, so be it they are controls which are related to efficiency and, in the course of human nature, capable of being soundly administered. (Menzies 1944: 179)

There was not, however, universal agreement about the meaning of full employment and the extent of state intervention and control to be pursued within the terms of the Keynesian settlement. Ross identified a range of qualifications to the full employment objective emanating from the political right:

Some want full employment only if it can be obtained without competition with private production of the goods which private employers believe to be their own domain. Some want full employment, only if sufficient unemployment is maintained in order to keep labour in its proper place. (Ross 1944: 199–200)

This position is mirrored in the statement of the New South Wales Institute of Public Affairs (IPA), a newly-formed employer-funded lobby group:

There is no need to pose employment as an objective in itself, as is now so commonly done ... To talk about promoting full employment is, for the sake of political kudos, to turn into an end what is only a means... The recovery and expansion of markets is the only way to the betterment of material standards. (IPA 1945: 25–6)

The IPA and other employer bodies did, however, accept the broad agenda of sustained economic growth and non-inflationary full employment; and, while continuing to express preference for a contributory social insurance system, they also accepted an expanded, general revenue-based social assistance 'safety net'. They cautiously accepted the legitimacy, based on Keynesian economic theory, of a more interventionist state which ameliorated the inequalities of and set the parameters for the operation of the market. They similarly accepted the attendant institutional framework, which included a stable international economic system set in place by the Bretton Woods Agreement, federal government retention of income-taxation powers, an effective national accounting system, a strong central bank (but not nationalized banking), counter-cyclical budgeting, highly protectionist trade and industry development policies, a centralized conciliation and arbitration system, and federal constitutional responsibility for an expanded social security system. Employers' endorsement of the Keynesian welfare state provisional settlement was based on a pragmatic balancing of concessions on questions of demand management against the promised benefits of guaranteed profits flowing from tariffs and from demand management itself. Employers continued, however, to express their concerns about inflation, and pressed for tighter controls on wages growth. In short, they were prepared to accept a conservative Keynesian presence in return for a growing and protected domestic market.

For their part, union leaders were generally supportive of the White Paper, the promise of full employment, economic development, the extension of central banking powers, and the expansion of the social security safety net. Left-wing unions were concerned that the Labor Government proceed with its policy to nationalize key areas of industry such as the coal mines and banks, and exerted pressure for the forty hour week and higher wage settlements. The ACTU and the State Labor Councils were, on the whole, prepared to accept some compromises on the nationalization and wages agenda, and to accept a less interventionist Keynesian presence in return for the promise of economic growth, full employment, the forty hour week and economic security. When the Left unions eventually pushed for higher stakes, the Chifley Government called in the army to break the 1949 national coal-miners' strike, and introduced a 'Penal Clause' into the Arbitration Act in 1949. The effect was to break Left union opposition to the cautious Keynesian agenda and to impose an effective buffer on wages growth.

The continuities with the turn of the century liberal/social democratic settlement are clear. At the turn of the century, employers were prepared to strike a strategic alliance with organized labour to secure a sheltered economic prosperity. In the 1940s, similar interests led employers to support significant expansion of central state intervention into trade relations, industrial development, wage determination, labour market regulation, and a system of social protection based on general revenue financing. Unionists, for their part, were prepared to accept certain constraints on their industrial actions and narrow their political agenda in return for the promise of job security, wage maintenance, and an extended social security system.

The extended system of non-contributory, flat-rate pensions and benefits was based on the principle of meeting *needs* rather than *rights* to welfare, and of alleviating poverty for those not within the primary allocation systems of the market and of family interdependencies. Drawing its revenue from general taxation rather than from earmarked contributions based on labour force participation, it represented a 'solidarity' compact between those in and out of employment. In short, the combination of centralized wage determination and expanded social security policies in the 1940s was well within the long-standing Laborist tradition. The commitment to full employment and expansionary public investment policies, however, represented a Keynesian development of the tradition of state intervention, effected in the name of equity and a 'New Order'.

Notwithstanding the defeats of bank nationalization and of concerted efforts to introduce a national health insurance scheme and develop a strong public-housing programme, by the time of the Liberal/Country party victory in the 1949 elections, the Curtin and Chifley Labor Governments, with the support of organized capital and labour, had been able to negotiate and set in place the institutional framework for the long postwar boom.

However, not all interest groups were involved in the processes which established the dimensions and terms of the settlement, and some significant population groups found their claims either ignored, or only marginally addressed.

In November 1943 an Australian Women's Conference for Victory in War and Victory in Peace was held in Sydney, with a view to adopting an *Australian Women's Charter*. Attended by representatives from every State and from 90 organizations, the Conference adopted a wide-ranging set of policies, including gender equality in all laws and regulations; equal-rights legislation to abolish sex discrimination; equal employment rights, opportunities and wages; a Women's Employment Board to evaluate the relative value and standard of women's work (which was introduced to bring some order to the wage rates for women engaged in the wartime labour market); a personal endowment for all mothers and/or homemakers; a comprehensive, free, preventative, and curative health service; free secondary, technical, and university education; a national public housing policy; child care and other social services; access to services and amenities for rural and isolated women; land rights and citizenship for Aboriginal Australians, and federal responsibility for Aboriginal affairs (Australian Women's Conference Committee 1943).

The failure of most of these items to be treated seriously by the major interest-groups struggling over the final form of the White Paper on *Full Employment* and in the eventual postwar configuration of labour market and incomes policies (and the absence of consideration of the *Women's Charter* in the major texts on the foundations of the Australian welfare state) reflect the prevailing male-centred assumptions relating to the place of women in the labour market, the family, and in public life.

However, outcomes for women were mixed and it is a mistake to focus on continuities to the exclusion of change. In 1945 the Re-establishment of Employment Bill was passed to ensure automatic preference for the employment of ex-service personnel, where possible in their previous positions (Baldock 1988). Many, but not all women left or were forced out of their wartime 'male' jobs and into the segregated 'female' occupations. In 1950 the Basic Wage decision handed down in the Arbitration Court, responding to ACTU and feminist organizations' claims for equal pay, set the female wage at 75 per cent of the equivalent male wage, stating that the granting of equal pay would disturb the traditional pay structure. Not only did the Court hold that men supporting families needed higher wages than single women, but that equal pay would cost too much, with the effect that if single women were to be paid more, then married men with families would have to be paid less (Curthoys 1988). The erroneous assumptions, that all employed adult men had dependents, and that all employed adult women were single and without dependents, expressed clearly the persistence of patriarchal assumptions in public policy.

For women, however, the elements of the 1900s liberal/social-democratic settlement were modified considerably by the Keynesian welfare state settlement. The basis of the wages system was still the family wage, although the gender gap had been reduced, and women received child endowment payments designed to supplement (and at the time to restrain increases in) the family wage. Nevertheless, the child endowment payments were an explicit and appreciated form of redistribution to women in their role as mothers (Cass 1988). The availability of age and invalidity pension, unemployment and sickness benefit, and of widows' pension (for which divorced and deserted women, as well as widowed women, were eligible) did mean a greater degree of security and reduced dependence on a man's market income, particularly since the social security system did not base its entitlements on prior labour force participation. Paradoxically, a needs-based social security system, one of whose basic assumptions was married women's dependency, gave women *independent* entitlement, although the progressive impact of this was lessened by the construction of the married couple as the unit for income-testing (Shaver 1992).

5. SHAKING THE KEYNESIAN FOUNDATIONS

By the mid-1960s the effect on social expectations of almost twenty years of full employment and strong economic growth was being felt. In many ways it appeared as though all the Keynesian welfare state chickens had come home to roost. The years of apparent prosperity contributed to the resurgence of confident social movements (specifically social rights movements) and both generated an expectation that all social groups would share in the economic security promised by the liberal/social-democratic settlements. Paradoxically, poverty was rediscovered, even in the era of full employment, and shown to be concentrated among the aged, the Aboriginal population, certain migrant communities, women-headed families, rural labourers, and small farmers; i.e. among those reliant on Australia's redistributive social security system and among low paid families, who were clearly not protected by the basic wage and child endowment. In 1966 a Referendum to give citizenship entitlements to Aboriginal and Torres Strait Islander Australians and to give Constitutional responsibility for Aboriginal affairs to the Commonwealth was passed by an overwhelming vote. Migrant communities rejected the official policy prescriptions to assimilate and integrate, and made claims for the recognition and respect of cultural diversity. The feminist movement was revitalised and in 1972 the politically influential Women's Electoral Lobby was formed, articulating claims with other women's organizations for 'equal pay for work of equal value', child care and the income support necessary to care for children without a male partner.

A succession of Liberal/Country Party coalition Governments attempted to come to terms with the social and political changes. It was the Whitlam-led Labor Party, however, whose social policies reflected the hope and optimism of the late boom years, and promised the realization of the progressive ideals expected of the Laborist Keynesian welfare state; thus introducing into political and public discourse the language of social equality, cultural diversity, political and community participation, and access to social welfare as a universal right.

Included in the Labor Government's programme was a commitment to extensive reform of the social security system, with promises to abolish the means-test on the old age pension, increase and then protect the real value of all pensions and benefits, and introduce a supporting-mothers benefit for those categories of female sole parents excluded from entitlement to widows' pension. These social security measures were to be accompanied by a significant expansion of health and welfare services, with promises to introduce a universal health insurance system; revitalize public housing and urban and regional development programmes; significantly expand public education at both secondary and tertiary levels; and develop a comprehensive system of child care services. The incoming government was also committed to equality of opportunity, and in some instances equality of outcome for women, Aboriginal people, and migrant communities: with promises to support the claim of 'equal pay for work of equal value' before the Arbitration Commission and introduce maternity leave; enact Aboriginal land rights legislation; remove the last vestiges of the White Australia Policy; and provide more adequate migrant settlement services.

From an Australian perspective these were considered to be radical measures, but by some overseas standards of welfare state provision they were moderate. There was no commitment to seek the creation of 'no less than a new social order' through the pursuit of 'socialist goals' including 'a fundamental and irreversible shift in the balance of power and wealth in favour of working people and their families' as there was from the British Labour Party election manifesto in 1974. Rather, there was an unstated assumption that Keynesian demand management, fiscal expansion, and policies aimed at ensuring greater competitive efficiency would ensure full employment and economic growth sufficient to pay for the measures without imposing any increase in the size of the public sector relative to Gross Domestic Product. Underlying the Whitlam Labor Government's programme was the 'differentiated' welfare state assumption that Keynesian macro-economic management had removed the shackles from the politics and economics of redistribution through social welfare measures.

A significant amount of the government's programme was achieved: in particular, the social security initiatives (although with only partial realization of the abolition of the means test on old age pensions); the introduction of a comprehensive, universal health insurance scheme; the public housing and urban development programmes; gender equality in minimum wage determination; the beginning of a children's services programme; expansion of education and the abolition of fees in higher education; the cessation of an immigration policy based on racial exclusion; and the introduction of Aboriginal rights legislation and Aboriginal community programmes (Patience and Head 1979). It must also be noted that, apart from the extremely significant reform of wage-determination for women, whose outcomes narrowed the gender wage gap substantially in subsequent years (Willborn, Gregory and Daly 1992), the Government did not introduce a comprehensive incomes policy and the expansionary fiscal policies were not accompanied by comprehensive taxation measures.

At the same time as the Labor Government developed a strong programme of welfare services through central state funding and direction, predicated on a significant re-conceptualization of what public investment in physical and social infrastructure might achieve, the long-maturing fractures in the Keynesian national and international institutional arrangement became apparent: the stable international trade arrangements set up in the postwar years collapsed; the long-term decline in Australia's terms of trade was compounded by the OPEC oil price increases and their aftermath; and inflationary pressures mounted.

The onset of international recession in 1973 was quickly transferred to Australia through a collapse in export demand and prices, and compounded by a marked reluctance by industry to invest—a reluctance sparked by the Whitlam Government's reforms to Restrictive Trade Practices legislation, the Prices Justification Tribunal, tariff cuts, and foreign investment controls. Simultaneous inflation and unemployment (stagflation) confounded the Labor Government which first attempted to spend its way out, and then in 1975 introduced the first budget predicated on fiscal stringency in the new era of rising unemployment. Keynesian economic theory appeared to be unable to provide an adequate solution to Australia's domestic economic problems in an increasingly deregulated world economy.

In short, the 1974–5 recession itself and the subsequent election of the Fraser Liberal/Country Party Government challenged the legitimacy of both Keynesian economic thought and the interventionist welfare state provisional settlement. The Coalition Government (1976–83), espousing, but to only a certain extent practising, revived neoclassical economic theories, claimed that Keynesian policies were responsible for the advent of both inflation and unemployment; rejected many, but certainly not all aspects of the expansionist Labor reforms, and placed further constraints on social expenditure, particularly in the provision of centralized community services, accompanying this with a very different language of 'individual responsibility' and rejection of the concept of the 'right to welfare'.

6. THE END OF FULL EMPLOYMENT

In the period since 1975, which covered the recessionary years of 1977–8, 1982–3, and 1990–3 with an intervening period of strong growth in 1983–9, a number of major labour market changes, similar to those experienced in many other OECD countries, challenged Australian economic, social security and labour market policies. These changes included a significant alteration of the distribution of employment across industries, with relative decline in manufacturing, and strong increase in jobs in the private services and community services; an increase in part-time employment as a proportion of all employment; a significant increase in labour force participation rates for adult women, particularly those with children; decreased labour force participation rates for older men, associated much more with labour force exclusion, particularly from manufacturing and construction jobs, than with voluntary early retirement; for young people, increased retention in secondary education, strong decline in full-time employment, rapid growth in part-time employment with about three-quarters of part-time jobs for young people filled by students in 1991, and very high rates of unemployment among those who leave school without completing 12 years of education and without acquiring post-school qualifications. Unemployment rates rose to almost 10 per cent in 1983, then declined to 6 per cent in 1989 following consistent job growth, but rose again to 11 per cent in 1992. The most significant feature of unemployment is the increase in long-term unemployment, a problem of considerable intractability even in the time of strong job growth, but exacerbated in each period of recession.

These labour market changes, in conjunction with increased population ageing and increased sole parent family formation (where the parents' employment opportunities were also reduced by recessionary changes until

1985, when sole parents began to benefit from the considerable growth in women's jobs), were reflected in complex social security trends of considerable political importance. Between 1976 and 1984, numbers of social security recipients as a percentage of the population increased from 13.3 per cent to 20.8 per cent, while, expressed as a percentage of those employed, the increase was from 31.3 per cent to 50.2 per cent. The subsequent sustained fall, to 18.7 per cent of the population and 40.8 per cent of those employed in 1990, was reversed by the recession, when these proportions again increased, reaching levels almost equivalent to those in 1983–4. Further, the proportion of all children aged under 16 dependent on social security recipients increased from 8.9 per cent in 1976 to 17.8 per cent in 1984, falling only very slightly by 1990 and increasing considerably to 20.4 per cent in 1991. This is a reflection of the concentration of unemployment and joblessness in families and of increased proportions of sole parent families, of whom 70 per cent received social security assistance in 1991. As a result of this increased reliance on transfer payments, outlays on social security as a proportion of GDP increased from 6.7 per cent to 7.4 per cent between 1976 and 1984, from which point there was a fall to 5.7 per cent in 1990, rising again to 6.5 per cent in 1991 (reflecting the 1990–1 recessionary changes). While these changes are hardly dramatic, and certainly do not provide much evidence for the allegation of 'burgeoning' welfare expenditures promulgated in conservative political rhetoric, they do reflect the significant increases in unemployment and joblessness flowing from the various recessions.

The significance of these trends is that since the mid-1970s Australia experienced a considerable increase in the number and proportion of people of labour force age reliant on social security for a certain period of their lives. This had profound implications for individual and family welfare, reflected in increased levels of poverty and vulnerability (Edgar *et al.* 1989; Saunders and Whiteford 1987), while effects at the national level included loss of industrial output, attrition of skills, and high budgetary costs, resulting as much from decreased tax revenues as from outlays on social security, health, and welfare (EPAC 1988; Dixon 1988).

These issues of reduced economic and employment growth, high levels of unemployment and joblessness, .and the increased necessity for jobless people of labour force age to rely on income support generated heated debates at political and public levels. These debates have centred on the respective roles of public and private sector investment, the extent of state regulation of trade, industry, and the labour market, the relative merits of state provision of health and welfare services or increased market provision, and the form and scale of social security programmes which might intervene most effectively and fairly in the distribution of economic welfare.

The policy priorities of the Hawke Labor Government from 1983 focused initially on promotion of strong job growth and the sustained reduction of unemployment from its highest postwar level of almost 10 per cent. Within the framework of the Prices and Incomes Accord with the ACTU (initially negotiated by the Labor Party before its election, and subsequently re-negotiated five times in the light of changing social and economic circumstances), the Labor Government established a reasonably integrated combination of wages policy and tax and social security arrangements, composed of market wage restraint accompanied by compensatory 'social wage' measures. These measures included universal health insurance, a more interventionist industry policy, increased and indexed family income support, expanded investment in community services with particular empha-sis on child care, considerably increased coverage of occupational super-annuation, and the introduction of a more integrated approach to incomes policy through wages/tax/benefits packages which simultaneously restrained market wage increases and redistributed to low income families (Harding and Mitchell 1992). These initiatives, complemented by strong job growth and substantial reduction in unemployment (at least until 1989), are con-sidered to be among the more progressive elements of Labor policy (Stretton 1987).

The onset of deep recession and very high levels of unemployment from 1990, however, followed at least four years of stringent fiscal policy and several years of tight monetary policy, characterized by very high interest rates in a de-regulated financial market and banking system. There can be no doubt that from mid-1988 the priority of strong employment growth was sacrificed to inflation control and to producing a more favourable 'balance of payments'. Well before this, however, fiscal policy had focused on the reduction of public expenditure as a proportion of GDP, in the belief that a reduced public sector would make way for increased private sector investment. These policies appeared to militate against the emergence of a new liberal-democratic/conservative alliance, with significant sections of industry apparently accepting, and certainly working within the Labor structures of tripartite industry policy; wages, taxation, and social security policies; fiscal constraint, and selective deregulation.

In the early 1990s, however, there was a strong resurgence of polarized political debate, partly in response to the depth and apparent intractability of the domestic and international recession, and partly influenced by the Liberal/National Parties' attempts to establish a more radical neo-liberal social and economic policy agenda. In response to the persistence of low rates of growth and increasing unemployment, with particularly high rates of long-term unemployment, the Labor Government initiatives outlined in the *One Nation Statement* (Keating, 1992) and extended in the 1992–3 Budget, indicate a new recourse to post-Keynesian policy. This agenda proposes a temporary counter-cyclical departure from the fiscal restraint characteristic of policies from 1987 to 1991, to be effected by considerable expansion of public investment in large physical infrastructure development projects, so as to redress previous neglect and to promote economic growth and job growth. Although this plan is predicated on the intermeshing of public and private sector investment to generate job growth, no commitment has been made to pursue full employment as the linchpin of public policy.

Counterposed to these initiatives is the Liberal/National Parties' economic and social policy agenda, influenced by the conservative public policies of the United Kingdom and New Zealand (Vintila *et al.* 1992; Garnaut and Viviani 1992). Whilst the *Fightback Program* (Liberal and National Party 1991), first published in 1991 and revised in late 1992, is ostensibly focused on the introduction of a broad-based tax on consumption, including all goods but food, and most services, with cuts in income tax and increases in transfer payments designated as 'compensation' for the ensuing price increases, the agenda is equally focused on the restriction of welfare state provision. The objectives are the reduction of direct Commonwealth Government social expenditures, particularly on health and community services; considerably more stringent eligibility arrangements for various forms of income support; greater privatization of health, welfare, and education services; dismantling of centralized wage fixation; and reduction of what is perceived as 'union power'.

A subsequent document, entitled *Jobsback*, outlines a programme of radical deregulation of centralized wage-determination and industrial-relations policies mounting an attack on organized trade union influence in industrial relations and in social policy deliberations, an attack which is redolent of the neo-liberal labour market and welfare agendas instituted in the United Kingdom (Deakin and Wilkinson 1991) and New Zealand (du Plessis 1992). This programme is predicated on strong opposition to the ACTU/Government Accord basis of welfare provision (the 'social wage'), characteristic of the neo-corporatist welfare state arrangements of the 1980s. The total project of radical restructuring is concerned as much with dismantling the institutional influences of the centralized trade union organ-isation on wages, incomes, welfare, and industrial relations policy, as it is with taxation, social security, and welfare arrangements. The expressed intentions are to alter fundamentally the labour market regulations and wage-determination systems which have constituted the basis of wage protection, particularly for low wage earners.

Public policy debates in the 1990s are therefore poised around Labor Government plans for the maintenance of a moderate form of Laborist corporatism and revived neo-Keynesian infrastructure development on the one hand, and on the other hand, conservative Coalition plans for labour market and wages deregulation, with significant reductions in public invest-ment in health and welfare services and labour market programmes.

7. RE-ASSESSING THE AUSTRALIAN WELFARE STATE

To return to the question of the categorization of Australia as a 'liberal
welfare state regime', both in terms of its history and its contemporary
policies, it is clear from this brief account of Australian social policy and
its intersections with economic policy that such a categorization is far too
simple, indeed too removed from the debates and the events to elucidate
the various alliances and conflicts and their outcomes at different points in
Australia's contested welfare history. To what extent, then, does the alternative categorization of Australia as a 'radical redistributive welfare regime'
better capture the characteristics of these shifting liberal/social-democratic
settlements?

The period of Federation set the parameters of Australia's liberal-
democratic and social-democratic settlement around the objective of securing the 'working man's paradise', based on the establishment of two
minima: the 'living wage' (for adult men), set by centralized wage fixation,
and a social assistance 'floor' for the aged and disabled. During the Second
World War and postwar reconstruction, Keynesian economic policy set an
agenda for high levels of economic growth and full employment, through
the central role of counter-cyclical public investment in physical and social
infrastructure. In the words of *Full Employment in Australia*, 'public capital
expenditure' was considered necessary to stabilize and maintain the totality
of public and private sector expenditure, and thus to maintain the level of
demand essential to strong employment growth. In addition, the consolidation of the social security system as a general, revenue-based, flat-
rate and means-tested system, confirmed the parameters of the mildly
redistributive, characteristically Australian, welfare state settlement.

Successive conservative coalition governments throughout the years of
the 'postwar boom' maintained these interventionist approaches, but with
more conservative Keynesian economic policies and a more restrictive
approach to the development of welfare services. The Whitlam Labor
Government's attempts to realise and to extend the progressive potentialities
of the Keynesian welfare state, particularly in respect of social security,
gender equality in wages policy, and community service provision, were cut
short by the onset of international and national recession in 1974. From
this point, the legitimacy of Keynesian policies was challenged fundamentally
by revitalized neoclassical economic policies, which redefined the objective
of full employment as contrary to, and able to be sacrificed to, other
economic priorities: the control of inflation, and the reduction of social
expenditures.

The strategic alliance between liberal and social democrats collapsed,
with the liberals rejecting what they saw as the Whitlam Government's
profligate concentration on the politics of redistribution at the expense of

the politics of wealth production, resulting in the formation of a provisional liaison between the liberal democrats and the neo-conservatives. The Fraser Liberal/Country Party Government from 1976 to 1983 embraced the neo-conservative rhetoric and constituted the 'fight against inflation' as its key policy priority. It was, however, only partially successful in the objective of reducing social expenditure, reducing investment in health and welfare services, but compelled to increase expenditure substantially on social security, because the recessions of the late 1970s and early 1980s brought increasingly high levels of unemployment and the entrenchment of long-term unemployment.

The Hawke/Keating Labor Governments' economic and social policies were developed predominantly within the context of the Prices and Incomes Accord with the trade unions, introducing for the first time in Australia's welfare history reasonably integrated wages, taxation and benefits policies. By 1988, the initial policy priority of economic and employment growth had been sacrificed to the control of inflation and foreign debt by the reduction of social investment and the imposition of a high-interest rate regime. Within the context of the ensuing deep recession from 1990, a 'battle of the plans' between the Labor Government and the Liberal/National Parties emerged. These plans proposed alternative futures for the Australian welfare state through substantially different market/state configurations: an extension of Laborist corporatism on the one hand, and a redirection of Australian public policies towards a privatized market-driven agenda similar to the neo-conservative policies of Britain and New Zealand.

There are some indications that, in response to what is perceived as the 'economic rationalism' of both the Government in the latter half of the 1980s and the Opposition, a new informal coalition of liberal democrats and social democrats outside of the party political process is forming around the objective of reclaiming the political, economic, and ideological agenda. Despite their different points of emphasis, the nub of the arguments put by this coalition of conservative Keynesians, liberal democrats, social democrats, and feminists is that social relations should not be reduced to the rules of commodity exchange, and that social policies should not be submerged by, or constituted as, mere supporting partners to the unequal allocations generated by unregulated markets (Disney 1989; Kemp 1991*a*, 1991*b*; Krygier 1992; Pusey 1991; Yeatman 1989). What is required, according to this argument, is not a radical repositioning of market and state, so as to 'free up' the market, but a renewed and long-term emphasis on strong public investment, better market regulation, strong employment growth, the concerted reduction of unemployment, and more adequate and extensive income support and community service provision (Stretton 1987; Cass and McClelland 1989; Freeland 1990; Head and McCoy 1991; Vintila *et al.* 1992).

To recategorize the characteristics of Australian market/welfare state relations, it is clear from the evidence outlined above that neither of the dualist categories of the liberal or radical redistributive welfare regimes captures the distinctiveness of the characteristically Australian liberal/social democratic alliances which have shaped Australian public policies. Although labour aspirations have been major determinants of welfare state outcomes, neither at the turn of the century, nor during the period of World War II and postwar reconstruction, nor during the period of the Hawke/Keating Labor governments, have the policies of organized labour been the only determinant of state interventions in market relations. Neither, on the other hand, has the traditional liberal reluctance to intervene in market relations, particularly labour market relations, been a central feature of Australian public policy. In the 1900s, the 1940s, and in 1983–92, Australia's distinctive combination of labour market regulation, centralized wage-determination, needs-based social security arrangements, and other social welfare provisions were shaped by the perceived imperative of maintaining the strategic liberal/social-democratic alliances which have been central to Australia's Laborist tradition. (It could also be argued that the liberal/social-democratic alliance broke down in 1974–75 in response to liberals' perceptions that the Whitlam Labor Government pursued its social redistributive agenda at the expense of fiscal responsibility).

The specific nature of the policy configurations differed with each period, bearing similarities with contemporaneous developments in similar capitalist welfare states, but deriving both impetus and policy frameworks from domestic traditions and imperatives (as evidenced by the Australian interpretations of Keynes and Beveridge during the 1940s). In the 1983–92 period, the market/state configuration was influenced partly by social corporatism derived from Swedish and Austrian models, as outlined in *Australia Reconstructed* (ACTU/TDC 1987). However, the Accord framework of economic and social policy formulation was influenced much more by the alliance forged between the peak trade union body and the parliamentary Labor Party, and the Labor Government, which integrated negotiations over wages, tax, health, and welfare policies; and by the institutionalization of tripartite economic and industry policy negotiations between the three major social partners—unions, industry, and central government. This Australian variant of corporatism also involved the welfare sector in public policy discussions, without endowing welfare organizations with equally effective partnership in tripartite institutions.

It must also be emphasized that in the latter half of the 1980s, the Hawke/Keating Labor Governments implemented policies which ran counter to the labour corporatist model, such as reductions in the size of the public sector, reduced public investment in physical and social infrastructure, and total deregulation of the financial system. These policies were resisted by liberal and social democrats concerned with maintaining a vital public sector and a redistributive welfare state, a resistance which gained impetus and some political legitimacy in the context of the more vigorous state interventions accepted as a necessary response to the 1990–2 recession. There is, at the time of writing, a strong possibility that the Australian corporatist experiment may be superseded by the neo-conservative deregulatory policies of the Opposition parties, which would reorient market/state relations towards an Australian version of the liberal-welfare regime. It might well be said that the polarities of welfare state regimes identified by Mishra (1990) and Mitchell (1992), a polarization in the 1980s and 1990s between social-corporatist and neo-conservative approaches, represent the ideological boundaries within which Australian economic policies and welfare state arrangements will be contested in the 1990s.

REFERENCES

Australian Council of Trade Unions/Trade Development Council (1987), *Australia Reconstructed*. Canberra: AGPS.

Australian Women's Conference Committee (1943), *Australian Women's Charter, 1943*. Sydney: Australian Women's Conference Committee.

Baldock, C. (1988), 'Public Policies and the Paid Work of Women', in C. Baldock and B. Cass (eds.), *Women, Social Welfare and the State*. Sydney: Allen and Unwin.

Beveridge, W. H. (1944), *Full Employment in a Free Society*. London: Allen and Unwin.

Black, L. (1984), 'Social Democracy and Full Employment: the Australian White Paper', *Labour History*, 46.

Cass, B. (1988), 'Redistribution to Women and Children: A History of Child Endowment and Family Allowances', in C. Baldock and B. Cass (eds.), *Women, Social Welfare and the State*. Sydney: Allen and Unwin.

—— and McClelland, A. (1989), 'Changing the Terms of the Welfare Debate: Redefining the Structure and Purpose of the Australian Social Security System', in P. Saunders and A. Jamrozik (eds.), *Social Policy in Australia: What Future for the Welfare State?* Sydney: University of NSW, SPRC.

Castles, F. (1988), *Australian Public Policy and Economic Vulnerability*. Sydney: Allen and Unwin.

—— and Mitchell, D. (1992), 'Identifying Welfare State Regimes: The Links Between Politics, Instruments and Outcomes', *Governance*, 5/1.

Coombs, H. C. (1944), 'The Economic Aftermath of War', in D. A. S. Campbell (ed.), *Post-War Reconstruction in Australia*. Sydney: Australasian Publishing Co.

—— (1981), *Trial Balance*. Melbourne: Macmillan.

Cornish, S. (1981), *Full Employment in Australia: The Genesis of a White Paper*. Canberra: Australian National University.

Curthoys, A. (1988), 'Equal Pay, a Family Wage or Both?', in B. Caine *et al.* (eds.), *Crossing Boundaries*. Sydney: Allen and Unwin.

Deakin, S., and Wilkinson, F. (1991), 'Labour Law, Social Security and Economic Inequality', *Cambridge Journal of Economics*, 15.

Disney, J. (1989), 'Government and Public Welfare', in P. Coaldrake and J. R. Nethercote (eds.), *What Should Government Do?* Sydney: Hale and Iremonger.

Dixon, D. (1988), *Unemployment: The Economic and Social Costs*. Melbourne: Brotherhood of St Laurence.

du Plessis, R. (1992), 'Old Wine in New Bottles: Social Security in New Zealand 1984–1990, Change and Continuity'. Paper presented at the Dept. of Social Work and Social Policy, Univ. of Sydney.

Economic Planning Advisory Council (EPAC) (1988), *Income Support Policies, Taxation and Incentives*, Council Paper 35. Canberra: AGPS.

Edgar, D., Keane, D., and McDonald, P. (eds.) (1989), *Child Poverty*. Sydney: Allen and Unwin.

Esping-Andersen, G. (1990), *The Three Worlds of Welfare Capitalism*. Cambridge: Polity Press.

Freeland, J. (1990), 'An Active Labour Market Policy for Australia: Rhetoric or Reality'. Paper presented at the ACOSS Annual Congress, Univ. of Sydney.

Garnaut, R., and Viviani, N. (eds.) (1992), *The Australian Quarterly, Special Fightback Issue*, 64/2.

Harding, A., and Mitchell, D. (1992), 'The Efficiency and Effectiveness of the Tax-Transfer System in the 1980s', *Australian Tax Forum*, 9/3.

Head, B., and McCoy, E. (eds.) (1991), *Deregulation or Better Regulation? Issues for the Public Sector*. Brisbane: Centre for Australian Public Sector Management.

Institute of Public Affairs (IPA) (NSW) (1945), *What Is Ahead for Australia?* Sydney: IPA.

Jangenas, B. (1985), *The Swedish Approach to Labour Market Policy*. Uppsala: Swedish Institute.

Keating, P. J. (1992), *One Nation: Statement by the Prime Minister*. Canberra: AGPS.

Kemp, C. D. (1991a), 'The Australian Economy: What Is to be Done?', *Quadrant*, 276/35: 5.

—— (1991b), 'Those Terrible 80 Years?' *Quadrant*, 281/35: 11.

Krygier, M. (1992), 'In Praise of Conservative Liberal Social Democracy', *Quadrant*, 286/36: 5.

Liberal and National Parties (1991), *Fightback: Taxation and Expenditure Reform for Jobs and Growth*. Canberra: Coalition Parties.

Macarthy, P. G. (1976), 'Justice Higgins and the Harvester Judgement', in J. Roe (ed.), *Social Policy in Australia*. Sydney: Cassell.

Macintyre, S. (1985), *Winners and Losers*. Sydney: Allen and Unwin.

—— (1989), *The Labour Experiment*. Melbourne: McPhee Gribble.

Markey, R. (1982), 'The ALP and the Emergence of a National Social Policy 1880–1910', in R. Kennedy (ed.), *Australian Welfare History: Critical Essays*. South Melbourne: Macmillan.

Marklund, S. (1992), 'The Decomposition of Social Policy in Sweden', *Scandinavian Journal of Social Welfare*, 1/1.

Menzies, R. G. (1944), 'Response to D. B. Copeland', in D. A. S Campbell (ed.), *Post-War Reconstruction in Australia*. Sydney: Australasian Publishing Co.

Mishra, R. (1990), *The Welfare State in Capitalist Society*. London: Harvester.

Mitchell, D. (1992), 'Welfare States and Welfare Outcomes in the 1980s'. Paper presented at a conference on 'Social Security Fifty Years After Beveridge', Univ. of York.

Parliament of the Commonwealth of Australia (1945), *Full Employment in Australia*. Canberra: Commonwealth Government Printer.

Patience, A., and Head, B. (eds.) (1979), *From Whitlam to Fraser*. Melbourne: Oxford University Press.

Pusey, M. (1991), *Economic Rationalism in Canberra*. Melbourne: Cambridge University Press.

Roe, J. (ed.) (1976), *Social Policy in Australia*. Sydney: Cassell.

Ross, L. (1944), 'A New Social Order', in D. A. S. Campbell (ed.), *Post-War Reconstruction in Australia*. Sydney: Australasian Publishing Co.

Saunders, P., and Whiteford, P. (1987), *Ending Child Poverty: An Assessment of the Government's Family Package*. SWRC R&P 69. Sydney: Univ. of NSW.

Shaver, S. (1990), *Gender, Social Policy Regimes and the Welfare State*. SPRC Discussion Paper 26.

——(1992), 'Focusing on Women: From Difference to Equality in the Australian Social Security System'. Paper presented at the Academy of Social Sciences in Australia Symposium on Market and State Relations in the 1990s, Australian National University, Canberra.

Smyth, P. (1991), 'T Bones and Television: Social Policy and Australian Economic Thought, 1945–1960,' unpublished Ph.D. thesis. Sydney: Univ. of NSW.

Stjerno, S. (1992), 'Norwegian Social Policy in Perspective', unpublished paper prepared at Social Policy Research Centre, Sydney: Univ. of NSW.

Stretton, H. (1987), *Political Essays*. Melbourne: Georgian House.

Vintila, P., Phillimore, J., and Newman, P. (eds.) (1992), *Markets, Morals and Manifestos*. Perth: Murdoch Univ. Institute for Science and Technology Policy.

Willborn, S., Gregory, R., and Daly, A. (1992), 'Women's Wages in Australia and the United States', *Nebraska Law Review*, 71/2.

Yeatman, A. (1989), *Femocrats, Bureaucrats and Technocrats*. Sydney: Allen and Unwin.

INDEX